I Am the American

I Am the American

Richard Skolnik

Library of Congress Number:		2001117350
ISBN #:	Hardcover	1-4010-1323-6
	Softcover	1-4010-1322-8

This is a work of fiction. Names, characters, places and incidents either are the product of the author's imagination or are used fictitiously, and any resemblance to any actual persons, living or dead, events, or locales is entirely coincidental.

This book was printed in the United States of America.

To order additional copies of this book, contact:
Xlibris Corporation
1-888-7-XLIBRIS
www.Xlibris.com
Orders@Xlibris.com

Contents

Preface

I met Earl Williams some thirty years ago when my son Seth and his son Scott both enrolled in the same nursery program at the Waldorf School in Garden City, New York. We struck up a friendship almost at once, one which lasted, without interruption, until his untimely death in 1996. I recall most vividly that one of the first events to which he invited me was a retirement party given him by his buddies on the police force. That occasion, I later came to realize, marked the conclusion of the "heroic" era of Earl's life. He then turned with obvious delight and considerable determination to raising his three children, Sandra, Scott and Tiffany, while his wife Dolores pursued a very successful career as a public school teacher. It was in these years that we saw a great deal of each other (our homes were less than a mile apart), each of us prepared to lend a hand to the other whenever the occasion arose. (I remember, for example, Earl attaching a rope to one of my constantly ailing cars and towing it through heavy traffic from Manhattan out to Long Island - no mean feat. Then there was the time he drove a rental truck down to Philadelphia to pick up my daughter's belongings at the conclusion of her graduate studies there.

Our conversations over the years ranged widely and often included vivid recollections and lively episodes from his past. As a historian, it was not hard for me to recognize the many treasures amidst these memories and to appreciate how adept he was in summoning up the details of that past. At some point along the way we both agreed to take these random conversations a step further.

A familiar routine soon developed. We'd have lunch together (drinks not included) then head over to my house, turn on the tape recorder and return for several hours, to times long past, with Earl patiently and thoughtfully responding to all manner of questions and follow-up inquiries that I directed at him. This went on for well over two years until we had accumulated hundreds of hours of interviews. After I had his story down on paper, Earl read and re-read every line of the manuscript, indicating when I missed his point, elaborating, emphasizing, questioning, but overall quite pleased with the end result. That he had produced a book was a source of great delight to him. It was for me a thoroughly rewarding and eye-opening experience. After all I had never, as Earl did, visited Cuba, served in the Army, collected garbage for New York City or been a cop. And of course I had never led the life of a black man in America.

Sadly Earl would never see the manuscript become a complete book. His passing produced a terrible void in my life and for a time the pages of a draft stayed stacked up on a shelf next to my desk. I had so much wanted to complete the project for him, have him proudly point to the book he had authored. But, what better tribute, I came to realize, could there be to his life and memory than to move forward and bring the work to its proper conclusion. And so I did, with the help of my good friends Professor Louis Masur and Bill Scher, both of whom read and corrected the manuscript with great care, and with the assistance of Mrs. Dorothy Hanley who typed and retyped it so diligently. I'm sure Earl would have been pleased with how it all turned out.

522-SKOL

Introduction

THE BAD TIMES AND THE GOOD

I worked this after-school job downtown on Broadway and 67th Street setting up and filling boxes, getting them ready for shipment—simple stuff. It was outside my neighborhood but a quick subway ride away, and it was steady work. This particular Fall evening, once all the packages were ready, I closed up and as usual started walking to the train station.

When I spotted them they were about a block away, Irish kids, who I'd seen before hanging around there. Just keep walking, I'm thinking. Never had serious problems down here. Some dirty looks, an insult or two—no big deal. But this time it was different."Let's get the nigger," that much I heard. That was enough to get the gang heading toward me on the run. I just took off. Maybe that was a mistake. Later I wondered what would have happened if I had stood my ground. Staying cool could have surprised them—might have worked. Maybe I could have made it back to my office and just waited them out. Instead I ran like hell, heading west along 67th Street.

So the chase was on. Along the street people just watched. Kids' play, the usual stuff—why get excited or involved? Besides, it's a black kid. Doesn't belong in this neighborhood. Serves him right.

I was fast and plenty scared. No easy catch. But I was heading west, toward Riverside Drive Park and the Hudson River. Then what? Into the park, and not knowing the place, I slowed up. Not them. They just piled on. "Throw the nigger in the water!" Ripping at my clothes, they stripped me bare. I kicked, shouted, fought back best I could. But it was hopeless. The air rushed by, then a slap, as the river hit.

I wasn't much good at swimming, and why I didn't panic I have no idea. If I splashed a lot, somehow I knew I'd go under and drown. "Do the dog paddle. Do the dog paddle." I did, because I stayed up and began drifting in the cold, choppy waters, the current taking me along. I tried screaming. But who in the hell was going to hear me? Anyway I was too busy, desperate to stay on top and keep from getting pulled away from the shore. But then I got lucky. I hit into what must have been part of a pier. I grabbed at a wooden post, all slippery and crusty, wrapped my feet around, practically hugged it. It saved my life.

Up and out of the water I climbed, covered with scratches and goosebumps but nothing else. The lamppost sign read 58th Street; I had drifted eight or nine blocks. And there I was, wet, freezing, and exhausted. Thank God it was dark now, no one saw me. Go back to where I had been tossed in—that made sense. The gang would be gone; maybe I'd find some of my clothes. No such luck. Probably dumped them into the river.

Naked, shivering, scared and a long way from 114th Street and home, you can imagine how relieved I felt when I spotted a policeman. Immediately I ran toward him. An Irish cop he was, most were then. He takes one look at me and breaks out laughing. I had to be some sight. But hey, this is crazy, I'm thinking—this is no joke. Well, he did help—sort of. He found some newspapers, (at least they were large-sized pages, not tabloid) and told me to wrap myself in them. "Where do you live?" he asked. I told him, but then all he said to me was, "Go on home."

That was it! New York's Finest—at your service! Nothing about what happened or who did it to me. Nothing about a squad car to drive me uptown. Did I have any money for a cab or a bus—not a word. A blanket? Forget it. "Go on home." Imagine a white boy naked in Harlem. Is the cop just gonna say, "Go on home"? Ain't no way!

I started walking, block after block, shivering, sticking to the darkest shadows. Some people stared; most looked away. I became real tired, (the walk was well over two miles.) I have no idea how I made it. The hard pavement, then the final shortcut through Morningside Park tore up my feet something awful. When I got home my mother was at the door. She was frantic. I had always been home on time. Crying, she just threw her arms around me. "Thank God you're alive. I didn't know what to think." Hot soup and plenty of tea, then under the covers. Exhausted, I slept long into the next afternoon.

I don't scare easily. Never have. I stuck to that job. Only now I carried a weapon with me tucked under my belt, a heavy pipe rolled up in a newspaper. Next time I'd take them on, do some real damage. Just brave talk, it turned out. Never saw them again.

* * *

Same job. Same neighborhood—several months later. On my way to work I had gotten into the habit of looking in the window of this restaurant, Ship Ahoy, one very fancy fish place. Some sight—the lobsters, snails, mussels, crabs and fish of all kinds, colors and sizes lined up by species, spread out in orderly rows on a thick bed of ice. A real work of art. Each time I looked in, a different arrangement. Imagine eating in a place like this? Fat chance. Downtown restaurants had no interest in Negro customers; we were not welcome there. No, they wouldn't keep you out but you'd be seated off in a corner and served in "good time" which meant after everyone else.

Each time I pressed my nose to the window there was the restaurant doorman watching me. Before long we got to greeting each other—his name was Peter, Peter Boyle—and chatting a bit. He knew I worked just a few doors down and I guess saw how reliable I was. And curious too because I'd always be asking him the names of the fish.

One day while standing at my usual place by the window, he asked, "Would you like to eat in here?" I think I said, "Maybe one day I might get to do it." "Why wait? You come back on Saturday night, get dressed up, look real good, and meet me here at eight o'clock." "You're not kidding?" "No, just be ready for a treat."

Was he joking? Who knew? Still on Saturday I got fancied up and headed down to Ship Ahoy. Sure enough, Peter's there, but he's not in his uniform. We walked in together, like regular customers. The *maitre d'* escorted us to the table and handed us menus. Anything I wanted, Peter assured me. Lobster, of course. crabs, that seemed fine, also some shrimp. Somehow the bartender knew to prepare a non-alcoholic drink for me.

Heads were turning. Who was this black kid getting all the attention? Why the fuss over him? Would you believe at one point the chef came over to our table? "How was everything?" Talk about getting the royal treatment. All the time Peter's there smiling, pleased with what he had cooked up, never actually explaining why he did it. Before it was over I had tasted lots of ocean creatures. What I couldn't finish, plus food I never got around to ordering, they put in a bag for me to take home. What a treat. Peter then walked me to the subway entrance and made sure I was safely on my way back uptown. Many, many years have passed but I've never forgotten that night.

So what about these memories? What black man doesn't have his share of ugly stories to tell? It comes with the territory, part of our being here in America. Christ, many of us are just plain lucky to be alive to talk about them. It's been that way right from the start and still going on. But for all the shit and abuse dumped on me, I've also met up with the Peter Boyles of this world—no small accomplishment.

So while I've always been on my guard—no sensible black

man could do otherwise, I also expected I'd catch a break somehow—discover America's better self. Turned out that way. Turned out I was one of the lucky ones.

* * *

1 SOUTHERN SHADOWS

Official papers, pictures, letters, the stuff that says: Here I am, this is what I did and when—there's not much left. I know folks like holding on to those things. I guess I should have; might have made it easier, but we'll make do. Also, don't expect me to remember much from my childhood. A few mental snapshots, a story here and there, sad moments and some of joy—those I still have. What's missing are firsthand witnesses from my childhood years, folks able to remind you of this or that. I have no one, not a single living soul to say, "Hey, Earl, you were always getting into things, givin' your Ma a fit," or, "I remember the time you and what's-his-name, the kid on down the road . . ." I'm on my own here. Been that way for a long, long time.

William Earl Foy Taylor Williams Washington, Junior. Memorize it, my mother insisted. And I did, figuring this name chain contained the history of the family. William Earl Foy Taylor Williams Washington, Junior. It got so that I could whip through it in an instant. I still can. But what exactly did it add up to? I don't know. My mother never spelled it out. Funny thing that is, too, because she would come to tell me about so much, insist that I learn, use my mind, absorb all that I could. The subject of family, however, never got filled in.

My roots were in the rural south, specifically New Bern, North Carolina where I was born on August 6th, 1929. My mother, Estelle Foy Williams (originally from Durham) not much past childhood herself—she was thirteen when I was born—would not many years later decide to leave the South. Just why she did I never fully understood. Was it on account of my father's death? I never knew him. I was a child when he died. He had, I found out, come as a young man from Barbados to the United States to better himself. What he hoped to do I have no idea, but what he did at first was take advantage of his natural talent for football, or at least for running real fast. According to my mother, a number of southern black colleges gave him scholarships recruited him to play for them. For some reason he never stayed long at any of them, moved on from one to another, each time with the same deal, tuition for touchdowns.

What a horror it must have been. It happened during a football game. There he was charging into the end zone, then smack into the goalpost. He never regained consciousness.

Maybe his death caused my mother to move on, to leave behind the awful memory. But maybe not. She was full of ambition, set on making her way in the world. Was this likely in the South? No, southern blacks were telling each other to go North—there it could happen. What might have made the north even more attractive was that her mother or possibly some other close relative already lived up there. When we arrived in New York I do recall that my mother and I traveled several times out to eastern Long Island and stayed on the Shinnecock Indian Reservation. What happened or who we visited there, that I don't remember. But more than once my mother reminded me that we had Indian blood in us. "You are Indian and you are Negro." And when some folks who were part Indian later moved in near us my mother made sure to visit them. More I can't say. Still I never doubted and always felt proud knowing that through me flowed the blood of America's earliest peoples, Aborigine and African. To my fellow Americans, however, that was reason enough to consider me "inferior" and to keep me "in my place."

In my time down South I never saw white faces. We lived in our own world. There was, I remember, even talk about a "line," and how we'd best keep to our side of it. Once there'd been fighting between "us" and "them," i.e., local whites, but then came some arrangement. Safe within our own territory, we could, however, expect trouble outside the borders. I saw what that might be the times my mother and I drove up north. Blacks had organized their own separate transportation network, a series of "stops" between points south and certain northern locations. It was not the fastest way to go but my mother preferred it. Segregated trains were not for her. Instead we used private car drivers who made their own arrangements with black homeowners to get us a bed and breakfast along the way—usually off the main highways and up some very dusty backroads.

These black drivers knew the score, knew what roads to take and how to avoid trouble. What trouble? The kind whites cooked up. These people resented blacks who drove fine automobiles and were independent types, not your "Yes, Sir" Negroes. They'd stop them, shake down the drivers and scare those inside. Local sheriffs or their deputies also were in on it. "Where y'all goin'?"—they knew damn well. Stay quiet, the driver would warn the passengers. "You know me. I'm just taking some folks on my regular run." Generally that worked; usually not before some palm greasing took place. My mother and I were never stopped, but just listening to drivers tell their stories and cuss out those whites told you there'd been some nasty run-ins.

It was no fun hearing that we couldn't just stop whenever I or someone else in the car needed a bathroom (when the distances were great, drivers would pull over and let us go along the side of the road) or because I got thirsty. Wait, I was reminded, until such and such a place where we knew colored people were welcome. Most service stations "allowed" us to get gas and buy bottles of Coke on sale out front. If they served food we'd be obliged to go to the back and then wait (blacks had best not be knocking or asking for service here) until someone came round.

When I was around five or so we left the South for good. Many years would pass before I returned. And then it was as if I had never left. The South had not changed its ways.

2 | BROOKLYN BOUND

When I moved on North in the mid-1930s so did many other blacks. But the "Promised Land" was no more. Thank the Great Depression for that. Had my mother and I stayed, life would have been tough but probably not as bad as those early years in New York City. Up from the rural South and practically alone in a huge strange city—what could be worse? Whatever relatives my mother might have had in New York, whoever else she might have known up here—no one showed up, no one helped us. Still we survived, living together with people just as desperate as we were. But instead of fighting among ourselves out of frustration and for the few available crumbs—people at the bottom act that way you know—we reached out and supported one another. That's how we hung on. Then came the miracle, the stuff of fairytales, except this one really happened.

Together with other newcomers to New York City, my mother and I ended up in a dilapidated railroad flat in Brooklyn. It was one family to a room, sometimes four or five people together. We were lucky: there were just the two of us. In the building were Polish, Irish and Germans (and others speaking languages I couldn't recognize). Our being black was no big deal; so were many of the people on our block.

The folks on our floor soon became "family." Say someone was short a week's rent, other tenants would step in and cover it (once the landlord would not carry you any longer). People did it because they cared and also because they weren't eager to have newcomers moving in. When those working as domestics came home with bundles of shirts to be washed and ironed, neighbors would sometimes pitch in and launder them. You'd see pressed shirts hanging all over the place!

Staying together helped us to survive. Certainly that's true when we went out "sneakin'." I'm talking about sneakin' food, snatching stuff off the carts of peddlers or running off with something to eat from a stand at the front of a store. We kids worked together; we were a team. Some did the actual lifting, the rest of us distracted. Fruits, vegetables, fish—we took them all. This was no sport; we did it so that we could eat. Some peddlers fought back, watched us like hawks. They'd shout, curse and threaten us, chase after us from time to time. Others, I think, understood we were desperate, and decided to look the other way when we came by. If we limited our sneakin' they'd live with the "loss." Of course all our loot would go into the community pot. Good sneakin' meant good eats that night. Sure we were thieves, but did we have a choice? The older folks knew what we were about but they never stopped us.

Before eating our food we all praised the good Lord for looking out for us. We appreciated what He had done so that we could eat. We also thanked "Mama," this old Italian lady who cooked for us all. She worked wonders, even with the smallest amounts of food—those were miracles.

No, we didn't starve, but not by much. Shoes, however, were harder to come by. There were times we walked barefoot in the streets and along the railroad tracks (where we'd be looking for pieces of coal). It was so unusual to be wearing shoes that sometimes we picked on those who did—they were "sissies"! Even when my mother managed to get me a pair of hand-me-downs (she would try to save them for the winter months) they soon were falling apart, especially in the rain. So she stuffed newspapers into the shoes and wrapped burlap around the outside trying to make them last. By that time though they were practically useless.

It's the God's honest truth. I mean what happened one day to me and my mother during our last winter in Brooklyn. I know you're gonna say, "It just couldn't happen this way. You're putting me on." Believe me, I couldn't imagine getting away with such a ridiculous story—unless it actually happened.

It was just before Christmas—already there was snow on the ground. These were bad times for us. My mother wasn't finding much household work and my shoes were the thinnest they'd been in a long time. On this particular day the coal in our community stove was running low, so I set out, as I usually did, to scavenge along the tracks and around the railroad yard. No police were around to chase me away, and I found several pieces of coal. Lucky me because my feet were freezing from the snow. I couldn't wait to get back home. About halfway across the street next to our building I felt something under my foot. I brushed away the snow at the spot, and sure enough there was a large brown envelope, folded over. I didn't give it much thought, didn't even bother to open it. But I did pick it up and when I got in handed it to my mother. She was angry. I had stayed out too long. With my wet feet I'd probably catch cold.

Once she saw the envelope, did her expression change. A gleam came to her face. I realized why soon enough. I think she'd first figured it was the kind of envelope numbers runners in our area carried aorund. There could be cash inside. Not cash but coins, gold coins just shining away. I had no idea what to make of all this, but then my mother started crying, tears coming down her cheeks. Over and over again she thanked God. These coins, she said, were from Him. He meant them for us because we were in such desperate need. It was a clear sign we would be saved. As honest as my mother was, I don't think she made any effort to find the owner of these coins. No, they were ours, to keep us going, to raise us up. Praise the Lord!

How my mother cashed them in I never found out, but clever woman that she was, she managed. We now had money, more than we'd ever had before, and just in time for Christmas. Being a generous woman, the entire house, not only our floor, got to celebrate the holiday. There were turkeys and plenty of food, enough for all—paid for this time. And new shoes too, for me, and some of the other kids. Don't go telling me now you don't believe in miracles!

After the holidays my mother made a decision—we were moving out of Brooklyn. She had found an apartment for us up on 114th Street in Manhattan. We were moving to Harlem! I wasn't thrilled. Sure we had known some very tough times in Brooklyn, but also some very good people. But my mother you see was no stick-in-the-mud, was not one to let a chance slip by. Movin' on up was her dream. If a higher power suddenly made it possible, she would not ignore the message. So it was off to Harlem, to the capital of Black America.

3 | IT WAS SOME HARLEM

My mother and I moved up to Harlem in 1937, and stayed there for the next seven years. I came to love this place. This was no ghetto. Here was pride and dignity, also hope—so what if it was the Depression. Most people I came to know stayed upbeat. Harlem, they'd say, might actually be the best place on earth for black folks. For sure it wasn't heaven, and even I, a youngster, saw that things were changing, and not always for the better. But I would have some terrific times here.

Some of what put Harlem on the map had happened years before. For example when I moved in Marcus Garvey clubs organized as part of his black nationalist movement were still around. For me it was quite a treat watching the annual march by Garvey's followers. Such uniforms—gaudy, said some, but to others simply gorgeous. Then there was Father Divine, a leading religious personality of the day. You'd see posters of him up along many of the streets. Now and then he'd drive by, riding in his big car along Seventh Avenue. I even remember hearing him at a rally in Mount Morris Park. He spoke very softly, but the crowd stayed quiet, listening to this man who said he was a messenger of God. My mother, skeptical of most religious leaders, believed Father Divine was sincere. The fact that we received assistance at a food depot he sponsored might have colored her judgment. You see, unlike many other spiritual leaders, he gave you something tangible, helped needy people. He arranged living quarters for the homeless and also jobs by setting up small businesses such as barbershops, grocery stores, restaurants (where he charged 15 cents for dinner) and a big laundry operation.

Father Divine attracted whites as well as blacks, which is what I think eventually got him into trouble with the government. He could bring folks together, even people of different races—that made certain people uneasy. They felt no better when he married a white woman (though to reassure the public he kept on saying it was a "chaste marriage".) But some now saw him as a threat. Blacks will usually catch hell, find themselves "discredited" if they challenge the "established order." Garvey, Father Divine, and later Adam Powell, Jr., Martin Luther King and certainly Jesse Jackson—all of them came under fire, had the rug pulled out from under them. We've always had a shortage of effective leaders, but then when some black dude does attract a following they slice him up. He's cut down to size one way or another by those who run the show. White folks are real vigilant. The game can only be played their way, with the people they choose.

Then there was the fighting 369th Regiment of Harlem, a troop of black soldiers who had distinguished themselves in France during World War I. What pride we took in these men when they marched by on parade. We were patriotic then, make no mistake about that. Damn it, we've always been that way—despite all the shit we've been handed. Tell me what other group has been so willing again and again to fight for this country? Name the war—we were there, dying like other Americans. We weren't always welcome, we got treated badly, were segregated in the ranks, given the worst and often most dangerous jobs and forced everywhere to take orders from white officers (and then caught hell again back home when the fighting was over). But no one ever questioned our bravery (that is, no one who knows the truth) or our sacrifices. When the 369th marched in Harlem, the people watching them understood such things.

No march, but it was some kind of parade. I'm talking about one of Harlem's most popular happenings—the Sunday stroll along Seventh Avenue once church was out. It took place even in winter, but the real show came along in the spring and summer. The route filled up from 110th to 125th Street along both sides of the avenue. Church left me fidgety, so the idea of getting out and walking up the avenue suited me just fine. (There was always the possibility we'd take in a movie afterward and then go on to Harry's Ice Cream Bar. It couldn't get any better.) You were expected to be in your finest outfit and to shuffle along the avenue, giving everyone a chance to see you. Folks took it real slow because you'd be needing to stop and chat with people all along the way. There was lots of standing around on the sidewalk. How else could you catch up on all the "news"? Here was a real community network in action.

* * *

Hard to think of a place our size that was so well known in the United States, also in parts of Europe, as Harlem. No wonder all sorts of blacks considered it home. Just think of the variety of folks living here, from pimps and hustlers, down-and-out bums, day laborers and porters to storekeepers, professionals, artists and musicians. Separate working class communities, middle-class areas and elite districts—that's the usual arrangement, but Harlem included everyone, people at all levels stayed scrambled, and out of that mix came tremendous energy and creativity. You'd notice this for example in many of the local bars. Not like in your white communities, here you'd find all kinds, all classes, all comfortable with each other. Because we weren't wanted "there" discrimination brought us together into an artificial community. Here we didn't separate out from each other as people usually did.

The cultural and entertainment capital of Black America—that was Harlem. It was our national showcase. We were proud when our stars performed for us and when those like Josephine Baker, Lionel Hampton, Hazel Scott, Bojangles Robinson, Ethel

Waters and Duke Ellington decided to live in our neighborhoods. Many an entertainer, black and white, also preferred staying in Harlem while playing downtown or at local jazz spots or clubs or at the Apollo or the Savoy Ballroom. Many stopped at the Hotel Theresa on 125th Street, as famous a place as we had in Harlem. Call him an entertainer, an athlete or a hero or just Joe, but the hotel's most illustrious guest (his "people" usually took up two floors of the place) certainly was heavyweight boxing champ Joe Louis. Humble, uneducated, a "country boy," but still he was our Joe. He owned Harlem. You'd see him walking the streets, talking to everyone or hanging out in some joint or other before or after one of his fights. Even in street clothes the Brown Bomber was one solid guy. (He had a beautiful complexion and despite all his fights never looked like he had taken much punishment). He represented us, struck blows for us underdogs, knocking out opponents just as we would have liked to do. Sure you might step on me but no one messed with Joe Louis!

We also had our Bojangles. Whether he was singing or dancing in musicals or playing alongside Shirley Temple, his was a big name in entertainment. And one smart man, that we knew. Sure he could play Uncle Tom and reassure white America that he was a "yes sir" black, but that wasn't the Bojangles we saw. For one thing, we knew he was no cheapskate. You figured that when you saw him drive through the neighborhood in his Dusenburg. We also heard how he built a park behind his house as a playground for the local kids. And we knew what he most liked doing—playing craps for high stakes on the sidewalk behind the Apollo Theatre—a deadly serious gambling marathon if there ever was one. There were his people. There he could be himself, be the "man". No smiling Negro now, he became this aggressive guy, one hard-assed gambler. Armed with his Derringer and a razor, if he thought someone was cheating, he'd pull his gun and have his way. No matter what he did the cops wouldn't touch him. So he pretty much ran the show, scared the shit out of a lot of people. White folks regarded him as a happy-go-lucky Negro but behind the Apollo he called the shots, was one tough dude.

Mention entertainment and Harlem, and you got to mean the Apollo Theatre. Downtown had its showplaces but for us it was the Apollo. Here black talent could get discovered and then go on to perform for the world. I loved the place, saw plenty of shows there. It wasn't all that impressive to look at; actually it was shabby and the stage real narrow. I remember being nervous whenever I went, afraid the building might actually collapse from all the noise and movement of the audience. You wouldn't find me sitting in the balcony. People up there were always jumping up and out of their seats so that everything bounced and shook. Downstairs toward the back—that's where I'd be. Easy to escape if the place suddenly came tumbling down.

Getting into the Apollo could be a problem. Lines formed early for the evening shows that featured live entertainment, especially on Friday, which was amateur night. Entire families would be out there waiting on line to watch tap dancers, singers, instrumentalists, animal acts, magicians and comics. If you wanted to perform you just signed up. If you had the guts to get up there you were guaranteed an audience, though not necessarily a friendly one. You wouldn't believe how quickly they'd could lose interest and begin booing, or from up in the balcony start tossing things, including empty beer bottles or bags of water, over the edge. Not that master of ceremonies Ralph Cooper discouraged this. Let him see that the audience was growing impatient and he'd call for the hook to remove the unfortunate performers. Some would beg for another chance or just a little more time. They might get it. Not usually though, because along would come Pigmeat Malcolm to remove the offending "entertainer" with this big hook. The audience loved this, went crazy in fact watching Pigmeat clear the stage.

Not all the acts faced the hook. Plenty of talented individuals got a chance to show their stuff. A lot was at stake. If you won for the best performer that night, (there were usually about ten acts) they asked you to return. If you were really good, you were invited back for two weeks, and now you were paid. Cooper himself was an impresario, booking black talent in Chicago, Detroit, and theaters located in other black communities across the country. Become a hit at the Apollo and you might land a spot in his road shows. That's how careers got started, why the Apollo deserved its reputation. Many of the performers eventually outgrew the place and headed downtown, to the "big time." But people in Harlem knew where it had all begun, took pride in having witnessed the start of yet another black entertainer who later would come back "home" to play the Apollo Theater.

* * *

Everybody knew Harlem was this famous Negro community, but what they probably didn't realize then was that there were other people around, white people who were also a part of the scene. I'm not talking about those whites who came up from downtown, who saw Harlem as their playground, a place to let themselves go. I'm referring to the Germans and the Irish and the Jews and Chinese and Italians and later on the Puerto Ricans who set up neighborhoods of their own up there, people who you had to deal with almost daily if you lived where I did in Harlem. Some of these groups, the Germans and Jews for instance, had been around for some time, while many of the Irish, Italians and Puerto Ricans had settled in more recently (as had the blacks, who had been pushed to the north along the west side of Manhattan).

As a kid ethnic distinctions didn't mean much to me. Were whites that much different one from the other? I would find out. One of the first jobs, if you could call it that, that I ever had was working for a rabbi on my block (114th Street). There was a synagogue next door from where I lived, or at least the first floor of a building was set up for religious services and for a school. I was, as I later came to understand, hired by the rabbi as the "shabbos goy" to take care of things Jews were forbidden to do on Saturday, their Sabbath. What a joke, I thought. All I had to do was sweep the stoop of the building and turn the lights on and off for him. For this the rabbi gave me a few nickels each time and a handful of candies. I was, I thought, being overpaid. The rabbi, a most congenial although strange-looking man, liked me. He enjoyed patting me on the head and was eager to teach me about life, at least as he saw it. Unfortunately I'm unable to remember any of these lessons which at the time so greatly impressed me. (I do recall one pearl which he urged me never to forget. In business, he would say, "it was all in the buy, not in the sell"—a bit of worldly wisdom I hadn't expected from a rabbi.)

Everyone who knew about the Germans found them oh so superior. To me they even walked differently—always erect when they came down the street. Such confidence. They dressed that way too, with their vests, watch chains, bowler hats, spats, mustaches curled at the ends and their trim beards. No one else looked or behaved like they did. Distinguished-looking, sure, but definitely haughty. Did other people even exist in their eyes? It was best not to be in their way and risk having them move you aside with their canes. I saw this happen, believe me. And the police respected them, that's for sure. No one fooled with Germans around Harlem.

The Germans owned many buildings in our area and made certain each had a superintendent (usually a black employee) around to maintain them. That they did. These buildings stayed immaculate. Germans also owned many businesses in Harlem, especially along 125th Street, the main commercial area. Everyone knew that landlords here would not rent to blacks, nor would these same white-owned businesses hire them. Not until black protests, led by the Reverend Adam Clayton Powell, Jr., put the heat on did the situation change.

The one German business that I knew well was Harry's Ice Cream Bar. It was an old-fashioned place, as clean as could be with its white marble walls always glistening, cut glass all about, a long counter and a deliciously sweet aroma. And there was

Harry looking typically German with his mustache and beard. His family had owned and worked the place for years, and it was widely known below 110th Street as well as to neighborhood people. It was always busy, (most times white customers outnumbered black) but there was no way you weren't going to wait around. It was just a great place to be—whether you ordered the homemade ice cream, a malted, the three-cent egg cream, the banana split or the candies. For fifty cents my mother and I had a wide choice of special delights. Would I be interested in going over to Harry's, my mother would ask. Some question! How were blacks treated, you want to know? All sorts of people went there, blacks and whites, and Harry catered to everyone. I never saw a problem there.

You knew there were Irish around. And that was a problem. The Irish have always been a problem for us. Ask me which group of whites have, over the years, been toughest on blacks, and I think an honest answer would have to be the Irish. I know the Irish themselves caught hell from other whites, were despised, exploited, labeled inferior. And maybe that's why we became a convenient target for them. Who else could they take their anger out against? Pushing us down and grabbing our jobs might help them move up even while standing on top of us. That's what happened. The Irish finally did make their way up, became respectable, accepted. If only that could have happened to us.

Struggles between people at the bottom play right into the hands of those in power. Encouraging such fights has got to be one of the oldest and most obvious strategies of division in the world. But boy, does it work. Meanwhile people on top are laughing themselves silly watching folks at the bottom tear into each other.

I learned soon enough it was best to stay away from the Irish. They didn't like us blacks, and, just as everyone else, were out to protect their turf, a block here and a block there, and see to it that all others, "outsiders," that is, stayed away. Enter their "occupation zone" and there could be trouble. So what you had to do is go around them. You needed to know who "owned" certain blocks and whether or not they'd challenge you. I figured out roundabout ways to get places when a direct line spelled trouble. Every kid learned this, kept a local map of safe routes in his head. It was part of growing up and making sure you survived.

And let's not overlook the police force, still mostly Irish then. Funny how some groups take over certain jobs, areas of the economy or parts of government. They penetrate, gain control and see to it that their own get preferred treatment while keeping most everyone else away. If only blacks had been able to do it. Now when we want in, they throw "reverse discrimination" at us and conveniently forget about all the years in which other groups used their control to keep us out. One day I overheard this conversation about the way the game is played. There were these Irish guys talking about how one of them was about to take the police exam. Now get this—he was taking this test for another Irish guy, someone still in Ireland! Once he passed, the plan was for the Irishman to come over here and join the force. Can you imagine that? Believe me, I've got a whole lot more to say about the cops in Harlem, but not just yet.

Sure the Irish were tough on us and on me personally (remember, it was a band of Irish kids who stripped me naked and tossed me into the Hudson River, came close to killing me, in fact) but then I met some Irishmen who were totally beautiful people. Remember the doorman at the Ship Ahoy and his lavish treat. There was also Mr. Welch, the owner of the local grocery store where I would work for nearly three years. He became like a father, treated me with great kindness, taught me so many things. There's just no forgetting him. He was Irish, all right, and I was black, but it made absolutely no difference to either of us. It was a warm human relationship. Race, religion—no such differences got in the way.

All the time you hear how people in groups do real bad things that as individuals they'd never consider. That's why you'll hear me preaching against groups (black groups included), how we ought not to be encouraging group identity, group neighborhoods, group separatism. Just creates too many divisions, suspicions and hostilities. Certain people I realize benefit from these groupings or count on manipulating them. Now I know groups can be important—for support, for influence, for holding on to tradition. But I just think overall, they're trouble—they pull us apart, keep us ignorant, encourage idiotic ideas of superiority and inferiority. We've got to let go, mingle freely, break down the barriers, interact, intermarry, allow the true American individual to come forward.

"The Guineas are taking our jobs." You heard that a lot in Harlem as the Italians entered the area east of Fifth Avenue in large numbers, then came to control a number of neighborhoods. We didn't hate them, but we certainly resented the fact that we were losing out to yet another group of "Johnny-come-latelys" who were taking over jobs in construction, paving, the Sanitation Department, places where we had made some headway, where there were openings for blacks. How the hell is it that we who've been in this country so long, who've worked so hard, been treated so miserably, are shoved aside again and again by newcomers who immediately take on a superior air and begin treating us like shit? No wonder we're angry! Just when it seems we might move ahead a new bunch of immigrants pushes in and begins elbowing us out.

And we get swept aside because we're black and they're not. Besides, they work cheap and, I got to admit, are often better organized than we are. Just makes me sick how often this happens. Talk about the Koreans, the Chinese or the Cubans or the Vietnamese or Russian Jews or certain Hispanics; they're all doing it to us again. And now there's fewer of the usual entry jobs to go around. So what the hell are we doing letting all these people in and hearing their bullshit about how we're all lazy and they're the hard workers who deserve a chance? We deserve that break.

Anyway, the Italians were a real problem for us, especially the younger ones I met up with. From what I could see the older folks were hardworking, conscientious people who pretty much kept to themselves. But many of their kids were trouble. Roughnecks, they ruled their neighborhood, intimidating and extorting money from just about anybody. They ran the junior high school I would go to, shaking down everyone who wasn't Italian, taking our lunch and our lunch money, letting us know just how tough they were. It got to the point that my mother had to sew secret pockets into my pants so I could hide my lunch money and carfare. The pool on 120th Street was in Italian territory, which meant you'd better think twice before deciding to go there. Either they kept you away, wouldn't let you in at all, or they demanded money before "allowing" you to use the city pool.

Today most ethnic groups who arrived several generations back proudly speak of their early years in this country, tell you of their hardships and struggles, and about the discrimination they first faced. That's true; it's part of their story. But you don't hear the bad stuff—the thuggery, the attacks on others. I got to see it firsthand. Me, along with a lot of kids I knew, got our butts whipped—not just black kids; the Italians went after just about anyone.

You could enter the Italian neighborhood east of Fifth Avenue if you had "business" there. If you were there to shop, no problem. I went with my mother many times to the market located under the New York Central Railroad tracks along Park Avenue. Those same toughs who usually beat the daylights out of me allowed us to shop and then to leave without any interference. If you were visiting an Italian kid in the area, you could expect "safe passage." "I'm going to see Joey," was enough to get them to give way. Word might even be passed down the line, "He's going to see Joey"—to guarantee security here in "enemy" territory.

There's more regarding the Italians. You can't mention Harlem in this period and ignore the Italian mob and how it took over and organized criminal activities here. As young as I was, I knew about drive-by shootings and saw an icepick murder that happened right under my apartment window. Harlem, I came to understand, was also a battle zone.

4 | ON THE BLOCK

I lived in Harlem, we all took pride in Harlem, but really our world, what most of us knew best, was the block. That was the neighborhood where we all looked out for each other, the community we were loyal to. It wasn't paradise, for sure there were problems, but it was a hell of a nice place to grow up. I miss it, and today when I run into those who were around then, I hear the same talk about what's been lost.

Over the seven or eight years my mother and I were in Harlem we lived in four different apartments, each a little bit nicer than the one before it. We moved up but not very far. Our first place was on 114th Street between Fifth and Lenox Avenues. We then moved to 116th Street and stayed on that street, although at different addresses, until we left Harlem in 1944. Naturally no block was the same, but they were so much alike that I can give you a general picture of this scene.

These streets looked good, were clean, not at all crowded. (There weren't that many cars around, so the blocks while not empty certainly were not congested.) Each building, about five or six stories high, had fire escapes in the front which people made full use of, and backyards with their tall telephone poles, each carrying layers of clotheslines. Just about every building had its own live-in superintendent. He kept the backyards clear, swept the pavement in front of the building, put the garbage out, mopped the halls. Let me tell you, those buildings and blocks stayed clean. You'd have been amazed. When, for example, a peddler or vegetable man passed through leaving horse droppings on the street, they'd be gone in short order. You know why? The older people in the buildings, especially those born in the south, loved the stuff, ran out and snatched it up, used it as fertilizer for plants in their window boxes high above the street.

People knew one another and frequently relied on each other. Borrowing was constant—flour, sugar, milk, needles—if needed, you just asked. If there was a fire in the apartment, which happened because people used extension cords all over the place, neighbors would chip in to help the family get back on its feet. Later you'll hear about all the rent parties that went on so that people wouldn't be evicted. (Naturally not everyone could raise the rent money and when they couldn't they'd just disappear to escape eviction. I'd see a kid one day, and next day he'd be gone. We'd get word his family had picked up and left in the middle of the night. With friends helping them, they'd be tiptoeing around and off they'd go.)

I witnessed plenty of evictions, too. It was sad seeing all those belongings on the street. But nobody touched them. They would be out there on the curb for days. People realized the owners were looking to relocate and might be back. After a time, when it became clear they'd had no luck, folks did start helping themselves.

My mother needed and got help from the people on the block because she often was away working long hours, sometimes even over weekends. She depended on others like Mr. and Mrs. Williams, who owned a candy store downstairs, and Frank the barber, who worked the next door down. If I was playing outside I'd have to report to Mrs. Williams (no relation) about every hour. If Frank looked out of his shop and saw me getting into a fight or crossing the street without looking, he'd stop cutting hair and come out of the shop. "You're not supposed to do that," and you knew he meant it. So much did my mother come to rely on Mr. and Mrs. Williams and Frank that when I was about seven or eight she left me alone for an entire summer when she went to work for a family outside of the city. I know people will say, "A whole summer alone—you're kidding," but it's true. It wasn't "desertion," and it sure wasn't "child abuse." Mostly I played with my friends, stayed in the apartment, read lots of comic books and listened to radio programs like "The Shadow." I didn't hear from my mother directly all summer, although she would call Mrs. Williams every so often, who would then pass along her greeting. It may sound strange, but I had a great summer—didn't feel alone, didn't feel abandoned, knew that there were people looking out for me, that I was safe on the block.

Besides adults looking out for the youngsters, older kids on the block did too. On my street the Chamberlain brothers kind of ran things. Mostly they hung around in the poolroom, but if they saw any kids misbehaving they'd be out there telling them to knock it off. And you listened or else. Every so often when the soda truck came onto the block, the little kids would scamper up on back, grab some bottles and pass them to friends running alongside. If the Chamberlain boys saw this mischief they'd put a stop to it. (They didn't practice what they preached. When beer or whiskey trucks came around they'd find ways to snatch a few bottles for themselves. I imagine they just didn't want us starting in at too early an age.) If the Chamberlains noticed you leaving the block they'd ask where you were going and remind you to be careful. It felt good having these guys watching out for us. We looked up to them; they cared about us.

If Mrs. Williams or Frank caught me doing something wrong they'd tell me straight out, even deliver a slap or two, especially if my mother wasn't around. What they did was not at all unusual. You'd see it happen all the time—adults on the block not ignoring but getting involved when a youngster was up to no good—even escorting the kid back to his apartment. Neighborhood adults had that "right" back then. And parents thanked them for taking the time and for caring enough. And then, behind closed doors, probably handed out their own punishment. Those days are gone.

And because of it today's world is not the "orderly" one that I knew.

We might "defend" our block against "outsiders," chase them off, even grab their jackets from them, but we were not marauders, going outside our territory to steal or fight. I think that's the point of the following story. When I worked in the grocery store for Mr. Welch I made deliveries using a big iron wagon that I pulled along. One day passing along 117th Street I was approached by some of the Social Dukes, the gang that dominated that block. When I wouldn't surrender the wagon to them they beat me up, chased me away, and stole the groceries. I went straight to the Chamberlain brothers, hoping they'd back me up. They listened, but decided that I was old enough and should not have been caught off guard. They refused to get involved in a matter concerning stolen groceries on 117th Street. Wait till the Social Dukes show up on 116th Street, our block. That's when we'll take care of them.

With or without the Chamberlain brothers, I was not willing to let it go. I wanted revenge, and so I decided to take matters into my own hands. What I did was to gather bricks when I found them laying about the area and hauled them up to the roof. It took several weeks to collect enough. The Social Dukes I knew usually hung out at night under a lamppost on 117th Street playing craps. Bunched together, they made an inviting target. I suppose by now you've guessed my intentions. Once I had anywhere from twenty to twenty-five bricks hidden away it was time for action. Lucky for me the roofs of all the buildings were connected. That meant that I could scamper all the way around until I was on a rooftop on 117th Street overlooking the lamppost. First I constructed a "launching pad," tying together two boards to create a large flat surface on which I placed the load of bricks. No one knew of my plan. What might come of it I hadn't considered but I couldn't forget how the Social Dukes had taken advantage of me and had not paid for it.

One night about a month after the incident I struck. Carrying several bricks at a time I made my way back and forth across the rooftops, piling them up on my launch platform. The Social Dukes were there as usual. Once all the bricks were on the board I went into action. It was over in no time. I lifted the board and pushed as hard as I could, the bricks tumbling toward the street. Even before they crashed down I was off, dashing back toward 116th Street across the rooftops. During my retreat I heard some shouting from below but nothing more. I was too far away and too afraid to look down to see what had happened. I never found out about any damage I might have caused. I asked no one. To my mind I had my revenge. I was satisfied.

My block was typical in that it contained stores of all sorts from one end to the other, which made shopping convenient and street life lively. Also, deliverymen and salesmen were always showing up on the block (many of them whites making a living selling to this heavily black community). The milkman of course came around each day. Usually Irish, he would climb the stairs from floor to floor, dropping off bottles and collecting the used ones. It was hard work. During the summer the iceman made his regular rounds, along with a man, usually Italian, who sold flavored ices, mostly to us kids. From time to time an Italian knife sharpener came by looking for business. The insurance agent, usually Jewish, went door to door selling policies and collecting ten to fifteen cents each visit. (My mother, I know, took out a few policies. If you missed the agent, he'd pay the premium for you and collect the money at a later time. You usually could count on him for short-term loans as well.) There was also a white guy who came around selling pots and pans and offering magazine subscriptions as a bonus for buying.

Then too there was the man who went floor to floor selling cloth from swatch samples he carried, and also a clothing salesman, usually a black man (who came around mostly at night or on Saturday on a regular basis with goods he had somehow gotten working downtown in the garment district). Word traveled around the building (my mother would shout down the airshaft that he was there) and people would gather, often in our apartment, to check out his merchandise. He carried shirts, dresses and shoes, all new, and his prices were good. People bought from him in part because it was so convenient, and because we blacks were never comfortable shopping downtown.

Out on the street horse-drawn wagons would come by two or three times a week. One would be carrying fruit, another vegetables, then there'd be the fish man and sometimes a guy selling cut flowers. Occasionally a man leading a pony would come around to take pictures of the children. When we heard, "Here's the gypsies," we knew we'd see a woman in gypsy dress sitting alongside a table with cards on top. She'd be there to tell your future. Nearby another gypsy, usually a man, was busy selling a variety of goods.

Every so often an open truck would pull onto our street with a makeshift bandstand featuring a musician playing an old piano organ, one strumming a banjo and occasionally a clarinetist as well. Once the truck parked the guys would begin to play—popular songs, some down South tunes and often the music of Scott Joplin. If a crowd gathered they'd stay, play and pass around a cup for contributions. If no one turned up, off they'd go looking for a better location. Probably the last person to use a horse and wagon in the neighborhood was the junkman, either a black guy or an Italian, who picked up whatever might be worth something. Finally someone else on the block had something to sell to us every day, and his business was as steady as they come. On sale here were hopes, dreams, or at least a way to get us from day to day. I'll tell you more about the numbers business and its hold on us shortly.

I enjoyed my years in Harlem. It was a terrific place to be for a kid. I don't ever remember being bored. And it was safe, certainly when compared to today. Sure we got into fights and the older folks worried about our being on the fire escapes and the roofs—but we occupied ourselves with the games city kids had always played or just enjoyed the life of the streets.

There was for us no better time than summer. I'd be out for hours playing with my friends. We had a few pools in the area we could walk to, but for cooling off there was always the fire hydrants. When someone would turn them on there'd be this tremendous rush of cold water. Stick something in the pipe and the water would spray wildly in all directions. Not for long, though, because the cops would show up, shut the thing off and start cursing the "little black pickaninnies" who opened it. Even worse, they might slap a few of us around or haul us off to our mothers for additional punishment. Our relations with "New York's Finest" were not very good; open water hydrants were the least of our problems.

Who could resist filling up balloons with water and watching them head toward our targets and then burst? We tossed them all the time from rooftops, and if they hit nothing but the pavement, it was enough of a thrill watching them splatter. As we got a little older and started riding the elevated lines near us, we occasionally brought water balloons along on the trip and let them fly at various points along the way. I wasn't a goody-goody, but I thought that was going too far. My friends though couldn't wait to see them come crashing down.

Playing out on the street was great, but there was another world open to us, especially during the warmer months. We were almost as likely to be up on the roofs as down on the streets. We weren't alone up there—adults joined us, to grow plants, to sit around, or to sleep on a hot night—but we considered it to be our second playground. My mother's only warning was that I not get there by climbing up the fire escape, but that I use the inside staircase. She also wasn't crazy about my jumping from the roof of one building to the next one (the gap was usually no more than three feet), but all the kids, she knew, did it. How could I not?

The roof became our own private world, a getaway out of sight of most of the older folks. For example, we had our "clubhouse" up there, a small structure that we built with scrap wood and into which we dragged a mattress. Here we would hang out, talk and puff on our corncob pipes every so often. It was fun being there when it rained. The clubhouse, of course, leaked; still it was cozy. We were always constructing something on the roof—carts, scooters, wagons or pushboards, which we then raced around with on the block. We would also spend time watching the pigeon keeper, who cared for about 100 birds on the roof. Where he kept them became pretty smelly and dirty, but the fun was watching him rouse the pigeons and get them flying off the roof in group formation. We saw him use the pigeons to deliver messages to a friend who had his own flock somewhere else. But the pigeons weren't always safe up there. Big rats prowled the roof. Also people would come up to steal, and later eat the birds.

No matter what the time of the year movies were always in season. What a treat. It was not like today, some coming attractions, a feature movie, and you're out in just over two hours. Back then the movies meant an entire day. Early day care centers. There were plenty of theatres in my neighborhood, and even more if I wanted to go up to 125th Street. (The older guys liked the ones on 125th Street. They were darker, they said, good places to take girls.) Not far from me on 116th Street on Seventh Avenue were the RKO and Loew's movie theaters, but I usually ended up right around the corner on Eighth Avenue at the Morningside Theater.

Saturday was movie day, all of us lining up just before 10 o'clock in the morning, big Jitney soda bottles in our hands. For a 15 cents admission charge you'd get four serials, fifteen cartoons and three, yes, three feature films. Okay, these were not first-run movies, but who knew the difference? Bring on Zorro, Frankenstein, Eddie Robinson, George Raft, Jimmy Cagney, Our Gang, The Dead End Kids, Ken Maynard, Hoot Gibson or Buster Crabbe and we were happy. I usually bought two hot dogs while inside and, believe it or not, they let you leave to buy candy outside at the candy store.

It always was fun; so what if a rat ran across your feet? It usually was not until 6:00 in the evening that we left. A day well spent. On Saturday nights not long after I got out, my mother and

Mrs. Williams usually went in. They'd see two feature films after which the lights would go on and the audience would start playing Bingo. And on the way out everyone received pieces of glassware. During these years going to the movies was a big part of our lives.

There were things to do besides playing games or hanging out with the guys on the roof. Heading over to the candy store and looking over the goodies was serious business. Today a penny may be a nuisance, but back then you could buy things with it—three gum-sticks, four candy sticks, a half dozen jawbreakers, a strip of paper with candy attached to it, or, if you could get away with it, two cigarettes. With a quarter to spend you were rich. Parents gave their kids money but there were other ways to put change in our pockets. Guys running the illegal booze business always needed bottles, so we started collecting them. They'd pay us for bringing them in. Kids also made money by putting up clotheslines in backyards. What a sight, all those lines strung up behind the buildings, attached to the telephone poles. (Just looking at the clothes flapping in the air told you a lot about a family.) To get a clothesline up you had to hire a kid to go up and knock a hook in. We charged according to how high on the pole we climbed.

There were times we just hung around, watching coal deliveries being made or looking on as painters or carpenters worked along the block. It was on just such a typical day that we were treated to this incredible sight. Well actually it was Halloween, but nothing out of the ordinary had happened until daylight began to fade. Then word spread that this Jamaican kid, the son of the bicycle repairman on the block, had spotted a weird object sweep across the sky at rooftop level. So sure was he that he had seen something that people began gathering and looking up. Several minutes passed. The sky was growing dimmer. Nothing. But what was that?

People said it looked like a skeleton whipping by, passing across the street above the rooftop. Seemed like something really was going on up there. Word spread and more people gathered. Then it happened again in the same general area. This time it looked like a body dashing across the sky. Many swore they saw it. Out in the street you wouldn't believe the number of people about straining to see what was going on. As the block filled up several cops arrived to investigate this public "disturbance." Once again another strange and eerie sight. Most people thought it looked like a witch's hat. There was—I saw it—real concern on the faces of many standing there. Someone, people said, should go up to the roof for a closer look. There were no volunteers. "Let the cops do it," people shouted—"Why don't you go up there and check it out? It's your job, you're police officers." But the police stayed put. They were, they said, waiting for reinforcements. They were also laughing a lot among themselves. The crowd now saw yet another object pass by overhead. Being dark, though, no one was quite sure what it was. I had never before seen so many people truly confused, trying to make sense of what was happening. Then it ended. In the dark no one could see much of anything anymore. The crowd broke up and the cops, still chuckling to themselves, left.

Had it ended there legends might have started, probably about extraterrestrial creatures. But the entire plot was exposed the following day. The conspirators, it turned out, were the Jamaican and his two sons. They had gone to the roof and rigged up a tight wire crossing the street. Attached to the wire were the various objects which, by turning a crank, they sent speeding between the two rooftops. It was an ingenious plan, well executed. But I suppose there are people who to this day are still not so sure exactly what was going on that one memorable Halloween night.

A lot of the kids used to enjoy hanging out and watching what the older guys were up to. When we could, we stood around just outside the poolroom on the block (practically every street had one), the usual gathering place for whichever gang ran that particular street. We knew the reputation of poolhalls. Certainly my mother warned me about hanging around there although it wasn't until I grew up some that I got a better idea of what worried her.

Pool, I came to realize, wasn't the only action going on there, no sir. Poolrooms were hangouts for your low level hoodlums. There'd be plenty of drinking going on (usually home made whiskey sipped from coke bottles. Coke bottles were then everyone's favorite container. All sorts of liquids went into these bottles—from the small amounts of kerosene that people could afford to buy to formula fed to infants). Besides the boozing you'd have your crap games and almost non-stop card playing. Poolrooms were also the main places to "fence" stolen goods and where you'd go to "order" items you wanted stolen. No wonder the cops made it their business to drop in regularly.

The older guys weren't thrilled by our presence, but I think they enjoyed the fact that we looked up to them, saw them as natural leaders. In fact some of the young men on the block not only didn't shoo us away, but took it upon themselves to look out for us, talk to us, guide us, sort of like big brothers. I remember there were two such guys who I really admired. One of them was Kessel Johnson. Kessel you would always find sitting out on the stoop of his building early most every morning, reading and studying. Living in a crowded apartment he had no privacy, no room to do his schoolwork in quiet. So the stoop became his desk, his office and his study. I'd look out my window early in the morning and there would be Kessel. The milkman would soon be leaving a bottle of milk with him, (he loved chocolate milk) and Kessel would then peel an orange while he sat there. He was so pleasant, always smiling. We kids gathered around and he'd tell us stuff and read to us. What a knack he had for storytelling, taking familiar tales and embellishing them so that we scarcely recognized the original. Kessel was going to college, and everyone on the block respected him for it. Even the tough guys who hung around the poolroom—they never bothered him.

No one talked about role models back then, but Kessel certainly was one; we all wanted to be like him.

Then there was McGee. McGee was "the body," as physically imposing as one could be, looked just like a football player. He couldn't have been more friendly to us. He would talk with us, play stickball, stoopball, share a soda with us, sometimes even go along with us to our all-day movie marathons on Saturdays. Can you imagine that—a man like McGee hanging out with us kids! We were thrilled. When I came onto the block McGee already had his reputation: just how he'd earned it I never found out. But no one messed with McGee. He would, everyone knew, never back down. Even the cops stayed clear; certainly the guys at the poolroom never showed him any trouble. What could be better for us?. He was our protector. What a feeling it was to be out on the street with him. With him there no one ever made any cracks. McGee worked much of the time and most every summer he was away at this job he had, teaching swimming at a camp upstate. Then one summer McGee didn't come back.

Eventually word came back to the block. McGee's body had been found in the camp lake. The official story had it that somehow he had drowned. Very few of us believed it. He couldn't drown, not McGee. He was a swimming instructor; the story didn't make sense. Most people in the neighborhood saw a darker picture, believed there was foul play. Talk had it that the Klan was active in the part of New York State where McGee spent the summer. Everyone knew McGee would never back down, that no one could push him around. It had to be, they said, that he had stood up to those Klan fellows and had been killed for it. McGee, our great "protector," would not be there for us anymore.

Life on the block was not violent, but every so often there'd be trouble. Usually it started at the J and J Bar & Grill, a seedy joint whose customers included habitual drunks, low level hoodlums, troublemakers, mostly men who had lost hope. Drinking went on day and night there (along with the numbers and the crap games) and where there's so much booze, trouble often followed. First, an argument would begin leading to a challenge, then a fight.

Usually the battle ended up on the sidewalk. Once out there it was serious—no question. I'm talking razors, sometimes icepicks, and even to the death. Naturally a crowd gathered but even if someone thought to, no one interfered. It was far too dangerous. The guys were raging and they were drunk—a lethal combination. Anyone might become a target for their razors. The cops, attracted by the large crowd on the street, would show up but usually did not interfere. They'd move the crowd back out of harm's way and that was it. Meanwhile the two guys went at each other, often too drunk to know exactly what they were doing. There'd be blood and real nasty wounds but they would keep at it—until one or the other or both collapsed onto the pavement, badly wounded, sometimes dead. Sure was exciting—if you were a spectator. My mother, however, always warned me about crossing the street to join the crowd. So I watched from a stoop on the opposite side. I didn't always get to see every blow but I saw enough.

There were other struggles taking place, some almost a daily fact of life. There was a pecking order on the block among the kids my age. You knew where you stood. A few got to boss the rest around; some tried to claim that right and others were the ones picked on most of the time. When kids joined gangs it was usually because they protected them from all this in-fighting. If you weren't part of one, and I wasn't, you became vulnerable, a target, forced time and again to prove yourself, establish your right to be left alone. I was no outcast, but then I wasn't much of a joiner either. I could be happy by myself; I didn't think I needed anyone. At times it cost me. Had I not been a tall kid able to box and wrestle, I probably would have been defending myself almost every day. As it was I fought plenty.

Mostly it would start with a taunt, a tease. "Sissy, fairy, chicken," or something said about your mother or that he'd screwed your sister (didn't even matter that you had no sister. It was an insult; you even had to defend your pretend "sister's" honor.) "Fancypants" was the term usually tossed at me, one that was supposed to set me to fighting. Why "Fancypants"? Because my mother made sure I dressed up when we went to church on Sunday or when we headed downtown. Once you got a name there's little you can do. You're labeled. It's up to you to prove that dressing up doesn't make you a pushover. "Fancypants" would have to show he could fight.

The taunt made, the challenge delivered, the two of you now approached each other. That was the signal for the other kids to gather around. Everyone loved a fight—so long as it involved someone else. I was never eager to fight, but bystanders often brought it on, pushing the two of you together. This contact made, it become all but impossible to back down.

Fights might begin as a boxing match but in little time they degenerated into no-holds-barred brawls. You couldn't stop: spectators wouldn't allow it. Surrounding the two of you they'd see to it that the fight continued, even if it meant pushing you back into the center to face your opponent. Your chances improved if you could avoid being hit too hard or too often—or squarely on the nose. Unless you've been hit there you've no idea what a shock it is, how it takes the fight out of you. If, on the other hand, you were on target and hit your opponent on the nose, then your chances improved considerably. Stunned and bloody, he might just call it quits. Take my advice—don't start anything until you've learned to take a shot in the nose. Then you can call yourself a fighter.

To know me back then, in fact to know me today is to appreciate the fact that I don't need too many people. I'm quite comfortable, actually prefer just being alone, reading a lot, getting lost in thoughts, occasionally in dreams. With my mother away so often I had to learn to be alone and on my own much of the time. Doing things by myself, taking care of myself—that became second nature to me. Alone in the apartment I read comic books and magazines, listened to the soap operas and tuned in to Gabriel

Heatter and Walter Winchell, my mother's favorite news commentators.

I also became a walker in the city. There were times, plenty of them in fact, when my curiosity and sense of adventure took me out of the neighborhood. I wanted to see more, and became a sightseer, a tourist in my own town. Mostly I went alone. Everything interested me; everything still does—the sounds, the smells, the people, the buildings, the shops. I wanted to see them all. I just might have because I covered miles and miles of Manhattan. Walking from where I lived on 116th Street down to Greenwich Village (about five miles) for me was a typical stroll. No shortcuts either. I preferred to cruise the side streets, walk along one avenue and then another—stopping, looking about, listening, open to everything. That was my thing. My interests were never narrow. I loved sticking my nose everywhere, understanding a little bit about a whole lot of things. Off I headed to Radio City, went up the Empire State Building (even though the elevator ride up and the view from the observation tower made me queasy), strolled about Riverside Park, took in the East River, haunted the Hayden Planetarium and enjoyed wandering about the Cloisters and along the Grand Concourse in the Bronx. It was enough for me just to sit and watch the cars passing over the George Washington Bridge. I got to know Manhattan real well, felt comfortable all around town.

I loved riding the subways, whizzing through the tunnels and leaving Manhattan for the Bronx, Brooklyn, and Queens. To be standing at the window of the front car was a thrill as the train rushed ahead into the darkness, me pretending to be the motorman, straining to see what might be out there beyond the beams of light. Once that train surfaced and moved along the elevated tracks what a treat to look out over the different neighborhoods below. I'd get off at the last stop, then board a train heading back the other way. Maybe it was because I was alone but I felt at one with the city as it passed beneath me, block by block. Being far from home never worried me. I felt safe.

I was a wanderer. Even a city as large as New York couldn't hold me. I don't remember how it came about. It might, I think, have been that McGee once did something like this. That would have been enough to recommend it. Or maybe I had read somewhere about hobos. Anyway, one day I decided to leave town, hop a freight train and go wherever it went. I was probably around ten years old at the time, mature enough, I reckoned, to travel the rails in search of adventure. It seemed easy enough at first. I had no trouble locating the train tracks along the west side of Manhattan, finding an open boxcar and getting on board. Now I was ready for adventure.

Trouble was I couldn't find much of interest. Alone in this huge, mostly dark boxcar wasn't my idea of a good time. The train moved slowly and stopped a lot. I did little more than stand near the opening, looking out, not seeing much of anything that I can remember. I slept on the train and ate food I had brought along. My "ride" took me as far as Philadelphia. It's there that some old guy, I have no idea who he was, spotted me and shouted what probably were words of wisdom. "Get your ass on home." I took his advice. I hopped another train heading (I hoped) back where I had come from. I got lucky. Sure enough I landed in New York City and made my way back home. My sudden disappearance had lasted between two and three days. Over and over I had rehearsed how to explain this to my mother. (I hadn't left her a note and had certainly not called.) I just couldn't come up with anything. So I took the easy way out; I told her the truth. No matter; she beat me, but good. Still, I had some story (no reason to stick to the truth here) to tell the guys. Few could top it.

5 | THE SERIOUS BUSINESS OF MAKING A LIVING

I might spend days wandering about, but all around me the much more serious business of life was going on—people out there struggling to make a living, support a family, just survive. For us blacks this had never been easy. When had we ever been allowed to compete for decent jobs or encouraged to run businesses, or been boosted up the economic ladder? No, the deck had been stacked against us a long time ago, the raw deal was nothing new. We didn't need a depression to slap us down, to bring us to our knees. Many of us had never had the chance to get up off the floor.

Living on the edge, hustling to stay above water—we'd long been forced to play that game. Harlem did have its upscale places, its Sugar Hill, Striver's Row, and brownstones where successful black entertainers, businessmen and professionals lived. Good thing, too, for it showed the rest of us that there was a way to beat the odds and have a shot at some of the better things in life. And plenty of people who lived around us believed they might get there. In Brooklyn I hadn't seen that; there desperation blocked out hope. But in that lower section of Harlem where my mother and I lived, many hard-working folks thought they still might make it. Certainly my mother was a believer, a striver, with faith that moving on up was just a matter of motivation and momentum.

You just needed to keep working at it. That idea she never let go of.

To make a living in New York City blacks had always to scramble, put up with a lot of rejection, take what little they could get and then work like hell. I wasn't much more than a kid then, but I could see what was happening, overheard people talking, knew what they were going through. To even get the crumbs, most of us had first to appear deserving, to behave properly, to show the right look, be polite, humble and submissive, to "Yes, sir" and "Yes, ma'am" every white person to death. Even then blacks were hardly considered for the better jobs in New York City. Today they talk about glass ceilings; back then we never got above the manhole covers. Even with jobs we were kept out of sight. Mailroom, messenger boy, elevator operator, shipping department—that was the extent of our climb up the corporate ladder. In the Jewish-controlled sections of the garment center we did get some chances though, got jobs as sewers, cutters and machine operators. (When Jewish bosses and foremen asked us, we did recommend other blacks for jobs.) While other working class groups found their niche in the city's economy—the Italians in construction, the Irish in transportation, on the docks and in the police department and the Jews in the garment center—we didn't. Ethnic connections worked for them, but we've never gotten much chance to play that game. Still we kept at it, found ways to get by, to feed and hold our families together.

If you had a steady job, and it didn't much matter what kind, you were a somebody. We looked up to those folks, knew what it took. We had our own job ladder, though compared to whites it had far fewer rungs on it. Mostly we were in service jobs. To be a maid or a butler for a well-to-do family counted for something. Working as a doorman at a good downtown hotel was a big deal; nothing wrong with waiter or bellhop jobs either. A position in the mailroom or as a messenger was not small potatoes. Even operating a freight elevator had its advantages, gave you a shot at some side cash. "What building you at, man?" was a question

I heard lots of times. If it happened to be an active building with lots of traffic you stood a chance to make extra money when manufacturers and truckers needed goods out quickly. It was the elevator man who often decided whose shipments moved, and in what order. That was worth something. (So were those goods that somehow "fell" off the racks and into his hands.) Everyone I knew envied the railroad porter, especially the Pullman car porter, also the skycap out at the airport or the stevedore on the docks—all real solid positions. They paid the kind of money folks could live on. For us, government jobs were hard to come by. Those lucky enough to get them, whether in the post office, sanitation department or sometimes in the schools—they were the privileged ones.

Service jobs were tough. The hours were long, with schedules set to meet the needs and convenience of others. Such jobs might force you to be away from home for long periods of time. Pullman porters could be off on a run for up to a week or two. Maids and butlers working downtown or in Westchester or out on Long Island could be gone all week, back home only on certain weekends. Doormen, bellhops and waiters usually worked late into the night. Providing services meant catering to people, staying pleasant and cooperative at all times. As I've said, white people expected us to behave that way; besides, wasn't it part of our simple, dependent nature? We knew what was expected of us and most understood the need to play the game. It brought bigger tips and more job security. It meant also that the families for whom we worked would offer us food, used clothes, discarded furniture to take home.

"Show 'em your teeth and put your hand in his pocket." Many of our people understood the advantages of a smile. You needed to "charm the shit out of them." Blacks have always been great actors; we've had lots of practice. Anyway to offend was dangerous. Surly blacks created problems; they would not be kept on for long. My mother and her friends would talk about making sure when leaving a job not to antagonize anyone. We blacks had this part all figured out; "explanations" came easily. You'd be amazed at how many of us got word of a close relative who had taken sick. What choice did we have but to head down south to be with them?

Getting started was tough and once you got going the pressures were enormous, still blacks operated all kinds of businesses in Harlem. There were ways, even without black banks, to get start-up cash. Numbers runners and numbers bankers lent money out, so did certain black bar owners. A credit club Marcus Garvey had set up years before still operated, loaning money to members. A number of local churches, the Abyssinian Baptist Church for one, provided money to congregants, and I recall my mother telling me that when she belonged to the local Episcopal church, the minister there would accompany a member to the bank and support an application for a loan. All over Harlem you could find blacks in real estate, owners of brownstones and other buildings, living in one of the apartments while renting out the others.

Some businesses naturally belonged to blacks, like funeral parlors, always a part of any black neighborhood. The beauty parlors and barber shops we went to also were black owned. Here we felt most comfortable, were treated properly. White haircutters generally were not interested in our business, couldn't cut black hair, some of them said. (You still hear this. Just recently my son and I went into an Italian barber shop and got the same story—he couldn't cut "our" hair.)

All around Harlem were black carpenters, electricians, plumbers and painters. Because whites wouldn't always come when called and when they did, charged a lot, these black workers kept busy. Black owned bicycle repair shops and auto mechanics were easy to find. They'd be repairing cars right out on the street.

There were plenty of bars around in those days, some real swell places. Many were neighborhood centers where a particular crowd enjoyed hanging out. Some of those black owned bars attracted a mix of people, black and white—professionals, pimps, gangsters, strivers, hustlers of all kinds. Like a club, it was a place where one belonged (bars would compete against one another in sports) and came back to even after you left the neighborhood. Blacks generally didn't have the cash to open up such bars, and no bank would lend them the money. Jewish money people sometimes did though. The go-betweens here were usually the insurance agents, mostly Jewish, who went as I mentioned door to door in Harlem selling policies and collecting monthly premiums. Let me say here that I'm a great admirer of the Jews. I've read their history and know how they've suffered. Blacks and Jews, our two peoples have been through hell—we're both survivors of Holocausts, both of us became tough and shrewd—just figuring out a way to get past all the shit we've faced. For a long time in America we felt comfortable working together, understood that despite differences we were, in many ways, in the same boat. The Jews weren't angels but they did reach out to us, when very few others did.

I don't believe there is any other group in America, in fact I challenge anyone to name one, which over the years has been as helpful, as aware of our condition. Sure they needed us, often made money off us (all the pawnshops in Harlem were Jewish owned and there were plenty of Jewish landlords) and didn't necessarily like us, but they did reach out, offer assistance and occasionally friendship. In Harlem often it was only Jewish lawyers who would take our cases. No one else would touch them. It was Jewish-owned garment companies that employed blacks in my early days. Jews, as I said, lent money to blacks to open businesses. (And my mother frequently borrowed money from the many Jewish employers she had.) Jewish families hired us to work in their homes. (My mother considered them nice but demanding. They'd want you out there doing the windows, no matter what floor of the building they lived on!) Often it was only in Jewish neighborhoods where we stood the slightest chance of buying a home or renting an apartment. (Blockbusting realtors often "introduced" blacks into Jewish areas, knowing there'd likely be some "acceptance.") Jews as Communists and Socialists worked for the cause of black workers and as Liberals certainly were up front in the fight for civil rights. Jewish philanthropy supported black education. I can't read their minds. I don't know exactly why they did it. But who else was making that kind of effort?

Having said all this I can't tell you how troubled I am by what seems to have happened to black-Jewish relations. I've heard some of the reasons. I know blacks weren't happy playing second fiddle, and maybe they were told too often what was expected of them. Maybe we were too close for too long and ignored some of the strains that developed over the years. To many blacks the Jews were just another group of pushy, insensitive immigrants who had jumped over them, who ignored the fact that blacks were Americans who had arrived back at the very beginning of America. Certainly some big-mouthed blacks saw they could get mileage and plenty of publicity out of picking on the Jews, making them into demons. That's always been an attention getter. In America anti-Semitism always had its place. Say nasty things about the Jews and you can join the crowd. It just might get you accepted. Besides, the Jews are in a way an easy target—there's just not that many of them.

The Jews are not blameless. They've made it in America and along the way absorbed some of the racist bullshit of the culture. I mean the Jews once controlled much of Hollywood. Sure, they didn't invent the black stereotypes, but how much did they do to challenge or soften them? Uh-huh,—they kept right on presenting that crap to the public. And then after lots of them made it, some prominent Jews went conservative, began voting Republican even when Republicans played the race card again and again. And then there's that quota thing that really gets my goat. I understand Jewish sensitivities here. I know quotas of Jews were used in colleges and in the marketplace to limit their numbers. To limit their numbers, not exclude them! We need a little affirmative action just to get us in the doors, doors that for us have usually been shut tight! Dammit, it's not the same thing, and Jews should understand that. And don't give me that merit stuff. A lot of it (not all) is bullshit, just another excuse for favoritism. Tell me now how many people you know have their jobs just because of their smarts!

Blacks and Jews had better work out their differences or just accept them and get back together again. If these two groups stay apart, forget about moving America in the right direction. We got the numbers, we got the votes, and we have right and justice on our side. With Jewish money, smarts and influence, imagine what could be done. This worries many of those in power. Black-Jewish tensions suit them just fine, draws attention away from their own power games. They'll even "accept" additional Jews into the ruling circles if it helps undermine black-Jewish coalitions.

There were jobs for blacks in Harlem, but there should have been more. Take the situation along 125th Street. Here on our main commercial street, in our neighborhood, blacks could not rent space for businesses or get jobs in German, Irish or Jewish owned stores. Even when they shopped here blacks were made to feel uncomfortable. So most of us preferred taking our business elsewhere. Thank God for Adam Clayton Powell because he challenged all this, held rallies along 125th Street demanding that blacks get jobs in those stores. Local church people and political organizations also demonstrated, marching in single file up and down 125th Street, carrying placards. I remember the black newspapers gave it plenty of coverage. Up to that time who thought blacks would risk standing up like that? Powell showed us that we could raise our voices, let out our anger. No wonder Harlem loved him. Of course the white community saw it differently and had little patience with a black man who challenged things and was outspoken and aggressive. He had a big mouth, they said. He was slick, he was smooth, he was causing problems, he was trouble. You bet he was.

There were other businesses, sometimes black owned, that

you couldn't miss in Harlem. The local pawn shop was one, owned not by blacks but by Jews. It was a business most of us welcomed (except when you didn't get the money you had hoped to for an item—"That Jew bastard took me again.") They were all over Harlem, actually they were all around New York. For some, the pawn shop became their department store, especially those uncomfortable shopping in downtown stores or along 125th Street. It was a "convenience store," too, a place to get quick money, especially for thieves looking to cash in some of their loot there. Same with the cops. When they stole goods or took them from us, off to the pawnshop they'd go—no questions asked.

To stock up on booze we might skip the local liquor store and check out the illegal stills, usually operating in a nearby apartment building basement. Superintendents earned extra money by putting aside space, providing "cover" for producers. It wasn't much of a secret. You could smell the stuff from way off. Making "white lightning" was something we had long known how to do down South. I was no "hooch," drinker but people I knew liked it, said it was decent stuff and real cheap.

In Harlem there was no other business like it. No, we didn't have horse parlors like the Irish, Polish and Italian neighborhoods did but we sure had the numbers. Just about everyone I knew played. That meant jobs, lots of them, just keeping the system going day to day. It was not legal, still it ran wide open, was obvious to everyone. Hardly a conversation went by without someone mentioning it. "Hey, man, did you find out the number today? I didn't hear it." Harlem people read the papers each day, stayed up on the news, but first we looked for the numbers, (although they usually were posted at the newsstands). Without the numbers some people would have had trouble making it from day to day. Watching for "signs," interpreting dreams (dream books printed up by local blacks explained that certain dreams meant particular numbers), deciding which of your lucky numbers (everyone had them) to play, waiting for the number of the day to come out and then starting all over again—there was plenty to do. Mostly, you expected to lose, but there were winners. Plenty of people around you "hit" (or better yet had a "big hit" or a "big bang.")

Not everyone welcomed the numbers. Some black preachers condemned it as gambling-a waste of money. What they left out is that they didn't like the competition. Money for the numbers meant less for the preacher. But some "good" people agreed with them and kept away. Most folks, however, found nothing wrong and played day after day, week after week, hoping a hit might change their lives for the better. We kids didn't play; it was just for the adults, though many a time we were told to look out for the runner so the grownups could get their numbers in. Blacks ran the action here, but whites could also get in on it. Black porters and elevator operators working downtown, for example, would handle their business. Black maids sometimes played the numbers for the lady of the house. This was her thrill—gambling, doing something naughty.

The system depended on numbers runners out there on the streets recruiting customers and handling their action. Some worked their territory by foot; those you'd see walking about during the day. Others with larger areas and bigger lists got around by car. Usually they respected each other's turf. Customers, however, might switch runners either because they felt they were being cheated or had decided the guy simply wasn't bringing them any luck.

In Harlem we didn't look down on numbers runners. We saw it as a way for a guy to get started, a chance to show off his energy, enterprise and to make it up the ladder. A successful numbers runner could make a decent living, be an excellent family man, even a community leader. These guys (though there were a few women in it, too) had better be trustworthy. To run off with a customer's money meant disgrace. They had also to be accommodating, giving credit or, if you weren't around, holding on to your money. Smart too, able to conceal customers' names with codes and memorize large sets of numbers instead of using policy slips which the cops were always looking for. Your numbers runners could tell you your number (three-digits) the next day, and those played by dozens of others. Dummies they weren't. Even so you'd try crossing them up—"I had 505, I hit." "Yeah, you played it Monday. Tuesday is when it came up." "How about paying off on the weekly number?" "No way, man. You didn't play it with me, so I didn't put it down!" Sure you could try, but outwit them—no sir.

Backing the runners were bankers who financed the operation and paid off the winners. (Some runners tried bankrolling their own operations but this was real risky. If they got hit hard and couldn't pay off, they were out of business and probably on the run.) Bankers stayed behind the scenes but you knew they were there, especially when newspapers reported cops busting up a bank. Even so, they'd be right back in business. Bankers kept runners in line and stayed close to the action, moving some of it around to other banks if a certain number was getting heavy play. (Sometimes runners were ordered not to accept any more money on a number or, if a particularly popular number did win, payoffs got shaved. Blacks worked out the technique of "laying off," i.e., spreading the risk around, a practice the Italian mob later picked up.)

Because numbers were big business, and completely illegal, trouble followed. What on the surface seemed like a smooth operation was more of a battleground, complete with corruption and political pressures and backed up by violence. Because blacks were involved and what's more were making good money off the system, the situation became, as it always seemed to, attractive to certain whites. Now don't let me get too far off the track, and I'm not forgetting we're talking of an illegal business here, but over the years the same sort of shit always seemed to happen to us. Read the history books, or at least those that have bothered to uncover certain facts, and you'll understand what I'm talking about. In place after place blacks managed, after hard work, to gain a foothold, set up businesses, get themselves established in the community. Whites took notice and didn't like what they saw. "The goddam niggers are making too much money. We gotta put a stop to this." Next thing you know they're concocting some reason or maybe not even bothering to explain why they're busting into the black section of town, burning down the place, destroying shops and scaring the shit out of everyone. End result: much of the area is ruined, black stores are out of business, and the niggers are put back in their place. Check out this slice of American history particularly look up Tulsa Oklahoma in 1921—I'm not bullshitting you; it's true—you just gotta look closely to find it.

The point being the numbers business in Harlem became "too good" for blacks, too rich for their blood! They had to go. During my years there the mob moved in and took over much of the action. Not by themselves; they found partners and collaborators. Both the politicians and the police joined hands with the Mafia to pluck the golden goose that was the numbers racket in Harlem. After the smoke cleared (some of it gunsmoke, some from arson fires) they squeezed us out, put us in our place, forced blacks to surrender much of the profits from the numbers. "Blacks just aren't enterprising." How many times have you heard that? How long will white folks continue to get away with this self-serving crap?

6 | HARD AT WORK

I sure wasn't your feckless, lazy Negro. I was a worker from early on. I enjoyed working, always have. You can't imagine all the jobs, part and full-time, I've had over the years. It started, I guess, when I was nine or ten when I became a businessman, an independent shoeshine boy. Before hitting the streets I did research, hanging around the shoemaker on my block, watching him handle different shoe dyes. I learned how to put on paste wax and then add water. Moving that cloth, knowing when and how to use pressure, applying different dressings around the shoe—that made all the difference. From me you got yourself one hell of a good shine.

Then it was time to build myself a shoebox, no big deal. We kids were always constructing something, always whittling away with our pocket knives. So a small crate became a shoebox, and on top I put a shoestand made of wood. When that didn't work well, I invested some money and bought myself a regular shoehorse. Now I needed a way of getting around. The solution—a scooter, again something we kids were used to making. A wooden crate, some two by fours, the wheels off a pair of roller skates, a little assembly, and there it was.

Back then shoeshines were real big. Someone was always around to shine 'em up—at barber shops, near newsstands and hotels, at separate shoeshine parlors, or from kids with shoeboxes wandering about. People liked getting shines; it made them feel good, feel important, especially with someone bending down working over their shoes. Whites especially liked getting shines from black folks, probably saw it as the proper relationship between the two races, blacks working away happily at the feet of white people—smiling, shining up them shoes, accepting a tip and sometimes a pat on the head. Those blacks who then brushed off the clothes and made sure to say, "Yessir" did even better, enjoyed repeat business.

Most shoeshine boys liked to head downtown to the hotel and entertainment districts to catch the well heeled customers. I figured there'd be plenty of business right in my own backyard, in Harlem. Well off or poor, most folks here tried to look good, to dress up, and stay sharp. Certainly our "hustlers" did, those slick dudes surviving off their wits, their tricks, their looks or whatever else they used to make out, usually at the expense of other working class stiffs. Whether a gambler, a pimp, a booze or numbers runner, hood, crap game organizer or wannabe businessman, this guy was wanting to be lookin' good all the time and worked hard at it. Naturally that meant wearing high-priced shoes—Whitehouse and Harding or London at $40 a pair—shined to perfection. I knew lots of these guys and tried to be around, shoeshine box ready, wherever they might be.

I got to be known, could count on plenty of customers. Usually it was five cents a shine and on top of that a five-cent tip, though some guys tipped much higher. Where other kids pulled in maybe a dollar whenever they went out, I'd make four to five. Working after school and on weekends I could earn some real good money.

I became a hustler myself, hanging around the bars, ginmills, hotels and crap games, and dashing over when I heard—"Hey, Earl, come over here." "Earl, how about a shine?"—"Shine 'em up, kid." Eventually I had my own customers including some of the big-time and little-known hustlers of the area. I was not shy. I got to know their names—"You're looking sharp today, Mr. Edwards," "Mr. Taylor, a shoeshine and you'll feel just perfect." I learned the come-ons that worked—"Did you miss your shine today, sir?"—"You're wearing beautiful shoes, they should look even better," or "What a great suit." Some liked me well enough to take a shine even if they had just gotten one elsewhere. On rainy days business was especially brisk once it stopped. When it snowed, out came the galoshes. You might just as well go home.

Business, I figured, would be real good around the Theresa Hotel on 125th Street. But the doorman there kept chasing me away. Could have been a shoeshine man inside whose territory he was protecting. Things changed, though, once I got to know this guy. He let me set up outside, and sometimes looked the other way when I snuck into the hotel itself. Once inside, customers were not hard to come by. I was a pleasant kid and, if anyone bothered to look, I gave a great shine.

Nights could be lively at the Theresa, but this one time sticks in my mind. Joe Louis was staying at the hotel then, about to defend his heavyweight championship. If he won, and we knew he would, Harlem would celebrate that night and probably for days after. It had happened before. At such a time and with the kind of people who came up to Harlem for a Louis fight, there would, I knew, be lots of calls for "Shine 'em up." All went according to plan. Louis won the fight and returned to the hotel. The place was jumping packed with all sorts of sharp-looking, shady types. (Everyone was relaxed and had their jackets open. I spotted many a gun that night.)

I got into the hotel and began working my way from floor to floor, doing a lively business. I began doubling as a messenger boy with guys asking me to get word to rooms located on other floors. People were all about the halls, celebrating everywhere. And then it happened. There he was, Joe Louis himself, looking all fresh and fashionable, standing outside one of the rooms. He spots me waiting with my shoeshine box and motions for a shine. Joe Louis wants me to give him a shine! I rush over and in no time I'm all set up, taking care of Joe, hero of Harlem, Heavyweight Champion of the World. I won't tell you that we talked and became buddies. That didn't happen. He was busy at the time speaking to so many people who were coming up to congratulate him. But the point is, he asked me for a shine, paid for it himself, handed me a tip. Ten dollars—can you believe it? Now, that's a champ for you.

Joe, I found out, had other conquests in mind that night. Now some people may challenge me and say it never happened or that I didn't understand what he said. Maybe so, but I did hear him and heard others talking about it. He wanted, he said, "all the Rockettes," and I think I knew even then what he meant. The guy was out to prove he had what it takes, that he was King of the World entitled to anything he wanted. Around the hotel people were buzzing about Joe and the Rockettes. He "was going to go through a half dozen tonight," someone said. "How is he going to last?" others wondered. Okay. I can't be sure it was the Rockettes; but I did see some fancy looking white chicks heading to his suite. Joe Louis certainly had his hands full that night in the Hotel Theresa.

I roamed the neighborhoods, heading off to wherever I thought I could sell me some shines. Often that meant showing up at rent parties or working the buildings where they were going on. These parties brought in plenty of people, many moving around from one to another. In between they were sometimes willing to have me "Shine 'em up." Other times I headed over to 126th Street, one block north of the Apollo Theater, where the odds were a big crap game would be going on outside the Apollo's backstage door. Now crap games went on all over Harlem, but none of them stacked up with this one. It was, people said, probably the biggest game in the city. Musicians, entertainers, Pullman car porters, blacks and whites, sometimes as many as fifty of them got together for some real hot action. Guys came into this game with pockets stuffed with cash, flashing amounts that even today would knock your socks off. It was an organized game, this one fellow controlling things, supplying honest dice and making sure all the money was down. Not an easy job. The Apollo crowd was noisy and excitable, players cursing up and down, wary of cheaters and loaded dice. Many packed pistols. If not guns they were almost certain to have razors. And they'd be using them if they spotted or caught a cheater, someone who'd slipped loaded dice into the game. Such slashings happened regularly. It was a real tough scene, and I saw some ugly stuff, but I kept coming back—business here always was real good. Most of the regulars knew me, liked my spunk, saw me as a hustler like most of them. (Some of the older shoeshine guys were there, too, and resented me for cutting into their business.) I learned never to bother people who were losing. Winners, on the other hand, were on a high, were in another world. A shine or even a second one made them feel even better, might even bring them more luck.

My shoeshine business probably lasted about three years. The money was real good. Besides, how many kids my age saw the sights and met the people I did? I was on my own here, living off my wits, cocky as hell. And even after I stopped there'd be another payoff years later during my Army days. Believe me when I tell you no one around then could match the spit shines I gave to my shoes and boots.

7 | SEX DRIVES

What an education it was growing up and working in the city. Plus I was a curious kid, always interested in watching, snooping around, asking questions, trying to figure out what was happening. Being tall for my age and looking much older, too, also counted for something. It meant that I could hang out with people who were older and more experienced and that I got to do certain things ahead of time.

Like sex. Ah, that's something with which blacks are supposed to be quite familiar, even obsessed with. Whites certainly think so, making us out to be little more than simple sexual creatures, yes, even animals. Our sexual appetites, even our sexual organs—both oversized I've heard. So what were we really like? To my mind probably far more modest than most whites. If there was an obsession with sex in Harlem I sure missed it. Hell, there was little or no pornography around. That stuff came out of the white community. On the streets I never saw open sexual display or obscene gestures. Female virginity was the way things were supposed to be, and an unexpected pregnancy meant a visit to the "get-rid-of-the-baby lady" (there was usually one in every neighborhood). The sex talk I heard was how the white people were really into such things, and how indecent their behavior was. I'd hear some of that from women working for white families as maids and housekeepers. "They ought to be ashamed of themselves, walking around the house with practically nothing on." "You know why they're always asking me to take the kids out to the park? They can't wait to screw!" And these same women would tell you how they always had to keep an eye out when the husband was home, because his hands had a way of roamin'. With the white cops in Harlem came more trouble. These guys considered most every decently dressed black woman to be a prostitute, and I suppose that was their excuse when they practically demanded sexual favors from them. Now you tell me where the sex stuff comes from.

We certainly took an interest in sex. For many of us young kids it was difficult not to notice, living in small rooms with lots of different people about. I remember how upset my mother was when we were in Brooklyn and later when we rented one room in an apartment in Harlem. In both places there were couples living in the next room who had sex regularly and openly. You'd hear the bed creaking and the usual breathless sounds of love making. This upset my mother. "Don't these people get enough?" (Although my mother was a single woman and dated other men, she never once had them stay over when I was in the apartment.) I'm sure this was one reason she worked so hard, so that eventually we could afford our own place.

As kids, an interest in our bodies led us to compare penis sizes and compete to see who could piss the furthest. There we were up on the roof, directing parallel streams of urine as best we could. Hanging out near the poolroom, we hoped the guys inside would get around to boasting of their sexual exploits and would let us listen in. Yet with all their bragging and exaggeration, these guys had limits, asked for no more than straight conventional sex, and, even then, spoke with some pride about girls who "gave them nothing." Mention anything other than that (blow jobs or anal sex, for example) and you'd discover that these guys not only didn't dig it, but wouldn't do it. "Man, that's what dogs do." The poolroom guys had their standards.

I was as curious about sex as the next fellow and did get my chances to brush up on the subject—and after one particular relationship, to pretty much complete my education.

What I needed first was greater worldliness, a little more sophistication. That couldn't come from messing around with girls from the neighborhood. But it might be something you'd get at the Savoy Ballroom. Downtown had its Palladium, but for us in Harlem the Savoy was where it was at. It was on the second floor of a building that ran the entire block from 144th to 145th Street on Seventh Avenue. Seen from the street it was nothing special, but inside you had to be impressed by the huge dance floor. Bands played in the center of the room against the wall. A few tables and booths were scattered around the place, but mostly you either were out on the dance floor or standing along the side walls waiting to be asked or checking out the talent. It was two dollars to get in, so it wasn't cheap; expensive enough to keep out the riffraff. They served liquor, drinks going mostly for sixty to sixty-five cents.

The place could get packed, especially Thursday nights and on weekends. (It was closed one day a week.) Figure it could hold something like 400 people, but I it seemed to me that on busy nights they'd just keep selling tickets. They could do this because people got so hot dancing (at times the place did smell like a gym) that they would leave, at least temporarily, to get some air and cool off. Also most of those who came were single, so when boys met girls there and coupled off they'd often split for a party in the area (and if not a party then for a room in one of the small hotels nearby—actually converted brownstones which rented rooms by the hour).

Generally young people showed up and most times things were cool. Besides, the bouncers usually managed to hustle the troublemakers out onto the street where some pretty rough stuff might take place. The Savoy scene was not just for blacks. Whites came, though not in large numbers. (Blacks from the Caribbean usually were not Savoy customers. They preferred their own small clubs, usually in area basements. At the Savoy you wouldn't hear Jamaican music.)

People, of course, came to dance and to listen to the music.

There'd be one or two bands a night, and featured singers. Even in my day some "names" were still showing up. Count Basie, I recall, brought one of his smaller groups in there, and Chick Webb and Fats Waller had their combos swinging away. The big places downtown usually booked bands like these once they'd made their reputation at the Savoy.

Talk about being in jitterbug heaven. These weren't professionals, but man could they shake a leg. Some, it's true, came directly from the Apollo Theater jitterbug contests. Winning at the Apollo meant you'd be featured on the Savoy dance floor. "Here they are, your dance winners from the Apollo," went the announcement. Most every time they played a jitterbug (or the slower Lindy for guys who didn't want to fling the girls over their shoulders) certain slick couples just naturally took over the floor, and sure enough, just like you'd see in the movies, the other dancers would stop and circle these star performers. There might be three or four clearings like that with everyone else looking on. Sometimes just one couple was in the spotlight usually because of their fancy footwork and flashy jitterbug outfits.

The jitterbugging was for athletes; the slow dancing for lovers. That's when they turned the blue lights down real low and when you hoped to be dancing with the girl you'd been eyeing all evening. Slow dances always packed the floor.

The Savoy contributed to my growing sophistication, but not as much as the following real life experience. It came out of nowhere, and after it was over I was, as the cliché says, no longer the same. It was the stuff of fantasy—something boys my age and older guys as well dreamed would happen, never figuring that it would. But it did to me.

I was then working as a delivery boy for Mr. Welch's grocery store that I first met her. Some woman had placed an order, which I made up as I always did, put into the a wagon, and off to Manhattan Avenue I went. I was impressed; it was a very nice building, and such a pretty apartment. Two sisters lived there, both in their thirties, one a nurse, the other a hairdresser. They were very pleasant, offered me a soda (I said no) and on the way out, one of them handed me a fifty-cent tip. The following week the same thing happened. I looked forward to going, having been treated so nicely the first time, especially the fifty cents tip. The week after that it was the same story. This time, though, I noticed that the beautician, just as the previous time, was still wearing a bathrobe, though it was then midafternoon. Also why was it open more than it should have been in the front? While I was still wondering about this there comes this invitation: "How would you like to have dinner with me and my sister tomorrow afternoon?" Why not? I accepted. My mother, when I told her, saw no reason not to go.

I showed up right on time the next day. Would you believe Renee (the hairdresser) was still in her bathrobe? And once more wore it in a way that left little to the imagination. Then after just a few minutes the other sister announced she was leaving for work. That's strange, I thought (it was, after all, Sunday afternoon). Why was I being left alone with Renee? It makes no sense, a thirteen-year old kid and a woman in her early thirties. Why am I having dinner there?

Before long I found out. While tending to the food she was preparing, her robe parted even further. The next thing I know Renee asked me if I would sit next to her on the couch. By this point I'd stopped looking away from the parted folds of her robe. Why not take in the sights? After all, Renee was an attractive woman with full, shapely breasts. Had I ever kissed a girl, she wanted to know? I mumbled some answer, at which point she got up to check the stove. Dinner, she declared, was ready to be served. She was some cook. It was delicious. She even served wine. We talked about my job and other matters of no great importance.

Dinner over, she brought me back to the couch. This time she exposed her breasts completely and encouraged me to kiss them, which, after some hesitancy I did. But that was not all. It turned out this was to be an instructional lesson—how to kiss them, where to kiss them and for how long. You bet I listened: for once I was a most diligent student. She was conducting this like a class, she the teacher and me the pupil. Was I really doing this? No, I was just following instructions.

She was a patient and understanding tutor. I had known what it was to get aroused before but nothing like this. It went no further that day. She tightened the bathrobe around her and we headed back to the table for dessert. Before I left, however, we arranged a date for the following Sunday afternoon. Only when I headed out the door and onto the street did it hit me what had happened. Up in her apartment had been a fantasy world; maybe I had been dreaming. Outside reality returned, making me excited but also scared. I never kept secrets from my mother. But what could I say about this? I would just mention the dinner was fine and certainly not say I had ended up alone with this woman. It came off easily; my mother had no reason to suspect anything. But I'll tell you, I felt guilty as sin. Couldn't wait for the week to pass though.

Sure enough next Saturday there were groceries to deliver to Renee and her sister. "Did you remember our date?" Renee asked when I got there. I had not forgotten. But what would I tell my mother about this one? One dinner invitation by two "nice ladies" may not be unusual, but to be asked back the following week—that was stretching it. Yes, it was strange, my mother remarked, for a second invitation to be extended so soon, but I don't think she suspected anything. These were, I assured her, very nice ladies, trying to make "ladies" sound as if they were considerably older women.

Renee's sister wasn't even in the apartment when I returned on Sunday. "She's out of town for the week." Now even I realized this was deliberate. I had for days, as you might imagine, thought of little else but this get-together. Who knew where it would lead, but by this time I sure was interested in finding out. If she wanted to teach me about sex and a woman's body and how to enjoy them, I'd have no objection. I suppose you'll say that she seduced me, and that this was child abuse, my performing acts unnatural for my age, for her pleasure. I sure was a willing "victim." Besides, she went about her seduction in such a loving, tender way that I didn't then nor have ever since considered myself to have been abused.

Renee seemed determined to reshape me in every way, to make me into the complete cultivated young gentleman. We never left the apartment (and in the many times that I was there her sister seems to have disappeared). There were books all over and she had, over the years, done much traveling, especially in Europe. She was anxious to pass on all sorts of information. I was by nature a curious, inquisitive fellow, which she must have sensed when responding to my questions. She taught me how to set a table. She instructed me in wines. She would wind up her Victrola and we'd listen to some great jazz. Mother, lover, teacher, a friend—she was all of that.

Sex, of course, was the highlight for me. All week long I looked forward to that part of our get-together. I had long since stopped telling my mother where I was going just about every Sunday afternoon. Instead there was one lie after another—out with my friends, a movie, playing ball, a long walk. Never before and not again after that would I lie so shamelessly to her. What else could I do? As much as I wanted to, I didn't dare tell any of my friends, either. Bragging about such matters in general conversation was one thing, but this went beyond anything we might ever have imagined. Besides, word might just get back to my mother this way.

Was I becoming addicted to sex? If, when I arrived, Renee was fully clothed, my disappointment clearly showed. "Haven't you seen enough?," she'd say. "No," and you could see how much that delighted her. Some Sundays she'd let me know she wasn't in the mood, which I understood meant there'd be no sex. But then there were the other times. Nothing I had ever done before had been as thrilling. It was all here—an older, attractive woman looking out for me, teaching me all about sex, giving me full play of her body, allowing me to enter it. I never stopped to consider why she might be doing this, what pleasure she found in it, or why me, not much more than an oversized kid. I questioned nothing, wanted nothing to get in the way. It lasted nearly a year and might have gone on even longer had I not moved to Queens with my mother. I promised Renee I'd be back to see her, but that never happened. Where, after all, could this lead? But there was no forgetting the times together when she had taken me from childhood to maturity with little effort and so much pleasure. Years later I would, every so often, notice a woman on the street who reminded me of Renee, and in an instant I would get this flush of excitement and warmth and then remember back to my growth spurt, when in a very short time, I came a long way to becoming a man.

8 | MEAN STREETS

Growing up involved more than just having one's way with a woman. It meant facing the realities of life in Harlem. It was my mother and me, just the two of us, trying to keep our heads above water. It was no different for plenty of others. I shined shoes at rent parties where people were trying their best to hold on. And when they couldn't, I saw the results—their belongings out on the street, piled up. I saw hustlers, all flashy and fine, hanging out in the bars and the poolrooms, playing cards, rolling dice, talking the talk, letting everyone see who they were. But these men, slick on the surface, often stood at the edge of desperation. That's why some were so quick to take offense, to fight those who challenged or, worse, tried cheating them. When they fought it was never pretty, their razors and knives tearing at flesh. I watched, usually terrified at the sight. (Growing up I saw how the weapons changed from the razor to the switchblade knife, then to the much larger stiletto of the Italians, and finally to guns—first widely used by the Italians.)

Not every one was a fight to the finish. Sometimes guys circled around each other, looking just to penetrate and cut. With such a wound and some blood, the fight could be over, if neither of them had a mind to do the other in, just needed to keep face. You could tell, though, when guys were not going to back off. They just plunged in, slashed away, ignored their wounds and the blood that poured out. One or sometimes both of them might then collapse on the sidewalk. And maybe even die there, since it was unlikely they'd be brought to a hospital in time. If either survived he'd have cuts on his face and neck, and that fierce scarface look you imagined went along with being a "bad" guy.

One time looking down from my fire escape I watched as two guys went after each other, not with razor blades but with icepicks. One, then the other, found his target. It was ferocious, hard to watch, worse than anything I had ever seen. Sure enough when it was over one man lay dead in the street, the other limped away, badly hurt. What made these people so desperate, so willing to fight to the finish?

If on the other hand you'd asked me what brought white policemen to Harlem, I'd have the answer. Most every cop, I came to understand, was in Harlem because no other post in the city could make them as much money in graft and corruption. Any wonder why cops paid to be assigned to Harlem? Yes, they bought these posts and why not—they were as good as gold! Harlem was the promised land for New York's "Finest," for those Irish cops (and some Italians and Poles) who kept us down, then robbed and beat us.

Back then, and it was not only in Harlem, you just didn't challenge cops. They represented authority, had a kind of power not possible today. They walked beats by themselves and could take charge of and control most any situation. No way you'd defy them or try to run away. They thought nothing of getting physical, of kicking the shit out of you. And they'd get away with it; not a word would be said. "Police brutality"?—it didn't exist then. If a cop needed an arrest, he'd bring you in. If he witnessed a crime he'd beat the guy up right on the spot with his fists, his nightstick or a blackjack. If he didn't batter you on the street, chances were he'd do it back at the stationhouse.

Most all black parents made sure their kids knew how to behave in front of cops. To question their authority, to say something stupid or do the wrong thing could be dangerous. Black kids, to survive, had better be respectful, quiet, do exactly as they were told by the cops. Not only parents but many of the older kids on the block taught this lesson, tried to protect the younger ones. The police meant trouble. The cops in Harlem were among the greatest menaces we faced.

We hated them and for good reason. White liberals later learned about all those southern sheriffs and how brutal they were, but the white cops in Harlem that I saw were just as bad, maybe worse. (And I should add, the sloppiest looking guys you will ever see on a municipal police force.) In the South, sheriffs beat up on those blacks who challenged or broke the law. Most others, if they kept to themselves and "behaved", would ordinarily be ignored. Up in Harlem it often didn't matter if a black broke the law or not. When the cops came around anyone could be in for shit. They had no respect for any black. Even black clergymen were not exempt. A cop thought nothing of using the worst racial epithets. Everyone was a "nigger" or "boy," and first names were all you could expect. Worse, they took what they wanted. You'd see them walk into a bar, stay there for a good part of their tour and expect all drinks to be on the house. They paid for nothing and asked for everything—fruits, vegetables, fish, clothes, from neighborhood stores—it didn't matter. Even our women. In their eyes all black women as I've said were fair game, were prostitutes, available for the asking. They propositioned them at the bars and even out on the streets. Some black women for all sorts of reasons accepted, thought it better not to say "no." Most black men looked on, said nothing, but seethed inside.

Did we, could we, do anything about the situation? We cursed those "Irish bastards," not so much because we hated the Irish, but because most of the cops who mistreated us were Irish. We tried setting them up, getting them to accept money, then phoning the incriminating information in to the local police station. It didn't work much. We did it anonymously because we were scared, had good reason to worry about retaliation. All were in on it, were part of the same system. Who'd be crazy enough to upset such a profitable setup? It was well known that police, off duty in plainclothes, would beat you up in the hallways or up on the roofs if they believed you had in one way or another been causing trouble. Who could you complain to? The rules didn't matter in black neighborhoods.

Sure, there were a few blacks on the force at that time. I would like to be able to tell you that had more black cops been around we'd have been better off. Some, it's true, were fair minded, not out there to bust our butts and fatten off Harlem, but those they got rid of real quick, one way or another. That left black cops who were fully part of the rotten system and who were just as vicious toward us as their white buddies.

What helped sometimes were not the rules as much as a little pull. Blacks who worked downtown for white companies usually carried the business cards of their bosses with them. That provided some protection. It helped if you knew a cop and carried his card with you. For a time the police made it their business to harass the followers of Father Divine until they went out and got themselves some lawyers, Jewish lawyers, and that seemed to work. Blacks who were Catholics could expect some consideration from the Irish Catholic cops. And if you knew someone with a little political pull, the cops would probably back off. All this helped some, but still blacks were vulnerable, always afraid of catching hell from the cops in Harlem.

Occasionally we retaliated. Every so often guys would go up on the roof and wait for a cop to pass by. When he did, bricks or garbage would come flying down. No mistaking the message, but not much came of it. Yet the cops could never feel totally secure. And they could never catch these guys, who knew the roofs well. But there were few such acts of defiance. Mostly they thought they had our respect. In fact we hated them, but quietly.

Harlem, thanks to the police, became one big "pad," corruption and payoffs at every turn. An honest cop in Harlem— I don't believe there was one! Cops operated both for themselves or for the higher ups on the force. Also they served as henchmen for the politicians and gangsters who pocketed the profits of Harlem. Organized up and down the line, everyone got a piece of the action. The cops divided up the territory, kept records of monies "owed" and paid, ran it just like a business. Always their hands were out. No one even asked or dared to ask how this came about. "Why do I have to pay you off?" "How come you're a cop and you're demanding money from us?" No such questions. Instead you paid off whether you were involved in a legitimate business or otherwise and hoped they wouldn't expect more.

Cops knew where people gathered, when there'd be some "action." That's where they showed up. There'd be cops dropping in to rent parties. (Many had card games with money around to be "collected.") At Morningside Park where I would go to watch baseball games on Sundays there'd be guys off to the side shooting craps with a lookout posted, watching for the cops. If he sounded the alarm, they'd pick up the money and dice and run like hell in all directions. If the cop managed to get close without being spotted they'd drop the money on the ground and take off. He'd come over, pick up the money, pocket it, throw the dice as far as he could, and not bother chasing after the players. Everyone benefited, I guess you could say. When I was shining shoes behind the Apollo near the big time crap games, cops would come by like clockwork to get their "cut." The guy running the game knew to have the money ready. Cops didn't even have to break stride (except for those in the squad cars who pulled up along the curb and waited for someone to deliver). A new shift of cops brought on a new bunch of takers, their hands out.

All the illegal activity in Harlem meant big dividends for the police. Say you didn't pay off. Then they'd just do their "job," and run you the hell out of there. Those basement booze guys couldn't stay in business unless the police had a reason to look the other way. The guys who ran the big card games (card games as a business probably was invented in Harlem) in the poolrooms, at rent parties or in the social clubs or hotels couldn't operate for long without letting the cops in on the action. No way the numbers business got so big in Harlem without the police as partners. They kept close watch to make sure they got theirs. Cops went after those trying to go it alone and forced them out of business. It could be quite a cat and mouse game. Mr. Williams, who with his wife ran the candy store downstairs on 116th Street, built a connecting passageway over to Frank the barber, whose shop was right next door. Williams took numbers, and unlike others didn't memorize all of the action. Instead he wrote the information down on policy slips. Now when he'd spot a cop what he'd do is grab the slips, rush to the wall area and stuff them in for Frank, who would then take hold of them. When the cop passed and headed toward the barber shop, Frank would slip them back through the wall to Mr. Williams. Numbers banks, which collected and distributed funds, were raided every so often—a double message there. The general public saw cops enforcing the law, but it was also a warning to folks who were holding out—better not "cheat" the police.

The cops were in business for themselves, but also did some of the dirty work for others. Thanks to the police, well connected businesses didn't have to worry about competition. The cops would uncover "violations" and harass the hell out of them. Once the Italians took over fish and vegetable operations, for example, blacks found it almost impossible to continue in those businesses. A bunch of summonses usually did the job.

Even in those depression years lots of money floated around Harlem, a situation that attracted the Mafia. And so it began to muscle in on the Harlem rackets, to go after the numbers and the bootlegging, gambling, prostitution, bars and nightclub businesses. Try resisting and chances were good you'd be rubbed out. Those simply stubborn were "persuaded" to change their minds. On the other hand, local blacks who cooperated and let the Mafia take over got police protection and were allowed to carry on and keep a share, certainly a much smaller share of the take.

The mob had taken over, and every so often we'd get a taste of how it operated. Twice I witnessed how vicious the struggle for control could be. It was early one morning that I climbed out onto our fire escape, something I would do when it was too warm in the apartment. Also I enjoyed just watching the comings and goings outside. Not this time. What I saw at first did not seem at all unusual. Out on the street this black guy was counting out and handing over money to someone sitting in a parked car along the curb. But then the scene turned ugly. I could tell an argument had started. Then the back door of the car opened and this white guy holding a machine gun stepped out. It was over in an instant. He opened fire at point blank range. God knows how many bullets hit the guy who, as he fell, grabbed on to the fire hydrant alongside. The gunman calmly climbed back into the car, which then slowly drove off. I'll never forget the sight of that guy sprawled over the hydrant, face down, hands stretched out in front of him, another victim, I found out, of the gang warfare that had come to Harlem.

A second round of gunplay could have cost me my life. It happened while I was out on Seventh Avenue and 135th Street shining shoes in front of the Renaissance Bar. I considered this a prime location; the place was a favorite hangout for fancy dudes. In fact I was giving a shine to one of them when all hell broke loose. I probably saved the day when out of the corner of my eye I spotted this really long black Buick limousine driving along slowly on the far side of the street. I mean this car was immense, so I looked up once or twice to glance over while I was buffing the guy's shoes. He must have noticed me looking, because he did, too. Some reaction. He jumped right up, left me squatting in front of the shoebox, and ran into the bar. I turned around now and saw that the car had made a U-turn around the island in the middle of the avenue and was now moving north on Seventh heading right toward the bar. Who hasn't watched such a scene in the movies? That's exactly how it happened. The side windows front and rear both slid down and out came the barrels of two machine guns. I hit the pavement. Falling in the direction of the car I could see that the guys inside were white. Then they blasted away, the shots smashing into the front of the bar, shattering the windows. I was sure I was about to be shot. But then in a matter of ten, maybe fifteen seconds it was over. The windows had just about disappeared, pieces of glass scattered all over. I ran like hell but then realized I had forgotten to take my shoebox, so I stopped and headed back. No one had yet come out of the bar, probably figuring the guys might be coming back. Two cops who had been posted a block away made no move at first. Then instead of chasing after the car they strolled over to see the damage. (The local police station itself was only a block away.)

I grabbed the shoebox and took off. I had no idea if anyone inside was hit. Probably not. My customer's warning had given them time to duck for cover. Besides, I heard people talking later that this had been just a message to whoever owned the bar. I got the message, too—that there was a battle going on to control Harlem. I came real close to becoming a casualty of that war. You know, I never got to finish that shine.

9 | SCHOOL DAZE

I've talked about the streets and the roofs, the games, the cops and the mob, but what about school? For me that meant P.S. 10, and then the junior high school. Mostly I had black classmates, because whites by that time were leaving the neighborhood. The teachers were, of course, still all white, Irish and Jewish. P.S. 10 was a great place as far as I remember, real orderly, the teachers interested in educating us. (I never heard anything derogatory about the students from them.) Actually they watched over us in ways most folks today couldn't take. Notes, notes, always there were notes from the teacher back home. "Your child needs a new shirt"—"Your child should come to school with better shoes." I remember one to my mother about my needing another pair of knickers. When a teacher sent a note home in those days it had the force of law. Parents listened. If you deserved to be spanked, you got spanked. My mother, I knew, never questioned them, felt that teachers truly cared. I remember one, Mrs. Keyes, an Irish lady who was almost like a mother to me. Believe it or not, teachers came to the home then, visited parents, just to chat and talk about their kids. I also remember quite clearly that my mother and I once visited Mrs. Keyes. She had invited us to come, so we took the subway all the way to Flatbush in Brooklyn, where she lived. If I have any quarrel with P.S. 10 it's that somehow in those years I never learned how to spell. I don't know why that was or what needed to be done. All I know is that starting then and up to today my spelling ain't worth a damn. To me it became a fundamental failing, a disqualification that would always hold me back. It sounds crazy, I know, and some people will say I used this as an excuse for my poor school performance, but I never got over the feeling that spelling counted for something important and that I couldn't get it right.

Next came Cooper Junior High School and the shock of my life. Gone was the order and seriousness of P.S. 10. Here was dangerous territory. Tough Italian kids terrorized the place, both in and around the school. Everywhere there was fighting. The "good" kids were black and, more often than not, the victims. The Italians applied themselves only to shaking down and beating up on the rest of us kids, taking our lunch money or our lunches, even our shoes and clothes. These were hulking sixteen and seventeen-year olds roaming the halls, many of them having been left back. What could we do against these toughs who usually carried stilettos with them and scared the daylights out of everyone. Things became so bad that four cops, the "Four Horsemen" they were called, two blacks and two whites, were assigned to patrol the school. The cops took to slapping the kids around a lot, especially the Italians. While most of us were afraid of them, the Italians generally wouldn't back down—that explains the beatings!

The women teachers had little chance of controlling their classes; some of the men managed, although the gym teacher actually got into physical fights with his students until the police would arrive to break them up. Just getting kids into the classrooms was a problem. Many just hung out in the courtyard or on the street surrounding the school. The cops were always pushing kids back into the building and escorting them to their classrooms.

Learning was just about impossible here. Most of the teachers (again largely Irish and Jewish plus a few Italians) couldn't have cared less. We were dumb, they'd tell us, and would never amount to anything. One of my teachers, Mrs. Goldstein, couldn't have made it clearer. Much of the time she'd bring a newspaper into class and read it up at her desk after ordering us to copy material she put on the blackboard. There were other problems. The desks were too small for the big kids, so they sat on top of them. Imagine running a class under those conditions. Goldstein was real strange. She'd sit in front of the class, her legs spread apart, letting us see that she wore no underwear. Word was she invited the older boys into the clothes closet with her during the lunch recess, but I never saw that. Because of these lousy conditions many kids just didn't show up much. I liked skipping school myself, heading downtown with a group of guys to catch the early shows at the Roxy, Paramount and Astor Theatres. We were not alone; there'd be plenty of other "students" lined up waiting to get in. Trouble was, truant officers knew this too. They'd be all over these places, figuring to round up all the truants they could handle.

I got an education in junior high school but it had mostly to do with sex, courtesy of the Italian hoods. They talked about little else. They bragged about the size of their sexual organs and mostly their conversations had to do with pimps, broads, who was getting screwed tonight, and who were the "good" and who were the "bad" girls. When one guy swore he'd had sex with someone's sister it guaranteed a fight.

Also, these guys were always trying to sell you—something they just happened to have with them, usually liquor. Some of the "good" kids couldn't take all this; their parents pulled them out of Cooper and got them into Catholic schools. Who knows if I would have survived. Fortunately I escaped this hellhole when my mother decided to move to Queens. People, I suppose, have reasons to romanticize the good old days, but let me tell you that no way were those school days of mine good. Say what you want about conditions in many junior highs today, but it's hard to imagine a situation worse than what I saw. So maybe it wasn't the spelling after all. Maybe Cooper Junior High School is to blame.

10 | ONE INCREDIBLE WOMAN

I considered myself street wise. But what I learned there wouldn't have meant much had my mother not sorted things out for me. I haven't said much about her yet; it's time I did. No one was more important in my life. She shaped me, guided me even while she was herself looking for a way to lead her life.

Talk about guts and gumption, she cut her family ties, struck out on her own, left the South where she was born, and headed north to New York City. She was, you see, a loner, an independent person, much as I'd be. What she managed to do was absolutely remarkable, and to this day I cannot put all the pieces together to explain her drive, and savvy. All I know is that it was just the two of us, trusting to God that we would survive and later being grateful when somehow it turned out right.

Sure I would have loved having a father and in certain of my relationships that's what I must have been looking for, but then I didn't much miss having one. My mother did one heck of a job—being both a father and a mother to me. Somehow she understood to combine guidance and control with enough freedom so that I would stay close even while making my own way in the world. How she figured all this out being so young herself I'll never know. She was, as I've said, one capable human being. There was very little she couldn't do. Still she would always say, "I have to do better," and by God, she meant it. Not a person to wait for things to happen, she was a pusher, a planner, yes, a dreamer.

She never fully revealed that dream of hers to me, but so far as I could tell it was about self-improvement, dignity, independence and making our lives as comfortable as possible. Quite a big order for a young Negro widow. I never saw her depressed or seem overwhelmed. Did she understand how great the odds were against her? I don't know, but what she did accomplish had to bring her great satisfaction.

She began, as did so many young black girls after coming north, by working as a housekeeper. She was good, she was reliable, so there was pretty steady employment. But it meant she had to travel from Brooklyn, where we first lived, to jobs elsewhere, including Queens and Manhattan. She left early and came home late, or not at all when an employer asked her to stay over. If she cleaned their homes anywhere near the way she kept ours, they got their money's worth.

Because she got along with most all the people she worked for, you can't imagine what they gave her. Lamps, towels, glasses, pictures, throw rugs—you name it. She was always bringing stuff like that home. Now it wasn't junk; my mother wouldn't let that into her home. Sometimes she asked me and my friends to meet her where she worked to help with a chair or table, whatever she couldn't manage by herself. I'm sure my mother's good taste, and she had very good taste, came in part from what she saw in those white homes where she worked. Not realizing it, white middle-class families were passing on styles and fashions to working class blacks. Those moving up already knew the "basics."

Housekeeping jobs helped us to survive the early years up north. I don't know who suggested it or if anyone did, but she decided somewhere in the middle of the 1930s to take classes to become a practical nurse. My mother had a way of knowing what might be out there for her. Sure enough she heard about a New Deal program, I seem to recall it was the WPA, where she could get the necessary training, and so she signed up. She couldn't have had much of any schooling in the South, so this must have been quite a challenge. But she got through, became a practical nurse. Goodbye housekeeping. She went to work in various hospitals and took a part-time job with a private physician. She wasn't finished though. How she did it I can't say, but one day she announced to me that she had become a registered nurse. After that, jobs came easy. Plus I never saw a doctor when I was growing up. She took care of me, got me whatever medicine I needed.

For a time she worked for several doctors whose offices were in the Essex Hotel, a swanky place downtown on 57th Street. Actually they weren't your usual doctors' offices, but rented hotel suites. These doctors, I learned, were abortionists whose customers were rich young and pregnant college girls from places like Vassar and Wellesley. They would check into the hotel, get it done, sleep over and then leave. I met her there several times but I never saw any of the patients. "We take care of wealthy girls" is about all she told me. At the time I understood little about what was going on, and didn't think to ask her about it. (Later on, however, when my mother got around to teaching me the facts of life, she reminded me of these abortion doctors while making a strong case for using contraceptives.) I'm pretty sure that sometime later while we were still living in Harlem my mother either performed abortions herself or assisted with them. Every so often she'd receive telephone messages (we had no phone; the calls came into Mrs. Williams' candy store downstairs) from this fancy madam living in the neighborhood. Usually a taxi then pulled up and off my mother would go for several hours. Somehow I came to understand what she was doing. What mattered to me was that it brought in extra money.

For every item she bought there was another she made herself. She could sew expertly, and was some knitter. She made many of her clothes, and took to restyling her coats. Put cloth in her hands and there's no telling what might come of it. When something caught her eye in a decorating magazine, drapes, for example, she'd set out to make them. So what if we already had attractive drapes. The new ones appealed to her—that was enough. No wonder our apartments looked so fine and finished, were always bringing my mother compliments.

And were they clean, squeaky clean. I don't believe that any part of any room we lived in went untouched, unscrubbed, unwashed or unpolished. That was after she had just painted the rooms herself. Naturally she scrubbed the floors regularly. She'd soak a rag in vinegar and water and then rub away. The walls would be washed down and of course the stove scraped clean.Ammonia and C-N she couldn't do without (the C-N for the toilet and also into the kitchen trap). A fumigation can was always on hand.It contained, my mother told me, a bedbug and roach mixture. Every week she'd be spraying away. Now there was no building in which we ever lived that didn't have roaches, but my mother took them on, determined to keep the upper hand. She sprayed everywhere, under the refrigerator, behind the stove, and into every hole she saw or imagined was there. The beds were stripped clean, after which she'd blast away at the frame and the mattress. To keep the roaches on the defensive she'd spray out in the hallway and also take baking soda and pour it across the doorway and along whichever pipes were heading into our apartment. Cleaning was no casual matter for my mother; it was war.

Of course she was a good cook. It was an experience sitting down to one of her meals. She had her favorite dishes; she could for example prepare any kind of beans you could think of, but she was always experimenting, consulting cookbooks, forever clipping recipes. She prepared fish of all kinds and various vegetables, especially mustard greens, collard greens and kale. She made her own dressings and was a whiz at soups, especially cream of spinach, curry and celery. She made the greatest pancakes you can imagine, her own ingredients going into the mix. She wasted nothing, reusing grease and Crisco, even making delicious carrot clippings soup. My mother didn't like store-bought bread, so she baked her own—white, wheat and corn, along with ice box rolls. Her home made pies and cakes were super. Because she was away from home so much she would prepare several meals in advance that I would just need to heat up. She also taught me how to cook and I did learn, really enjoyed doing it.

For providing for us even during real bad times my mother deserved all the praise in the world. But as I've said she was no ordinary woman. Even while she struggled day and night her interests in the world around her expanded. She read a lot, listened to the news, knew what was going on. She was one sharp lady with a mind of her own. It's not that she sat me down and preached, but she was always passing things on, answering my questions, telling me what I should know and read. To my mind she got things just about right.

Not outspoken and forceful, my mother would not organize others or take the lead. That's not to say she wouldn't speak her mind, but her style involved quiet suggestion and indirection. It was, she knew, a tough world; survival was not guaranteed. It made no sense to burn bridges or say things that might cause resentment and bring retribution. There were, she'd tell me, "all kinds of ways to do things." She read books, newspapers and magazines, kept up with developments—her power would come from knowledge. "The more I know the less you can hurt me," she often said. She had a talent for drawing others out, for appreciating what they had to say. She listened, and for that reason always attracted people to her. Estelle, they knew, would offer a sympathetic ear. She usually chose her words carefully, was not one to shoot her mouth off. "Your mouth," she would say, "can get you into trouble while your brain can get you out of trouble, so why use your mouth?"

Sweet and kindly on the outside, still she was one tough woman. She knew the score, knew that in her work world at least, she'd have to depend upon whites. Her employers assumed, I'm sure, that they could read her mind. She seemed so open and sweet. But I doubt if they ever could. (Occasionally she'd let me know how she felt. "They don't want to pay nothin' and they want to work your ass to death," she would complain.) But if there was to be a parting of the ways it had to be friendly like. She would never quit in anger; future employment depended on past recommendations. But she did leave many jobs, sometimes complaining, "They're too hard and cruel," but usually it was for a more attractive position. "I got a better job" is what she'd tell me.

My mother certainly was a liberal, and a strong supporter of the Democratic Party. She took an interest in politics and later when we moved from Harlem to Queens got involved in political activities. Franklin Roosevelt she loved. He, after all, gave her the foodstuffs and the classes so that she could become a nurse. My mother put up a picture of Roosevelt in our apartment because he was, she believed, the greatest president we'd ever had. If my mother liked Franklin, she adored Eleanor Roosevelt. Her name was always in the news, and my mother often talked about Mrs. Roosevelt and what she did for blacks. It was Eleanor, she said, who visited black orphanages, got money for black higher education, and persuaded the President to do what he did for Negroes.

That she believed in God was never in doubt. She kept a family Bible in which she placed all sorts of stuff and made many notes. But sometimes the Bible troubled her (even though she was always quoting this verse or that story). "This couldn't be," she'd say when questioning a particular chapter or passage.

Hers was a personal faith; organized religion interested her much less. "You don't have to go to church to believe in God," she'd tell me. She never went to bed without saying her prayers out loud, usually personal statements to God about particular concerns and needs. Still over the years she joined several different churches and attended services regularly. Her taste in religious services, as she said many times, was for "a quiet service." The storefront congregations around Harlem didn't interest her; neither was she attracted to any of the exclusively black churches. She left the Baptists, I think because she disliked their emphasis upon singing. Later on, after being "disappointed," she quit the Roman Catholic Church, though I never learned why. She seemed most comfortable in the Episcopal Church (possibly because it had stayed on in a neighborhood that had become mostly black). Still there was, she felt, too much hypocrisy in churches. Black ministers, she believed, were far more interested in their own livelihoods than in serving God. For certain my mother was a seeker in many ways, and while the Bible brought her comfort and wisdom, none of the churches she attended ever fully answered her needs. Whatever her religious views, my mother was a very charitable person. On many occasions she'd make up packages for the church to distribute to the needy. "Keep enough for yourself and then give what you can away." Time and again she'd tell me that.

My mother had no illusions about the country's racial problems. Still her self-control kept her from showing open anger on the subject. You'd never hear her blaming the whites. All she would say was, "Things are not right, not fair," and she'd talk about how hard blacks had to struggle. She never said so but it wouldn't surprise me if her anger at segregation was the main reason she left the South. When we traveled north she would, you remember, make sure to use private cars and avoid the segregated buses and trains. News of lynchings brought her to tears. Black newspapers provided detailed coverage of these incidents, often including pictures. I suspected, although she never said a word, that she had herself witnessed these horrors in the South.

Early on my mother took an interest in black history and in Africa and stopped in at Michaux's bookstore on 125th Street to check out various titles on these subjects. I found that out one day back from the movies after having so enjoyed the story of Hannibal that I had stayed to see it again. "Had a white actor played Hannibal?" my mother asked. When I said yes she became angry. Didn't I know that Hannibal was a black African? They had no business using a white actor! She also hated Tarzan, and the way it presented the African "jungle." Even when black actors were on screen, my mother sometimes resented what they were made to say or do. She had very little good to say about "Gone with the Wind," and hated Hattie McDaniel in it. She was also angry over the parts Bojangles Robinson accepted in the movies. "He is," she said, "a very intelligent man, and he's a terrific dancer," but she didn't like watching him with Shirley Temple. Stepin Fetchit was not what she wanted to see. While I couldn't wait for Amos 'n Andy to come on each week and laugh myself silly, my mother never joined me in front of the radio. "I don't want to listen to that," she said, "those are not black people." She did allow me to tune in, however. While I did she'd be sitting nearby in her high-backed upholstered chair reading and paying, it seemed, not the slightest attention to the program. Every so often, however, I'd peek over and catch her smiling behind the book, at something that had been said. Lots of blacks in the neighborhood considered the show "comical" and were loyal listeners. It got a smile or two out of my mother but never her acceptance.

My mother welcomed Adam Clayton Powell, Jr.'s outspoken and aggressive ways, and when he organized several rallies in Harlem to protest the lack of job opportunities for blacks in the city, and especially along 125th Street, she came round. She hated racial injustice but she would not accept it as the excuse for blacks not making their way in the world. It hadn't stopped her, she said, from trying or from succeeding. "Don't speak of racial barriers," she told me. "Life is a struggle for everyone," she said. "If you want something you have to really work hard for it." "Don't take and don't steal," she warned, "but work for what you get. God gave you equipment, use it."

As I think back I am absolutely astonished at how good a mother she was. She got it all right. She didn't smother me or make me dependent. Rather she made sure I could stand up to whatever might come my way. She didn't let me run all over her. She was the boss. Sure I defied her, especially as I grew older, and we had our squabbles but not many. Somehow she had figured out how to be both a mother and a father, also a friend. I loved her for all the things she was to me.

She would let others guide me too, especially older men. For a time, if she had a problem with me, off we'd go to see Father Dodd at the Episcopal Church. He could be a kind and loving man but also something of a brute. He was not above slapping me around. This my mother allowed, coming as it did from a clergyman. But then, Dodd slapped me one too many times, the final blow coming when, as an incense boy I forgot to shake it at the right time. That did it. I quit as an altar boy and left the church, a decision my mother accepted. My mother, I know, appreciated the way Mr. Welch, my boss at the grocery store, took care of me and how Frank the barber and Mr. Williams downstairs looked out for me. She encouraged my making neighborhood friends and many of them ended up loving my mother and coming to her for advice (as so many adults did as well). But she didn't want her apartment overrun with every kid on the block. "If they're your friends, bring them home," she told me. "If they're your acquaintances, don't bring them home." To those I invited home she couldn't have been nicer.

It was, my mother understood, a tough world out there. I'm sure she wondered whether as a woman she could prepare me for it physically. But you know, she even managed that. "You'll have to fight for yourself," she reminded me even as she assumed a boxing position, raised her fists and showed me how to use them. When I fought back out on the street she was pleased. "Take the pain," she said to me. If for some reason I quit or backed away she might send me back. So long as I wasn't half dead she'd rather that I continue to fight. Fighting back, she figured, might mean fewer fights later on. She was right—I got the reputation of never quitting, so I wasn't challenged all that much.

My mother didn't back away from discussing sex with me, although I was already past fifteen when she got down to basics.

Being a nurse I guess made it easier for her. What to do, what not to do, where it all led—she left nothing to my imagination. "It didn't happen just 'cause you touched someone," she said, before discussing where male semen ended up. She did not stop me from bringing girls to the apartment. She was gone a lot and realized there'd be no way to prevent it. "I'll leave everything that you need," she assured me. She was quite clear about one matter, however. She would not sleep on the same sheets where I had had sex. "When you get out of bed you have the girls change the sheets."

Talking about sex, what about my mother? She was young, vital, pretty, and what's more she had a steady job. Men were drawn to her. Sure thing I got special treatment in the neighborhood because my mother was a looker and men took a fancy to her. What a fine lady my mother was—I heard that all the time. (Men often whistled at her on the street. It embarrassed the hell out of me.) And she was some lady. In all the years we lived together in the same apartment she never once had a man stay overnight. She had her boyfriends and they would be over at our place, but come night they'd be gone. Now I had no doubt my mother had sex, but ever so discreetly. There'd be nights she didn't come home and weekends when she went away. Some of these times she was working; others had obviously to do with her social life. Why exactly she felt the need to shelter me in this matter she never said, but in a way I appreciated that she did so. As I said before, my mother knew just how to handle things.

My mother loved me; I never doubted that. I loved her as well, and I think for the most part I turned out to be the kind of child she'd hoped to raise. She put a lot of effort into being both a mother and father to me, into instructing me, guiding me and also into allowing me the freedom to grow up by myself. I gave her some fits from time to time (although I also pleased her by bringing in money from my various jobs, keeping the house clean, even doing some of the cooking) but until the day she died nothing very serious ever came between us.

I think, though, that she had to be a little disappointed in me. She knew I was capable, some of my teachers told her that, but she watched me drifting along in school, certainly not distinguishing myself. Schooling and education meant a lot to her. I didn't quite see it that way. After World War II she saw American society opening up and sensed opportunities coming even for blacks. "You can be what you want to be," she said. Still she saw that I wasn't headed in any particular direction. She never showed any disappointment. "Just do better," she'd tell me. Well, I would, in time. My mother, sad to say, would not be there to see it.

11 | FAREWELL MY HARLEM

America joined in the war against Hitler, and Harlem, too, signed on. Recruitment posters came up all over. Blacks knew though what they'd face if they joined the armed forces—discrimination, segregated units—support and service roles, not combat action. On the other hand we had something to prove, not to ourselves, but to white Americans convinced we didn't have what it took to make it as soldiers. So many men of Harlem chose to follow the flag. We wouldn't be turned away, we knew that. Disabilities that might get a white guy out got overlooked when we had them. You're in the army now, boy!

Adults in the neighborhood signed up with the Red Cross and many became Air Raid Wardens, making sure we put in dark shades and observed blackouts. Scrap metal collections began (although it wasn't always just scrap that got turned in at the collection depots for money). We kids couldn't wait to talk to soldiers home on leave. Those uniforms were something. Even the guys in the poolroom were curious, especially about how black men were being treated. (The truth was, not all that well, but that was no surprise.) At the Savoy the soldiers became quite the rage, squeezing out the local boys and monopolizing the girls. It figured. These guys not only had money in their pockets but were out looking to have a good time.

The war brought better times—jobs, jobs for everyone. Tensions eased; groups stopped fighting one another. Some took jobs not so much to help the war effort but to get out of going to war. "Essential" jobs—police, firemen, electricians, ship workers, etc. kept you far away from the front lines.

What about the German-Americans in our area? The Bund was active on 125th Street, had an office near the Apollo, and held rallies in the area attended by their uniformed followers and plenty of reporters. Blacks for whatever reason didn't bother much with them. It was different with the Italians. Probably to show how American they had become the Italian kids beat the hell out of the Germans. Blacks, on the other hand, were asking about a certain double standard. Why were only Japanese-Americans being interned? "They're putting all those Japs in jail. What about those Nazis on 125th Street?" I heard Mrs. Williams ask.

As I said, the war brought better times, new opportunities. For us too. Since we had arrived in Harlem in 1937 we had moved several times to better apartments. Making life easier, moving on up—it was my mother's dream. Again opportunity knocked. You already know how she was always keeping up with developments, knew what was going on. This time she got word of a vacancy at a city housing project in Jamaica, Queens. I didn't know about it, but she must have gone out there to see for herself and liked it. One day early in 1943 came her announcement—we were moving. I'd love it, she assured me.

People moved in and out of the neighborhood all the time. Still I had become part of the scene there; I wasn't happy about leaving. I couldn't tell my friends; no, I'd wait until the last minute. Actually I was thinking about something else—finally getting back at Spider, the kid who usually got the best of me when we had our fights. It would be perfect. I had always had a hard time with the Lyman brothers, and with Spider in particular. The fights we had, Spider usually won. What if I were to take him? I could leave champion of the block!

How to do it though. Spider was a good fighter; tall and wiry, he'd bruised me plenty in the past. Just why I thought I had a chance this time I'm not sure. Still what could I lose? And winning sure would make up for all the other times. I avoided any other fights the few days before I would challenge Spider. I wanted to be ready.

The day arrived. I told my friends I would be moving soon and what was about to happen. They were, as you might expect, all for my fighting. As usual Spider and some of his pals were hanging out at the candy store when I walked right up to him and announced, "This is it." You could see he had been caught off guard, just like I figured. I mean, there had been no provocation; he hadn't expected to have to fight. He had to be surprised, probably confused too. Here I was suddenly the aggressor when, mostly, I had backed off. But he had no choice; he had to accept my challenge. Already my "followers" were into it—"Yeah," "Go get 'em"—"He's yours."

Street ritual required a specific verbal challenge. Almost any one would do—we knew them all. My choice: "Your mother doesn't wear underpants." Then while he must still have been collecting his thoughts, I hit him as hard as I could squarely on the jaw with my right hand. I hoped to box but Spider, I knew, would want to get in close and wrestle with me, a tactic which usually gave him the advantage. But each time he came forward I nailed him, stopping him in his tracks. Suddenly I saw tears in his eyes. Spider was crying, probably because he was hurt and also frustrated when he couldn't wrestle me down to the ground and do his dirty work. Damn, I'm thinking to myself—this is the way I should have fought him all the other times. But hitting him when he charged in still gave him the initiative. So seeing him stunned and hurt made me decide it was time now to wrestle him to the ground. I was on top of him in no time. Now he's really crying. "Enough, enough," everyone hears him say. It was not enough. "Who's the boss?" I shouted. I repeated—"Who's the boss?" The Lyman brothers and the other kids are all crowded around. "You are," he answered. I couldn't believe these words. I couldn't believe the feeling. Meanwhile my guys are jumping all around in triumph. They could now claim to be the "bad guys" on the block. Mr. Lyman, owner of the candy store, came out and handed me a soda as a reward. "It's about time," is all he said. I wouldn't have to fight again. I would leave the block a winner. My friends and I celebrated "our" victory, drinking sodas on the fire escape and retelling the story blow by blow. It got better each time.

It wasn't but a few minutes before the truck got underway on a Saturday that the Lyman brothers came across the street over to where I was standing ready to get on the back of the truck, my spot for the trip. "We're going to miss you."

It was off to Queens and a new life, but it would be unfair to leave without paying my proper respects to Harlem. It was there, after all, that I had spent six happy years, the place where my mother and I first really took root in the North. Sure, it was less than perfect—misfits, drunks, hustlers, criminals—all were there, but what I saw day to day were people very much like my mother, struggling to achieve, hoping for some comforts in life. No, blacks hadn't ruined Harlem. They had instead taken up this part of town from the Germans and the Irish and the Jews, added their own flavor and tone, and created within a section of Manhattan in just a short period of time an area known round the world. Sure were proud of what we had done.

In the years after we left, I came back to Harlem every so often. My work would take me back there as well later on. But it became more and more difficult. My Harlem was changing into something I could still recognize but not accept. It lost its good looks. It lost its confidence. It lost its self-control and, most sadly, it lost its children.

I never saw a gradual change happen as quickly. The signs were probably there while we lived on 116th Street, but not until I returned after the war did it just hit you over the head. Visiting some of my old neighbors told part of the story. Mrs. Williams, you could see, was suspicious of everyone now, muttered as to how the same kind of people weren't around anymore. Frank the barber no longer was his smiling, genial self. Now no community as vital as Harlem could have gone down for the count from one blow. No, it was a combination of shots delivered first to the midsection, then to the head, that brought Harlem low.

In a way the good times Harlem experienced during the war backfired. Southern blacks had been moving in before that, but then the flow really picked up because the war meant there'd be jobs for almost everyone. The Harlem that I knew had never seemed very crowded, but during and after the war it became congested. More and more people were jamming into apartments and buildings were becoming ever more crowded. The recently arrived southern black was different from most Harlem folks. I mean he needed time to adjust to city living, to develop the smarts and the skills to survive. It might work if he had a job. It would keep him going until he figured all this out, but without one he was lost in the big city. When you saw guys shuffling lazily about Harlem in their overalls and heavy work shoes, you knew these southern boys still had a ways to go.

The Harlem economy, never very healthy, had managed just barely to get through the Depression thanks to relief programs and New Deal construction projects. Then the war brought a big shot in the arm that put people in jobs that they never before could have gotten. Plenty of black domestics, for example, left their old positions and got work in the war plants during the early 1940s. But once the war ended lots of those good jobs disappeared. Harlem, lifted up off the ground during the war, was, after 1945, sent crashing back down, except now there was plenty more people out looking for work.

During my time in Harlem the houses were fine looking, the streets clean, and the people proud of their neighborhoods. It wasn't that way after the war. I'll tell you why. There was, as I've said, overcrowding. One way you could tell was the amount of garbage piled up along the curb. I'd never seen this much before. Of course one of the problems was the stuff wasn't being picked up as regularly now. It's an old story, but then I hadn't much considered it. Watch a neighborhood go downhill and you'll also see city services pull back. There had always been fires in Harlem, usually because people overloaded their electrical outlets with all sorts of plugs. Once the fire was out rebuilding would start almost immediately and neighbors would come round to help. Well, the fires continued but now when apartments or entire buildings were ruined, no one rushed to repair or to replace them. Burned-out families found fewer people able or interested in helping out. The numbers of fires actually increased, many set by bums or drug addicts who gathered in hallways and apartments to heat up their heroin.

Physical deterioration set in because many of the old superintendents were no longer on the scene to keep things up. Landlords were not hiring a super for each building but now expected one to handle several all at one time. It couldn't be done. Without a live-in superintendent it didn't take long before apartment houses began to fall apart. Also the old German and Irish landlords were leaving Harlem, selling off their property to new, more speculative types, many of them Jewish, who were ready to handle their property in imaginative new ways. The old ways, they figured, probably wouldn't work anymore, because of the overcrowding, the unemployment, and the numbers of people unable to pay the rent. Expensive maintenance would have to go, and that included most of the repairs superintendents once made in each building. When fire destroyed all or part of a structure now, insurance monies were pocketed and did not go toward reconstruction. Buildings that operated at a loss became valuable assets—offsetting profits from other investments. These factors all sent Harlem in one direction—downhill.

The sounds of gunfire, once common in Harlem, ceased. The silence, however, meant not peace but conquest. Organized crime had won, muscled its way into and taken over the numbers business, organized prostitution, gambling, neighborhood bars and nightclubs. Most blacks were forced out. The rest became front men for the mob. Money, which had once stayed in the community, left. And largely as a reaction to the white mobs, black gangs formed. No longer just street groups organized to protect turf, these black gangs changed, turned aggressive, wanted in on the action themselves.

The mob with its political shield was bad enough. But then came the decision of certain mobsters to get into the drug trade. Gambling, loan sharking, prostitution, numbers, illegal booze, all of them meant big money, but nothing compared to the profits possible from drugs. And in which community could you peddle drugs and not worry about the reaction? Why Harlem, of course. Who really cared what went on above 110th Street? What political clout did we have? So drugs began moving relentlessly block by block, first starting at 110th Street on the east side of Park Avenue and then heading north. Drugs were not new to Harlem. Musicians, entertainers and others had been smoking "reefers" way back when. Maybe that's why there wasn't much concern, no warnings when the new stuff showed up. Besides, we blacks (along with the Irish) took pride in our ability to handle liquor. There were always stories about guys puttin' on big drunks but still managing to get to work. If blacks thought they could do drugs and then carry on as usual, which is what I think many believed, they were in for one helluva shock. Drugs turned you into a zombie; once hooked you became good for nothing.

And more and more fell—the unemployed, the young, and the desperate. Recent migrants from the South and those selling drugs—so many got hooked. Pushers, once addicted, looked for new users to feed their own habit. Because it seemed to some that pushers were living the good life, others joined in to peddle the stuff. Before drugs came to Harlem we had had crime, but usually the nonviolent petty stuff, troubling, but not very threatening. Drugs changed all that. We were destroying ourselves and our own neighborhoods. We had survived slavery as few peoples had. We had suffered through centuries of economic exploitation and racist assaults, bloody but still on our feet. But drugs sent us down for the count.

After the war you couldn't help but notice a new attitude among blacks. Just why it all came about I couldn't say, but I saw it, all right. We had always been told, and many of us had "agreed" to be docile, servile, and smiling. But after the war many blacks stopped this charade, were no longer willing to swallow their pride and follow the white man's script. Anger replaced acceptance, compliance gave way to contempt. Returning black veterans led the way. Bad treatment, racial hostility, and segregation in the armed forces made those who had faced death on the battlefield for the United States real bitter when they returned home to face discrimination all over again. It didn't matter that many of the returning vets were well trained, highly competent people; they still couldn't get the decent jobs. High scores on civil service exams weren't enough to overcome a system set up to keep too many of us from getting in. These disappointments plus the loss of war-related jobs hurt real bad. But this time around protest was in the air. Blacks knew that people like A. Philip Randolph had threatened Roosevelt because of the hiring practices of various war industries, had even planned to disrupt Washington, D.C. if something were not done. Certainly blacks in Harlem saw Adam Clayton Powell, the Communist Party, even some Catholic clergy taking up the cause of black workers and knew that other protest actions against employers and unions that discriminated against blacks had taken place in other northern cities.

Whatever caused these changes and attitudes, I caught pieces of it in Harlem. Housekeepers, for example, took to bitching about their employers more than before. Many complained that while previously a well-to-do household once hired a butler, maid, and cook, many of them had now eliminated most of these positions but expected her to do all their jobs. "I'll be damned if I'm going to do all this work!" Then too many of the nouveau riche employers were hard to work for. Without a sense of tradition, they were largely indifferent to their "help"; it was no longer "my maid" or "my cook," but "my girl." Others were angry because all their hard work and loyalty still didn't bring in enough money to put bread on the table. What was the point of working this kind of job? Some began to question whether they ought to continue working at all. "What the hell, if the welfare is going to give me money, I ain't going back to work."

To whites, blacks were no longer contented and respectful. "If I was shining your shoes along Times Square you know I'd be giving you an angry shine." The guys who hung around the poolrooms in Harlem, who I remembered as usually upbeat and playful, seemed to have turned cynical and sour. Some of your typical happy-go-lucky hustlers now let some of their anger show through. Parents who used to shield their kids, to cover up the bitterness and despair they felt, began speaking about it openly. Listening and seeing what it had done to the older folks, many kids decided not to take it any more. Fewer blacks wanted to hear Amos n' Andy in these later years. Aunt Jemima became embarrassing. And surely the black gangs in Harlem, aggressive and angry, were part of this changed atmosphere. The anger felt good. When had blacks ever been free to express the emotions they really felt instead of play acting for whites? And if the whites were uneasy in the face of this black anger—and many were—so much the better.

Right on 116th Street where I had lived there were gangs now not only selling but doing drugs. That I had never before seen. (Once the gang scene had been a stage kids went through as they were growing up. The gangs then often matured, the members entering businesses together, buying up real estate, the guys turning into solid citizens. Now this wasn't happening. Gang members grew up all right, but remained hoodlums.) But then it wasn't my neighborhood anymore. Many of the old landmarks were gone. The local movie theater closed up, as did my favorite German ice cream parlor. It didn't feel right when I walked about. The streets were dirty and uninviting. Even walking over to Morningside Park where I had once enjoyed so many good times did not boost my spirits. Seeing all the benches broken up only fit the general mood. One incident summed up much of what had changed. It occurred early in 1954, soon after I had joined the police force. Here I was in full uniform looking real sharp, thinking what a hot shot I am and how I'd get a warm welcome when I returned to my block, to 116th Street. I should have known better, but I was feeling so proud about becoming a cop that I was sure everyone else would too. Not so. "What the fuck do you got that thing on for?" That one comment summed up the attitude of the guys in the poolroom. I got some nasty looks too when I walked past the place. The fact that I had a job, a good job, didn't mean a damn to them. In their minds I'm sure it was the wrong job. Now they saw me as the enemy. With many of them into car thefts, robberies and muggings, I was the guy they had to stay clear of. Still, I was hurt. I hadn't switched sides but I also was no longer one of them.

Living in Queens did not keep me from coming back to Harlem, but my trips became fewer and the time between visits longer. To see what was happening hurt me too much. The Harlem that I had once known and so enjoyed became harder and harder to find. The openness, the sense of neighborhood, the pride in neatness, even in dressing well, all this was passing away. No one in my day had ever called it that, but now you heard it all the time—Harlem had become a ghetto.

12 | OFF TO QUEENS—1943

My mother had done it again. Moving on we were—and up so she believed. Queens, though part of New York City, was separate from Manhattan, not nearly as crowded, with plenty of grass and trees. We were moving to the "country," according to my mother.

It was project housing, but built on a small manageable scale by the city and well maintained. Rental charges depended on your income. It was some find, but how my mother discovered it and got us an apartment there I don't know. Here she'd be right at home. It seemed as if everyone (the project was about 80 percent black and 20 percent white) was ambitious as hell, was working their butts off and had the smarts to make it. I mean everyone had plans, everyone was going to school—there was energy all over the place. It wasn't long before I got caught up in it, got a whiff of the idealism and optimism of the people here.

In no time my mother (who was now working as a nurse in Jamaica Hospital, not far from where we lived) made the apartment into our home with her personal touch and sense of style. Almost every day she'd be bringing in new stuff, collecting it from people who had been holding on to things for her. Plus she was paying off her lay-a-ways, which also ended up in our house. And I shouldn't forget the modern stove plus a refrigerator and, for the first time, our own telephone. This was livin'! When some neighbors told her that she had set up one of the nicest apartments in the project it sure pleased her.

It had happened before—there had been Kessel and Mr. Welch, but now I came under the spell of a whole bunch of strong-minded, intelligent, opinionated older guys who couldn't wait to "educate" me. They'd tell me how things really were, recruit me to the "cause." My mother and I soon were part of a circle of friends and acquaintances in the project, all progressive minded, some surely Communists. My mother stopped going to church, preferring to attend meetings of the local progressive Democrats and to listen to the discussions going on there and in the project. Progressives, Socialists and Communists, black and white, were all battling it out, seeing the times as ripe for change, each convinced they had the key to the future. Never before had I listened to such lively discussions, seen such a sense of commitment or heard such openly bitter attacks against conditions. We'd often get together on the benches just outside the project and listen to these politically active adults talk the talk. I loved these independent types, became excited by their insights and criticisms of the "system". This was the way, I thought, to get a real education.

A lot of this bold talk was coming from black guys. The war, as I mentioned, was changing the way they saw things and they were speaking out as never before. Black veterans in particular came home and started talking about their war, what they went through in the army. No matter that they had put their lives on the line, they still had to face all kinds of crap from fellow soldiers and officers. Those "boys" who survived came home "men," angry and unwilling to put up with what they once accepted. Take my friend Eddie Angelitti. His war service took him to Tinian, a Pacific island supply depot where ships continually arrived offshore with munitions and other cargo to be unloaded. According to Eddie only the black troops were ordered to remove the bombs and other live ammunition from the boats, then lug this dangerous stuff through the water. Sometimes the bombs blew up on the way in to shore. Why was it blacks wondered, only they got this job? Black soldiers more than once refused to obey orders to unload, but such "mutinies" were hushed up, according to Eddie. Little by little we found out that what happened on Tinian took place elsewhere, wherever blacks were serving. Want to know why these troops came back with an "attitude"? We also heard about black soldiers in England and the tensions that developed there, especially after English women started going out with these guys. To discourage this, word circulated that "niggers had tails." We laughed plenty about those tails, still we knew, it was no joke. Tails and all, plenty of black guys came back to the States with English wives.

Then there was Charlie, an older guy who also hung out with us. He didn't go off to war, but he too had developed an attitude. Charlie was a Redcap on the railroad, and what stories he told. White people, he had long ago concluded, were the dumbest folks in the world. You could, he was convinced, con them anytime. This he did while working with prostitutes he let onto the trains to service passengers. In "business" with them, he supplied stuff to knock out their customers. Once out cold the women would pick them clean, give Charlie his cut, and then get off the train. These guys said nothing, embarrassed by what had happened. Charlie also told us about crap games that went on through the night involving porters, some of the other trainmen and certain passengers. The dice, he assured us, were loaded, and the passengers almost always relieved of their cash, after which the train guys would laugh themselves silly. Charlie's anti-white campaign included another unusual feature. His opportunity came when passengers left shoes outside their doors to be shined. Charlie would shine them, all right, but he'd then take a razor and partially cut the threads connecting the uppers to the soles of the shoes. This bit of spiteful mischief would go unnoticed until some time, several days later perhaps, when the two halves of the shoe would separate. So it was in this very personal way that Charlie took his revenge, struck back against white society. But Charlie, as I've said, was not alone. The long era of black docility was ending. Even the cops realized this. Usually aggressive when dealing with blacks, they were more likely now to back off and show greater restraint. Then too racial controversies of all sorts were bubbling to the surface and hitting the newspapers. A different type of black was on the scene.

I became aware of this listening to some of the talk going on in the project. Neville Lake for one had no illusions about the way things really were. Neville, who lived near us in the project, was a brilliant, educated, strikingly handsome black guy with a gorgeous wife and beautiful kids. To me he seemed so worldly and knowledgeable. Sitting on the bench outside, he loved talking to us about the history of Europe, and about the black past, which he really knew. He was a commercial artist, owner of a successful company in downtown Manhattan. However well he was doing, race still affected his business. He made, for example, few sales calls himself, but instead relied on a white representative. If customers knew it was a black owned company, business, he assured us, would suffer. Neville was a Progressive, and often went to meetings with my mother at the local Progressive Club, in fact spoke there himself several times. Many considered Lake to be crazy, far out, certainly too militant, but not me. Here was another Adam Powell, demanding that blacks organize, shake things up, apply pressure. "You can't wait for the guy to give it to you," he would say. "You gotta get out there and do it yourself. You must experiment with life." But what if the doors don't open to you? "When we have our revolution you go and blow the whole goddam building up!"

Across the hall from us lived Stanley Diaz and his wife. Stanley was a Puerto Rican, dark, in fact just about as black as I was. Diaz and his wife both were Communists, openly so. Stanley was the only black union pressman (Amalgamated Lithographers of America) in New York City and earned a fat paycheck working for a company that produced cover page proofs for Time and Life Magazines. For a committed Communist, however, he had developed certain advanced capitalist tastes. He loved tooling around in his two prized Cord automobiles, also in a third car, a convertible. Despite this he had little to say in favor of the existing economic system. Capitalism, he was convinced, was at the root of the world's ills. Racism, poverty, immorality—according to Stanley, all came from Capitalism. "Do away with the big money," he used to tell me, "and you do away with the problems." Stanley was not just a talker. A member of the Amalgamated Lithographers, then controlled by Germans and the Dutch, he fought like hell to get minorities into the union. In fact he would later become my mentor, teaching me how to run the big presses and at the same time pressuring the Lithographers to admit me. He was a "troublemaker," but one union leaders had decided to play along with. That explains how I later became a union member.

Then there was Bernie Bender, also a self-proclaimed Communist. Back then such declarations were not quite as risky as they would later become. We were, after all, fighting against Hitler, the Russian Communists were our allies, and American Communists were calling for greater efforts to win the war. To Bernie, Stalin was larger than life, a true hero battling heroically against the devil Hitler. He also made sure to give me books on Marx and Engels plus other leaflets proclaiming the glories of Communism. Bernie was confident I'd come around in time to seeing things his way. He took me to Greenwich Village to attend Party meetings. He and Lake also brought me along to visit one of the Communist camps located upstate. I knew about them, having watched Movietone coverage of some angry demonstrations against these camps by local people. There were tense moments both times we drove up, thanks to State Troopers stationed outside. Their job, I guess, was to harass those heading in. They stopped our car, looking, they said, for liquor although I'm sure it was for some reason to mess with us. Meanwhile FBI guys are up there too, aiming their cameras, taking pictures of everyone going in. The local folks were out in force as well, picketing the camp and carrying signs—"Communists Must Go."

Once inside it looked just like a summer camp, with log

22-SKOL

cabins, picnic tables, a big lake and a speakers' platform. Young people mingled with older intellectuals and socialists. Bernie knew almost everyone there, especially the labor organizers. Speakers aplenty there were, singers too, most especially Pete Seeger, who soon had us singing along with him. I spotted a fair number of young mixed couples, which I'm sure didn't sit well with the locals. This, I'd hear people say, was part of the Communist strategy—using white girls to attract black men into the Party. I can't speak to that, but I'm not denying I saw plenty of action around the camp. Once the speeches and singing were over, everyone, it seemed, disappeared into the woods or crowded into their tents. If part of Communism involved screwing around, there were, without a doubt, plenty of true believers at that camp.

Bernie often included me in his family outings, and we would sometimes end up in places where blacks were not welcome. You had to see the stares I got. (Believe me, blacks are not blind. In fact over the years we've developed a sixth sense, an early alert warning mechanism. We've used this system so long it may actually have become too sensitive, caused us to see slights, even threats that weren't there. Still with so many dangers around, better to be safe than sorry.)

There was the time Bender, after packing us all into an old truck he'd rented, headed out to New Jersey for a camping trip. It was his wife and kids and me plus this young white woman who was divorced, and her two children. As we drove in we got a nasty stare from a State Trooper stationed at the campsite. We must have looked like a group up from Tobacco Road, with our beatup truck and shabby looking tents and equipment that we spread out on the ground. We had just managed to get set up when two State Troopers headed toward us. What was wrong? The problem, it turned out, was me. The campsite was not for blacks; my being there could cause trouble. (Especially when it seemed I was in the company of this white female.) Bernie became irate, his face flushed with anger. He could barely get the words out. "They want us to leave," he muttered., "but I'm not leaving.

It's because of Earl." Then he had second thoughts. "They'll arrest me, though, if I stay. You can bet on that." After a pause he went on, "But if I get arrested how are you all going to get home?" He hated to give in, but then decided we'd better pack up and leave. For weeks after though you just knew it was still eating him up.

It was quite an experience listening to all these guys, Lake, Diaz, Bender, and Mr. Williams, the leader of the Progressive Democratic Club in the area. All were what you'd call "lefties," but they saw eye to eye on few matters. Williams and Neville Lake both belonged to the same Progressive Democratic Club, but they were always arguing, with Williams convinced that Lake was off the wall. Williams wouldn't even talk to Stanley Diaz, the Communist, couldn't stomach his talking, always talking—about taking over the government, taking over the corporations, taking over this and that. However much they disagreed, what an education it was for me just listening to them discuss where the power was, who really ran things, and how the people were being exploited. Bernie Bender, the white Jew, was constantly pointing out instances of racism to me, a black kid, and reminding me about the exploitation of the working classes. I found Communism, the way Bender and others presented it to me, appealing. It seemed to make sense, to explain why things were the way they were. Communism got you thinking. Communists appeared dedicated, willing to stir things up, take risks, put themselves on the line, educate people. I wasn't ready to overthrow everything (although they didn't talk this way during the war) but I certainly had no trouble understanding how unfair the system was, especially to blacks. Even Mr. Williams, who was in many ways an old style ward politician, was anxious to break with the past by running a black candidate in our district. And of course Neville Lake was always ready to march on a moment's notice and to call for one sort of revolution or other.

All of us actually got a chance to do some marching. The very day we moved to Queens I had noticed a YMCA not far from our apartment. I planned on joining, just as I had the one in Harlem. Not long afterwards I walked over to the Jamaica Y, to sign up. That I would be told I couldn't join never occurred to me. But that's what happened—"We don't serve Negroes here." It made no sense; I had already been a Y member back in Harlem. Friends quickly set me straight. There were black Y's and there were white Y's. My mistake was that I tried to join the wrong one. I let it go, but not others. Soon afterward local blacks decided to bring pressure on the Y to change its admissions policy. Naturally Neville Lake took up the cause, as did Bernie Bender and other Communists. Here was an issue they could sink their teeth into. It started as a small demonstration but then grew once the Y decided against any change in policy. Delegations from various other organizations, black and white, including the Harlem Y, labor groups, the NAACP and the Communist Party then joined in the picketing ("Two-Four-Six-Eight, the YMCA must integrate!"). On some days maybe 200 to 300 people were showing up. This brought out the cops and that's when the scene began to turn ugly. The police themselves started harassing the demonstrators and looked the other way when hecklers arrived to oppose and intimidate the protesters. I joined the picketers on several occasions, though my mother warned me to stay away. It could get out of hand, she said. Blacks in the area were divided on these demonstrations. Many got involved, but others, like my friend Sy Rooks, held back. Some suspected the Communists, many worried about the police, while others warned direct action was too provocative and might backfire. "Let it be"—that's what I heard from these people. Still the protest went on, weeks stretching to months. By the time it ended with the Y agreeing to end its racial exclusion, I was off elsewhere and certainly was not part of the final victory, But the message got through; changes in race relations were acoming.

Want to know where I was? I went off to fight in World War II! Seriously, that's what I did. But you were just fifteen and a half years old in 1944, you might say. How in the world did I get to join the army? Well, I may have been fifteen, but I was a big fifteen. Besides, no one asked for my birth certificate! They saw this big black kid who wanted to enlist, they needed bodies—"You're in the army now!"

Why did I enlist, you say? Why did I walk around the city by myself? Why did I hitch a ride on a boxcar several years before? I do believe I had a well developed appetite for adventure. This was no personal crusade against Hitler and racism, although I certainly was as patriotic as the next guy and was rooting for us to win. I was close to Benny Rollins, Eddie Angelitti and Wilbur Spell. They all had either been drafted already or had volunteered. I felt alone, left out. Besides, the uniforms on the guys who were back on leave looked real sharp to me. Imagine how I'd look in one of them! And what was keeping me home? School? It was just okay, nothing more. Going into the army—that was exciting. So off I went. I told my mother about my plans. I had to be kidding, she thought. When I next spoke to her I was in the army. I just didn't mention where I was stationed.

Let me tell you about my glorious war service. For me it was off to Fort Dix (we were given lunch money and carfare and told to travel to New Jersey on our own) for basic training. I was a big kid, five foot ten inches, so it was no problem passing for an eighteen-year old. Of course what I mostly ended up doing didn't take size, it took endurance. I spent more time on K.P. than with any kind of soldiering. Just how they got down the roster so fast and so often to me I never figured out. I mean, my name was Williams, that's a "W," a long way off from A, B and C! And K.P. work was a bitch—peeling potatoes, shucking corn, carrying out the garbage, cleaning the place, washing the dishes. Plus the cooks treated us like shit. They ruled the mess hall. No, they didn't just pick on me; they mistreated everyone.

Even the uniform turned out to be a disappointment. Mine didn't fit, and it was nothing like some of the snazzy ones I had seen, back at the project. And being winter the little soldiering we did was not for me; I never much cared for cold weather. I hadn't given it any thought, but what a surprise when I found myself training in an all-black unit—except for the white officers. My uniform didn't change my color or white attitudes. When I left the post to wander around a nearby Jersey town I felt the unfriendly stares. On a bus to Washington with a weekend pass I sensed hostility, and certainly Washington meant an all-black hotel or nothing. So what if I was preparing to fight for my country—I was still a nigger.

I never did get to fight. My mother, once she realized that I really was in the army, took action. She wrote a letter—to whom, I have no idea—explaining what had happened, and letting them know that I was just fifteen years old. It took three months for the letter to get through channels and for them to track me down. But then I was quickly mustered out of the army. "You're only fifteen and a half," my commanding officer said after calling me into his office. "It's great to know you're that patriotic, but you gotta go home." But, "Don't worry," he said, "comes the next war we'll call you number one." And so my service in the epic struggle against Hitler came to an abrupt halt some two months before our unit was scheduled to ship out overseas.

From Fort Dix and World War II it was back to junior high school, P.S. 40. Even though it was a new school for me and I was a transfer student, I fit in easily. Italian kids were here too, but unlike the situation in my previous Junior High, these Italians (and the Polish kids as well) were alright; there wasn't much trouble. My problem simply was with school itself. I still hadn't learned to spell worth a damn. Nothing new here. There was this one teacher, a black lady, Mrs. Himmescheimer, who believed in me, said I had a lot of potential, and tried her best to light a fire under me. But when I didn't come around, when I continued to stay away from classes, even she began to lose hope. Same with Mr. Lynch, the gym teacher. He actually came to my home a few times and spoke with my mother, both of them wondering what it might take to get me to get serious, as a student. But I was a good student—curious, attentive and critical, but my focus was not on school but on life.

For example there was the week that instead of going to school I accepted an invitation from one of the older guys in the project to drive with him to Cleveland. Seeing new places appealed to me, but more exciting was the fact that he was going to visit and stay with an old buddy and teammate from college days—Jesse Owens. Now Owens wasn't nearly as well known as Joe Louis, but many of us knew he'd been quite a star. Sure enough, we drove up to his home, located in a black neighborhood outside of Cleveland, and there was Jesse Owens, waiting for us. He was happy to see us, gave me a warm hug, and announced that I "must be a good kid." He lived in a large house that had a porch in front, and there were a lot of people inside who I imagined were part of his family. (Even more arrived the next day for a backyard barbecue.) Mr. Owens was very pleasant, well-spoken—and smiled easily. I didn't say very much, since most of the conversation concerned the good old days and the times the two of them had shared. We stayed two days and slept (my bed was the living room couch) over at Jesse's house. Mostly I walked around his neighborhood, and couldn't get over how clean the streets were. I also stepped into a local barber shop there—got myself a haircut. Nothing exceptional happened—just a pleasant trip and visit. But I had now shined the shoes of Joe Louis and slept in the house of Jesse Owens (in neither instance had I asked for an autograph!). Now how many other people could make such a claim?

At this time much of my traveling involved leaving the "country" scene in Queens and heading off to Manhattan—the "city." Most especially to Greenwich Village. I usually went alone, seeing it as my private adventure, a separate area of my life. I was eager to meet new and fascinating people to satisfy my hunger for stimulation. Back in Harlem I had often spent lots of time in the Village. I wasn't a "regular" then, like many of the people I ran into, but I was there often enough that folks included me almost automatically in whatever it was they were doing. While I would almost always end up in the Village, many an evening began in one or another of the midtown jazz clubs. I loved jazz, could listen for hours. The improvisational bursts, the competitive edge, the individual techniques of these guys—there was plenty to hold your attention. Geniuses some of them were, able to create intricate pieces, even those who couldn't read a note of music. The jazz joint itself was no ordinary place. Here was an audience that was serious and real appreciative—when the music played, all conversation stopped. And jazz encouraged a certain camaraderie even extending to blacks.

Here I was a young black kid and yet I had absolutely no problem getting in and becoming part of that scene. I'd hang out at several jazz joints that were located at the basement level of the many brownstones along West 52nd and 53rd Streets. I ordered drinks—no one ever asked for an ID because the logistics made this impossible. The place would be packed. There'd be five deep at the bar when I'd shout from somewhere along the fringe at the bartender. Often he couldn't even see who I was. Then I'd pass the money along toward the bar, thanks to a number of willing hands. A return trip carried my drink. Later in the evening, people at a club would usually have a place, a party, an apartment to go to. "Come on along with us, Earl"—invitations came all the time. The night was just beginning and the destination, I knew, was almost always the Village.

I loved the Village, saw it as an oasis of tolerance (it was probably the only area of the city where the racism of the cops stayed under wraps), a meeting place for people of all sorts and, not incidentally, a hell of a place to pick up girls. Everywhere we went people just opened up their apartments, invited us in and let us stay for hours on end—sometimes right through the night—drinking, smoking pot, discussing, making love, sleeping, actually just about anything we wanted to do. Now my strategy in such circumstances had long been to play the part of an interested listener, to ask questions, to hear everyone out and not say much myself. This technique worked well because there was never any shortage of talkers. People here were well informed, willing to listen to others, but mostly eager to push their own ideas. Young, old, men, women, academics, professionals, artists, street folk—all mixed easily.

Then there were the ladies. Not like any I had ever seen—so open and aggressive, so indifferent to ceremony or convention. Cursing, smoking, talking about sex without the slightest hesitation or caution. And it was not just talk. No one seemed the least surprised or paid the slightest attention when a couple, almost at any point in the evening, left the living room for one of the bedrooms. If you wandered across a twosome making love in one of the rooms you simply ignored them, went about your business. At first I couldn't believe how natural and casual sex was here. If the mood hit you and a partner was available, it was no big deal to take pleasure in one another. No elaborate strategy, scheming, or preparation. It just would happen. This was wild, and not something I was entirely comfortable with at first. But I learned. Soon enough I was approachinig a woman letting her know she turned me on. She'd look me straight in the eye and I'd have my answer—either way. If we clicked we usually arranged to meet later on in her apartment. If she was out of liquor or food she'd suggest that I bring some along. Many pleasant "sleep-overs" were arranged this way. It was all so casual and cool and uncomplicated. Those were real good times.

You may wonder how my mother took to me roaming around the Village and hanging around the jazz joints. It was in Queens just as it had been in Harlem. She went off to work and had her own social life, and I went my separate way. She trusted me. Our relationship couldn't have been better. Even as I grew more "worldly" she continued to tutor me, brought books and magazines into the house that she hoped I'd read, and took me along to meetings of the Democratic Progressives in the area. We agreed on most matters, although she found my indifference to school hard to accept. So many possibilities were opening up to blacks, she said, that I should prepare myself. But even when I made no obvious "preparations," she didn't lose patience. "I'm not going to sit here and be your judge," she told me. "You'll find out later."

Differences over school didn't lead to fights, but I'd be lying if I said we didn't tangle occasionally. I was, after all, pretty headstrong, independent minded, and a teenager, no less. There'd be times we stopped talking to each other, usually because of something I did. Eventually I'd own up to it and apologize. It took a lot for my mother to blow, but she could—especially this one time. What I did, I don't recall but I'm certain I challenged her, probably was fresh, too. Well, she exploded and threw an iron at me. Had it not been plugged in, it might have done real damage. Instead it snapped to a stop—just before hitting me. We just stared at each other, then both of us burst out crying as if on cue. Nothing like this ever happened again.

So you see, my mother wasn't perfect. I found another "fault"—her taste in men. As I've already told you, my mother was always discreet about this portion of her life, never once allowing any guy to remain overnight in our apartment. She would every so often, however, go off for the weekend, and while she said nothing, I figured it had to be with a man. With the exception of one or two, the men I did see were not the kind I would have wanted for my mother. To me they were hustlers, attracted I'm sure by her good looks and good job. But there was this one fellow, a commercial artist, a really nice guy who I think I might even have started calling "Dad". He'd take me to the zoo and for bus rides, while at other times the three of us went on wonderful outings. He spent lots of time in our apartment doing his artwork there. My mother, I knew, enjoyed being with him, and he treated her fine, always sending gifts for her birthdays and on holidays. But that relationship, so promising, somehow didn't work out. I sure missed him. My mother too. She was not herself for quite some time after it ended. Later on when by chance I'd mention him, tears came to her eyes.

Then one day my mother remarried. It was to a guy who worked in Jamaica Hospital as she did. Once the war started he had gone off to the army but they exchanged letters regularly while he was away. I'm not certain what drew my mother to him, although it might have been the fact that he was a religious man and, like her, a really meticulous individual. When he returned off they went to Elkton, Maryland, to get married. He then moved in with us. Early on there were problems. He was not the same guy who had gone off to the war. Where he was once easy going and considerate, now he demanded that things be done his way. I doubt whether she had seen that side of him before. I certainly was not about to knuckle under to him. "You're the sergeant but I'm not the corporal," I reminded him each time he demanded I do things his way. He also proved very tight with money, reluctant to pay his fair share of the household budget. It was not a happy family; then it turned far worse.

One day I came home to find my mother crying, her face all puffy. He had slapped her, and during the course of their argument, lost his temper and smashed a vase. I knew what I had to do. He had to go. No one was going to put a hand on my mother. He was her husband, but who the hell did he think he was? I knew he kept weapons around the house, guns he had returned with from the war. That's probably why I thought to get myself a butcher knife from the kitchen. "Pack your bags and get out of the house or I'll kill you," I shouted. When he didn't move I changed my terms. "Get the hell out now," I screamed at him. "I'll pack your bags and you can come back for them." That got him moving and he headed straight for the door. But then once out in the hall he turned on me. He may have been in the Army but it was no match. He left all right, but not before I had punished him real good.

I put all his clothes and belongings into suitcases and left them in the hallway outside our apartment door. He returned sometime afterward to pick them up. He never came back.

Marrying him, my mother later admitted, was "the worst thing I ever did." For my part I had defended my mother and rid myself of a stranger who had, I decided, no place in "our" home.

13 | THE SCENE IN QUEENS

Moving to Queens and living in the project had worked out real well. Still, I should have known my mother wasn't about to stop here. Her dream of moving up still had a ways to go. She had said nothing to me about it, but her heart was set on buying us a house. No pie-in-the-sky dream; she had already put money aside for a down payment. Her goal—a house in Levittown, Long Island where this builder, Levitt, was putting up row after row of affordable houses for veterans and other first time home buyers. Ads for his homes were all over the newspapers.

So one day there we were, the two of us setting out, first by train, then by bus—destination Levittown. Imagine the thrill of looking at a house that could actually be ours. We found the place all right and headed for the office. Other than some salespeople, there were few folks around. Perfect. We'd get us a look at some houses. Could we see the model? Not possible. The explanation—"Too many people were looking at it." Instead we were taken to a large empty area far from the construction sites. Just what we were supposed to see there wasn't clear. It didn't much matter, our escort explained. No telling when they'd start putting houses way out here. Still, we stayed to look around after he headed back.

My mother's spirits sagged. We had been led out to no man's land. That was the message—we weren't wanted in Levittown. What else could we think when, after returning to the office, we saw the salespeople laughing themselves silly—at our expense, we guessed. Undaunted, my mother asked if we could now visit the model house. "Sorry, it's closed for the day"! That did it. It was not often my mother cried, but I couldn't help noticing the tears that came into her eyes as we left. On the way back home we didn't say much to each other. Sadness had turned to anger though. "There it is again," she muttered, bitterly. There was no mistaking her meaning. This woman had played the game fair and square—worked, sweated, saved, dreamed, waited, and now they were telling her that it didn't matter a damn. We were black—there was no place for us there. It was, I'm certain of it, one of the unhappiest days of her life.

I didn't share my mother's pain. Life in the project couldn't have been nicer. This was one well run place, a black manager enforcing the rules, checking all the time to make certain things were in order. Complain about something and he was right over. Likewise if there was something a tenant wasn't doing or a problem a tenant had caused, he got right on top of it. And you'd better listen. Otherwise, being a no nonsense guy, he'd have you evicted. No one in the project fought him on this. He was keeping the place right and most everyone welcomed that.

It's hard not to believe that if public housing had been built this way and run like ours, it would have made some difference. The high rise prison-like public projects that came later were a disaster. It could have all been so much better.

Typical of the good times we young guys had together was this one incident that kept us chuckling for some time. It all began when my friend, Roger, one day asked if I wanted to "see something." I would not, he assured me, be disappointed. Only from his bedroom window could you see "it," he said. His window, I knew, faced a church and alongside were several buildings in which nuns lived, but that didn't sound very promising. But when I showed up at his apartment he announced that we would "see nuns doing things." "That's crazy," I said. Nuns didn't "do things." Still from his window you could look over to their residences, and if the blinds were up, into their rooms. At night you got the best view, he said. That's why I had shown up after dinner. But still the blinds, though mostly open, blocked much of what was going on.

Binoculars might help. So we asked around, explaining that it was for watching birds. Soon we had a pair; now we were in business. The next time I headed over to his apartment conditions were perfect. The light was on, the blinds were almost entirely open, and there were people in the room. With binoculars we had ourselves a good look. "Wait till you see this," was Roger's only comment as he crouched motionless alongside the window. I grabbed the binoculars. He was right. There were two nuns, one unclothed, sitting in a bath, and the other taking off her clothes. What I saw next I couldn't believe. One began sponging the other in the bath, but then she stopped to kiss her and also fondle her. Roger had not exaggerated. It was our private show. Neither of them was in any rush. We took turns with the binoculars, each of us describing the scene for the other. When the "bath" came to an end, both of them dressed and left the room.

Not long afterwards, I was back, asking if I could "play" with Roger. Now I know people are going to find the whole incident upsetting and some are probably going to say I'm making it all up—typical adolescent fantasy. No way. And believe me, I had excellent eyesight back then. They were doing just what I have described. At various times different women got into the act, all behaving affectionately toward each other. Lesbians? I never even heard the word. To me these were girls, taking off their clothes and doing things to each other that I never expected girls to be doing. And imagine our excitement watching them in secret!.

Naturally Roger and I couldn't keep this to ourselves. Actually we couldn't wait to tell the others. The problem was finding an excuse for these guys to be visiting the suddenly popular Roger. What we did was pick one or two kids at a time, so as not to arouse suspicion on the part of Roger's parents. No one was disappointed. Most times it was exactly as Roger and I had described it. Amazingly word never got back to any of our parents. These were, after all, trustworthy and reliable kids that I hung out with.

I haven't told you much about P.S. 40 in Queens, but by now you probably know why. School was not, never would be a major interest of mine. Still I stumbled through and completed junior high school. Next obstacle—high school. Where was I to go? One of my teachers, Mr. Lynch, had the answer—a trade school—Food Trades, to be exact. I wasn't thrilled, but I wasn't opposed. After all, I had enjoyed working in Mr. Welch's grocery. Maybe this was the field for me. A friend from the project, Shorty Tillman, had gone to Food Trades, then gotten himself a job at the Waldorf Hotel (later becoming pastry chef there). Plus, Lynch assured me spelling would not be part of the curriculum. Still, I didn't consider my choice of high school to be that big a deal since I didn't expect to attend on any regular basis.

In its favor Food Trades High School was located in Manhattan on 13th Street off Sixth Avenue in the Village, my second home. The school seemed all right. And for a time I actually enjoyed it. I had figured it to be a dumping ground for dummies, but I was wrong. This was a serious program that trained you for real jobs when you got out. True, the butcher teacher was a real slob, and I didn't much like tbe cooking classes, but the baking was something else. Then there was Mr. Citrano, a terrific guy, who taught commercial grocery. He was tough, but he knew his stuff, was easy to talk to and treated us all like adults. We learned where foods came from, how they were processed and canned. He introduced us to teas and had us drink and savor each one as if it were a fine wine. Class was great because Citrano was always doing something or other to hold our attention. Citrano was so good and my grades in his classes so strong that for a time I seriously thought I might be cut out for this stuff.

But it was not long before I returned to form. Up to this point my attendance, while certainly not perfect, had not raised problems. Then came this one day when I headed over to the playground near the school expecting to play stickball with some of the guys. When I got there, however, they had already chosen up sides and started the game. So I wandered off, walked a few blocks, and discovered a movie theater where some French film was playing. French movies, everyone knew, usually meant there was a good chance you'd see nudity and sex on the screen, more than you'd ever see in our films. In I went, and sure enough, was not disappointed. The "good parts" were there. I became hooked. The place changed movies frequently, and from that time on I didn't miss many, taking off from school for several hours at a time. These absences plus my usual stay-aways and stay-at-homes led to a crisis, then a letter from Citrano to my mother. "You have the brightest boy we have in the school," the letter went, "but he won't stay put all day." Forget graduating, Citrano added, unless I changed my ways. He asked my mother to talk some sense into me. As she read the letter to me there were tears in her eyes. "What's the matter with you?" "Mom, there's nothing to worry about. I can always get a job. I'm going to be all right."

When Citrano handed me my walking papers I wasn't all that surprised. "We got to suspend you," he said. That they did in April. I never again went to school. September arrived and I remained a truant. Not a word from the school or in fact from anyone. I had been turned out, forgotten, one less dumb black kid, probably a "trouble maker." The system didn't much care about such kind.

Fortunately I had a job. A part-time mailroom job at Reynolds Metals I had been working at after school now became full time. Despite my good work I eventually got into trouble there too, however. It was all quite innocent, although that's not how some others saw it. Reynolds occupied the entire building except for one small office which belonged to Honeywell, a manufacturer of thermostats. Salesmen dropped in to this office now and then, but it was really a one-person operation run by a secretary. She was a lovely Italian girl and before long she and I became friendly, and nearly every day I'd be in her office and we'd be chatting. Also when I was there I'd take out a cigarette and smoke. We weren't allowed to smoke in the building. (Only the president, Mr. Reynolds, could smoke. You'd always see him walking around with a cigar stuck in his mouth.)

How I looked forward to going up to Honeywell where I could light up without worrying about being caught. Besides that, this girl was great company, real pretty, sharp too. She enjoyed my talking to her about jazz, and I provided a sympathetic ear when she started telling me about her boyfriends. This was not a romance; we both enjoyed the conversation and the chance to pass the time. Then one day my supervisor let me know that I'd have to stop going there. He had, he said, received word that I was not to be seen in the Honeywell office. What prompted the memo I had no idea. It didn't take him long to offer his interpretation. It wasn't being in that office and not working that bothered some people, he said, but the fact that "you, a black boy, were seen doing a lot of talking with a white woman." Despite the warning I didn't stop entirely. Now though I had to be sneaky. I'd go to her office and she'd give me the key to the ladies' room on the floor. That's where I smoked. Sadly we were no longer able to talk much because folks thought it wise and proper to keep the races separate.

I left Reynolds not long afterward. So I needed another job. In fact, lots of people did now. World War II was over, war employment was ending and the veterans were returning home. It became quite a scramble. In fact two of my friends, Benny Rollins and Eddie Angelitti, had just come back from service and were looking for work. The three of us therefore decided we'd do it together. Each day we'd all pack a bag for lunch, go and get the newspapers and head off to apply for whatever was advertised. We were prepared to do most anything. But whenever we'd get to a place they would have nothing for us, even though in several cases it was clear they were still hiring. Neither Benny nor I were ready to say it was all because of race. But not Eddie.

He was convinced everyone but blacks were being hired. Having been in the army and run into serious racial bias there, he expected the worst. Tired of being turned down, Eddie dropped out of our job hunt. He was married, with two kids; he had to do something. So running numbers became his occupation. He was a bright guy and great with figures: he did real well. Later on Eddie took the civil service exam for the Sanitation Department and got himself appointed to the job. Not that he ever stopped doing numbers. I always felt sorry for Eddie. What a mind he had. It should have brought him more.

It was just me and Benny out there now. Then one day we hit it lucky, or so we thought. An ad in the papers listed this job opening—helpers in a glass factory. That was us—we'd make great helpers. Amazingly after we arrive at the place the job is still open. "You guys want this job?"—"Yeah, yeah." Who noticed that there was dust all over the office. "Okay, you guys got it. Just come back tomorrow in work clothes and boots and a hat and scarf." Seemed a bit odd, but we had the job—that's what counted.

You bet we were there the next morning, 7:00 a.m. sharp, in overalls, rubber boots, a hat and a scarf and carrying our lunch bags. What a sight we were. We'd be working in this pit. Our job was to feed the furnace, one of us shoveling in sand, the other broken glass. Our lunch break would come at 11:30. Geez, it looked simple enough. It was, but only if you ignored the conditions under which we'd have to work. Once we climbed down into the pit and got to work feeding the furnace it became obvious why the job had been available. It was hot, and boy was it dirty! All our covering, especially the scarves and hats, were necessary because little particles of glass were constantly breaking off and floating all about.

Were we treated nicely, the boss obviously hoping that we might decide to put up with the heat and the dirt and stay with the job. Sure it was a paycheck, but Benny and I both agreed it was just too much. The heat from the furnace—the constant sweating—the heavy clothes and boots and all the filth—were a pretty nasty combination. We couldn't take it. We quit the next day. Blacks I know are supposed to take jobs no one else will, but though the two of us were desperate we weren't suicidal—not just yet anyway. "Well, you lasted two days," the guy told us, almost proudly as if we had set a new longevity record for that job.

14 FLYING HIGH

So it was back to the classified ads in the *Times*, the *Tribune*, and the *Telegraph and Sun*. Benny temporarily dropped out, so I was strictly on my own at this point. That's when I spot a newspaper ad for a "baggage handler," the office located on Fifth Avenue and 46th Street. Why not? Guys were already handing in their application forms when I got there. I started filling one out being real slow and careful, hoping my spelling wouldn't do me in. I'm still working on it when I noticed everyone else had left. Then this young woman in charge of the office says, "You look healthy. Do you drive?" Surprised by the question, I blurted out, "Yes." Good thing she put it that way. Sure, I could drive; I just wasn't old enough to have a license. But I looked old enough—that saved the day.

"You're hired"! I couldn't believe it. I hadn't even turned in the application. I was used to hearing, "We got nothing for you," so you know I was surprised. Next thing she's handing me a uniform, some leather ties, a white coat and a cap. The coat and the cap fit! Maybe that's why I got the job? What would I be doing? I hadn't asked. Why, I had just become the newest employee of Resort Airlines, an operation flying out of LaGuardia Airport during the summer months to and from several vacation areas upstate. I'd be working at the airport because while Resort's offices were in midtown Manhattan, its terminal was out at LaGuardia. Well, "terminal" was stretching it. Resort Airlines rented a "closet" out there. There, she told me, I'd find a cart, a luggage carrier, and a little stand. So what if it was not a major enterprise. I was now an airline employee.

Out to LaGuardia I went to check out the place. I couldn't believe my good fortune. She trusted me, in fact gave me the key to the closet, yet she had never seen me before, asked for no references, made no background check. Nothing. I mean aren't blacks supposed to steal and be unreliable? This young woman must have come from another planet! Out at LaGuardia it took me some time to find the closet, and that was only after a number of skycaps pointed the way. I'm with Resort Airlines, I told them. They sort of grinned, didn't seem too impressed.

I was thrilled, though. Back in those days the airport was not like it is today with swarms of people of all kinds milling about. Then relatively few went by plane. It was a novelty. Those who did were the classy people (along with a lot of soldiers in uniform, because this is right after the war). Even the skycaps looked real sharp, almost like the pilots themselves. The whole atmosphere was different. To fly was something special. People even came to the airport dressed up, felt important, experienced a sense of adventure. I certainly did—especially in that uniform!

My job as "baggage handler" first took me to Resorts' 46th Street office each morning at 6:30 a.m., where I would get the list of passengers who would be flying that day. I headed out by subway and then by bus to the airport to set up for the day's schedule, which meant opening the closet and making certain the baggage cart was ready to roll. That was just one of my responsibilities. As Resort Airlines' only "ground personnel" employee, I had my hands full. The airline's single plane, a much traveled DC-3 with a capacity of about thirty passengers, was always parked along the edge of the airfield. One of my other jobs, I discovered, was to clean it up and get it ready for the day's flight upstate, to Lake George, Lake Placid, and Saranac Lake. That meant sweeping it out, mopping the bathroom floor, and taking care of the "honey pots". Now for flushing these "honey pots," into which passengers had evacuated, other airlines hired an outside service company. Resort Airlines figured it would cut corners here, save themselves a little money, so it fell to me. What's more I also had to dispose of this foul matter, dumping the stuff from the heavy, smelly pots out along the edge of the airport without being seen. Then I was supposed to hose down and flush these containers and place them back in the plane's bathroom. The job, you see, wasn't all glamour.

Before passengers arrived for the flight my next task, the one which I was most proud of, was to help guide the airplane into a position near the terminal where ticket holders could later board. I actually learned to do this thanks to Pappy Bryant, the plane's pilot, who flew throughout the entire summer that I worked there. He was one warm, wonderful guy, a Southerner, about 45 years old, short, bald, with a reddish face. He was always in good humor and the two of us got along real well. He positioned me out on the field, and taught me the signals to bring the plane in. You bet it was a thrill—me out there alone, controlling the airplane, directing its movements. It wasn't a very big plane, I know, but still that was me, a baggage handler, waving my flashlight with the glass tube over it signaling to Pappy. (With the propellers going you've never heard such noise.) The idea was to direct him into the loading area and to make sure there were no other airplanes nearby when I motioned him to move. How good was I? He never hit another plane the entire summer!

Soon afterwards passengers would start arriving. People always came early. (I don't remember a time the whole summer when someone dashed up at the last minute.) I couldn't get over those coming by limo—limos were not a familiar sight back then. And there I was, helping them out of those "boats."

The hard part was carting the bags out to the plane and loading them on board. Fortunately Pappy and his co-pilot pitched in. Still it might take us forty-five minutes to position the baggage. That usually ended my day's work—except those few times when I learned why I had been handed a white coat that first day. Three times that summer I became a "stewardess" when the regular one failed to show. There I was decked out in a white jacket playing bartender, serving drinks (Pappy bought the liquor, which was probably his own private concession) and giving out ice until we landed upstate. How many passengers, I wonder, recognized me as the same person who had greeted them at curbside, collected their tickets, and carried their baggage away?

And yes, I served as pilot this one time! Not for an entire flight, mind you, and there were no passengers aboard. It happened on a return run, the first leg of which I had served as bartender. Pappy asked if I might like to fly the plane. What a question! In no time I was at the controls, actually steering the plane. "Don't make any quick movements," Pappy kept saying. "Relax your arms—don't yank it"—"Use your hands and arms, not your body." Imagine my first flying instructions thousands of feet above the ground! Next Pappy called my attention to the braking system and the flaps. Sure I was thrilled but also scared to death. What a relief once Pappy took over, and we landed at LaGuardia. I dashed off to tell my friends. Trouble was, it sounded too improbable. No one believed me. Who could blame them?

When that summer ended, so did the job. Pappy flew off heading south, where Resort Airlines operated other routes during the fall and winter seasons. I locked the closet door for the last time, thus closing down our airport office. It had been quite a summer job, the kind you never forget. Only the tips failed to live up to expectations. Many passengers, I think, held back, assuming that with all the jobs I performed I probably was part of management. They weren't far wrong. "Baggage handler" didn't even come close.

15 | CUBAN HOLIDAY

There I was back chasing want ads. Benny rejoined me, the two of us once more checking out the daily papers, looking for anything that might be in our line of work, which meant just about any job around. Benny I think spotted it first—jobs, lots of them, available at the United Nations. "Mimeograph operator" seemed right for us. I once had worked a machine—actually it was a stamp machine, not a mimeograph, but how different could it be? So what if it said "experience required"; we'd learn on the job. The bigger problem, we thought, was getting out to Lake Success, where the United Nations was just getting organized. Luck was with us. It was the last stop on a bus route that ran from Queens.

Bright and early the next day it was off to Lake Success, the both of us looking just about as sharp as could be. Mimeograph machines were dirty, we knew that, but we had to make the right impression. And they were hiring, just like the ad said. After filling out forms we went into this building, where at least fifty machines were out on the floor. There'd be a test; we'd have a chance to show our stuff on the mimeograph. Some guys were already working the machines when we walked in. "What do we do now?" I asked Benny. We were on the spot. Lucky for us there was a line of men waiting to be tested. Watching them work the machines helped some, but there was no way we could follow all the mechanical adjustments needed to set up each job. The line kept on moving; we were still without a plan. Bluffing our way through seemed the best Benny and I could hope for.

But we caught a break. Just before our turns, lunchtime rolled around. A reprieve. Forget food; how were we going to operate those machines? They were I noticed all made by A.B. Dick, and I remembered having once operated a Dick stamp machine. The company, I knew, had an office in Manhattan. The idea hit us both about the same time—get down there and have someone show us how the damned machines worked. A brilliant plan! We ran for the Long Island Railroad, caught a train into the city, found the company's address and rushed over. Next came the bullshit. We were U.N. employees and responsible for making the final decision on A.B. Dick's mimeograph machines. First we needed a quick update on how they operated. Sure enough, some guy there bought the story and began putting the machine through its paces. Now Benny, being more mechanical than I was, instantly figured it out including how to adjust for different jobs. I got the general idea but not the fine points. No matter; we needed to get back. We hopped the train back to Lake Success showing up about twenty minutes late. A long lunch, we explained. Back to the end of the line again—no problem there. That gave me more time to watch and to listen to Benny run through each step with me. His turn came and he headed off with one of the supervisors. Even from a distance I could tell he was going to make it.

I was last on line. A black guy called me over. Actually he looked familiar, but from where? The machine, thank God, was the same as the one in the city. The idea was to set the stencil in, then ink it and adjust the guides so the paper would hit the stencil in the right position going through. I was nervous; plus, despite the tutoring, I didn't know exactly what I was doing. I blew it. I couldn't get the guides right and somehow I screwed up the stencil. But instead of sending me packing, the guy says, "Watch me closely," then goes through the steps very slowly. Second chance. I tried doing it exactly as he had. Just as I was about to start the machine up, he says, "Hold it"—and under his breath mutters, "Look at it again, turkey—don't you see what you're doing wrong?" He motioned me to the guides; they were upside down! "Now turn on the machine." That's how I passed and got the job.

I soon found out why. Of course the guy looked familiar. Only when Joe Jansen introduced himself did I remember him from 116th Street. An assistant supervisor in the printing facility, he was, he said, hoping to take on as many blacks as he could. But now that I was to be hired he thought it a fine idea if I could actually learn to operate the mimeograph. "Your friend," he said, "got it figured out, but you better put in some time here tomorrow." Of course he was right. His boss would be back next week when I was to start; he didn't want any questions about why I was hired. So the next day I spent several hours getting to know the ins and outs of the machine. I would be an excellent mimeographer from Day One.

It turned out to be quite a job. I was officially part of the United Nations Secretariat. We were there to prepare materials, usually transcripts from the previous day's sessions, in time for the delegates to have it the following day. What pressure! First off an army of typists went to work to get it all down on stencils. Then we took over to run off the sheets, collate them, staple them, have them ready for distribution. Even putting in twelve to fourteen-hour days and working two successive shifts wasn't always enough to keep up with the work.

That's why when the opportunity came I transferred over to the press room. Here they produced shorter versions of the transcripts and other materials for distribution to reporters. Working for the organization was exciting, gave you a feeling of importance. We were expected to dress properly and were allowed to walk about the entire complex and attend sessions of the General Assembly, which some of us did. Resort Airlines had been fun, but the United Nations—this was serious business.

I hadn't expected travel to be part of the job but one day word went around that some of us were being sent on a trip, all expenses paid, to Cuba. Havana was to be the site of an international trade conference, and naturally printed transcripts of the sessions would be needed. I couldn't wait to go. Everyone knew the reputation of Havana then—the brothels, the gambling, the beaches—it was one helluva playground. No one called it a vacation, but everyone expected there'd be fun times down in the Caribbean.

We would travel to Miami by train and then board a boat to Cuba. The ride down became one non-stop party. Even when we passed south of the Mason-Dixon Line, nothing changed. Blacks (maybe thirty or forty of us) and whites mingled freely in the same railroad car. This, I supposed, was permitted because we were United Nations employees excused from the local segregation laws. Once in Miami we got off the train and waited with all our baggage for taxis to get us over to the dock area. Sure enough they pulled up, but then reality hit us—the true South returned. The black guys would open the door of the cabs and then hear the drivers tell them that they could not get in. "White" cabs could not accommodate them. "Blacks only" cabs would have to be sent over. When they arrived we had no other choice but to get in, shaken as we were at this unexpected brush with southern hospitality. "That's the system down here," the black cab drivers explained apologetically. We Northerners had forgotten the ways of Dixie. Plus we had become almost color blind working for the U.N. Once we boarded the boat for Cuba, however, we stopped thinking about it. The good times and high spirits returned. No one had much information on racial arrangements in Cuba. They would, we imagined, be nothing like those of the South.

We were wrong. Our accommodations, we had been told, would be at the Hotel Nacional. It was there that we all went after landing in Havana. But then word came to all the blacks and Hispanics that they were being shifted to a cluster of villas some distance away. No one protested the move and no explanation was offered. We might, I suppose, have made an issue out of it, except that everyone was in such a good mood just being in Cuba. Who wanted to rock the boat? Besides, the villas were very nice and real private, which, as it turned out, worked to our advantage.

To call our stay in Cuba mostly a vacation would not be an exaggeration. There was work to be done almost daily, but usually we finished up by early afternoon. Several local people had been assigned to our department to assist and translate for us, and that simplified our job. We would not be paid until we returned to the United States but we received, in addition to free quarters, a generous daily allowance which was more than enough to cover our expenses plus a large number of "incidentals."

Havana had been cleaned up, at least the center of the city was swept clear before we arrived. While many of the downtown areas were generally off limits to the locals, we, together with the crowds of tourists, were free to go wherever we pleased. Wearing our U.N. badges we became VIPs around town, got special treatment and attention from just about everyone. Several bars near where we worked went out of their way to cater to us. Before we'd even set foot into these places ice cold beer would be heading our way. On a hot day in Havana survival depended on it. The cabbies couldn't have been friendlier. They'd rush to pick us up and then would wait for us, and later provide liquor, girls, whatever we wanted. We were Americans with some money—that was part of it. We might also be their ticket out of there. Could we, they were always asking, take them back with us to the States. They knew more about the United States than I would have guessed (especially the South and wanted no part of it). We were bombarded with questions about New York, Chicago, Boston, and other cities as well. We were forever getting papers to sign. Generally we did. What harm was it, we figured. Affidavits bearing the signature of Americans would, they hoped, carry more weight and maybe persuade officials to allow them to leave.

Security was real tight. Soldiers and police were everywhere, heavily armed, all carrying machetes plus their weapons. I never saw anyone actually use a machete, but even at the belt they sure scared the hell out of me and most everyone else. There were, we were told, "banditos" all about. But word had it that tourists would not be harmed. Locals "violating" this unwritten rule would, we heard, be shot right on the spot. Some beggars shuffled along the streets, but most, I think, had been cleared off or warned to keep out of sight. Many, it seemed, ended up living on the rooftops all over the city. I remember looking out from several high points in Havana and being surprised by this other world. The rooftop life I knew in Harlem could be pretty lively, especially in the warmer months, but it was nothing compared to what I saw here. People cooked, worked, ate and slept up there. Anyone could look in on their lives.

We found our pleasures on a fairly regular basis. Some were even memorable. That was certainly true the first time we headed over to the Hotel Nacional. Us colored folk could not occupy the guest rooms there, but we were free to spend our money in the casino. I bought myself some $15 to $20 worth of chips hoping they'd last long enough for me to have a good time. The place was loaded, mostly with Americans and Scandinavians; it was not easy getting over to the crap table. Once I squeezed in I heard a familiar voice, and sure enough, standing at the table was the movie character actor, Henry Morgan. Clearly the center of attention, Morgan was surrounded, mostly by women, I noticed. Totally at ease and obviously a regular at the casino, he was talking with everyone around him. Instead of playing right off, I just stood there watching him. He was gambling big and losing big time. Then, all of a sudden he stopped and turned to me. You can be sure I've never forgotten what happened next. "Son," he said, "come here a minute." I made my way over, as the crowd parted to let me through. "I hope you don't mind," he then said, and without my saying a word, he put his hand on my head and ran it through my hair. I stood there, stunned, embarrassed as hell. Here in front of all those people he was playing out one of those absurd superstitions whites had. Running your hand through the hair of a Negro brought good luck, that was the belief. Aside from this ridiculous idea, how dare he mess up my hair! I had combed it just right and now I was sure it wasn't the way I wanted it. But with everyone around smiling at Morgan, I pretended not to mind and just stood by as he began to gamble again.

What happened next is the God's honest truth, stranger, as they say, than fiction. Morgan took hold of the dice and let 'em roll. A "seven." "Double it," he shouted. Once more he rolled. This time it was an "eleven." "Double it." Another roll brought a pair of "threes." Next roll he makes a "six." The chips are heading his way, they're piling up all around him. His run of good luck has made me forget my embarrassment. But then he stops and looks my way. Once again he's asking me to come over to him. This time I'm not so sure. "I want to talk to you," he says. With everyone listening and watching it's hard to refuse, so I go over. He put his hand on my shoulder, then leaned over to talk so that no one else could hear. "I know what I did last time probably got you angry," he says, "but I'm going to take care of you, you'll see. I gotta touch your hair one more time." Even before I could answer one way or the other his hands are on me exactly as the first time-clean over the top of my head. "Don't leave," he then says. "Stand right here," pointing to a spot close by him. He starts playing and, would you believe, goes on a roll once more. "Seven," "Twelve," "Seven." He makes a four, then matches it on his next roll. Just how much he's betting each time I can't tell, but it must have been plenty, for the word has spread all over the casino. People are coming over and pushing in from all sides. Even if I wanted to leave, there was no way to get through the crowd. That was a shame, because I know my buddies are around somewhere in the room and they're missing out on all this. The main show, the center of attention is here; and I'm part of it and no one I know is watching!

He just stopped, even as the chips kept coming his way. "That's enough for me." That made sense, though I could see some of the people around seemed disappointed. Many had been betting along with Morgan and had watched their stacks of chips grow real tall. Now they'd be on their own. People came up to shake his hand and let him know that it was one of the greatest streaks of good luck they ever had witnessed. Others stood and simply applauded. It was quite a show, a triumph. Then Morgan broke through the circle of well wishers and approached me. "You're a good kid," he said quite sweetly. "Have a nice time, enjoy yourself." With that he placed a fistful of chips in my hand and walked off. I had no idea what he had given me, but I immediately headed to the cashier with my "winnings." He totaled it up, then started counting out twenty-dollar bill after twenty-dollar bill. I scooped up the money and counted it myself. Three hundred dollars. Wow! Not bad for just standing there and having your hair messed up. He could, if he wanted, run his hands through there anytime for that kind of money, I thought. Sure, I had sold myself, let myself be used. I realized that even then, but with such a reward I felt no regret. Whatever embarrassment, whatever my anger, it was all forgotten as I headed off to find my buddies. Of course, they didn't believe me. Then I showed them the $300. It was $300, incidentally, that I never would spend. I put it away and later handed it over to my mother when I got home. What she didn't get was the story behind it. That would not have pleased her.

Havana's reputation for wickedness was based largely on its famous red light district. It was a must see on any male tourist's itinerary. And a favorite destination for many of the local hot-bloods. (Now if all the men down there wanted to marry virgins, which is what you heard, yet were running around trying to screw anyone and everyone, open prostitution would at least solve one of these needs, maybe both.) Not that there weren't prostitutes elsewhere. You wouldn't find them on the streets, where they would be snatched up by the police, but rather working out of apartments. Many were girls who, for some reason or another, had been thrown out of the brothels. Unregulated, often desperate and frequently dangerous, they robbed lots of tourists. Far better was the red light district, an attraction the guys in our group put at the top of their lists.

There was no way you could miss this three-block heavily policed area jammed with scores of competing brothels. Nearly all the doors, which were huge, were painted red. Inside, the facilities were nicely decorated, immaculate, the places well run. "Patrons" were treated to a lineup of the girls (all under twenty-five, representing many different nationalities) when they first arrived. Wearing see-through gowns or chemises, you got a good look at what they were selling. A very capable madam supervised the operation and guaranteed satisfaction. Customers, if not pleased, could ask for a repeat performance, get to do it again with someone else of their choosing—a nice selling point but an option, I found out, not many exercised. None of the guys in our group came away disappointed. All explained they had performed well, up to expectations.

Also within the district was the famous pornographic theater with erotic entertainment that was supposedly world renowned. The theater seated, I would say, 60 to 70 people at a time, so everyone could be real close to the action. The opening acts featured a variety of sexual encounters including lesbianism, but most everyone was there for the "amazing" display that climaxed the show. Onto the stage comes a woman, unclothed, in obvious distress, who's then is tied to a round tabletop stood on edge. At this point a masked black man enters with two women who hold a cape around him. It's now that she begins to scream. Why, you wonder; what's the danger? What is behind the cape? He then approaches her, bends over, bites her on the neck, kisses her breasts and runs his hands all across her naked body. Now comes the big surprise. Once the assistants pull away the cape, you see that this guy's got himself an absolutely enormous penis. It's real all right—there was no mistaking that. Just to hold it up he needed both his hands. It blew the crowd away—oohs and ahs coming from all parts of the room, people popping up to take pictures of his giant genitalia. It's now obvious why the woman is crying. It gets worse once he approaches her, penis extended. With the drama building, the audience really gets into it, starts clapping as if at a bullfight, seeing him place his penis against her, shouting, "Push, "push," urging him on. Was this just an act? Not if you watched him trying to penetrate and heard her crying out in pain. Up to that point it had been sick but exciting, but now his efforts and her wailing and pain seemed all too real. I was disgusted and shaken. This was not titillation but torture. What a relief when she apparently passes out and he slowly withdraws from her. The show was over, the spectators probably having gotten more than they had bargained for.

I took in the bullfights from time to time in a rickety old stadium that shook dangerously with every cry of "Olé," but I couldn't get as worked up as most everyone else did there. I mean by the time the matador stepped into the ring the bull was, I figured, already exhausted, half dead. That didn't stop the crowds from shouting encouragement as he stepped ever closer to this wounded and doomed beast. What also spoiled it for me was the thought that were you to substitute certain human beings for bulls, there'd probably be the same reactions and cries for blood.

Cock fights around town weren't any more civilized though maybe somewhat more "fair." Never had I seen anything quite as ferocious. Sure it was "just" chickens but it took a strong stomach to watch. These roosters meant business. Just how they got that vicious I don't know, but jumping up and down they slashed at each other, refused to back off, gave no quarter. And their attacks were deadly thanks to razor blades attached to their feet. And as they battled, spectators went wild, screaming for one or the other, money exchanging hands, additional bets placed as the tide and odds swung back and forth. The fight would last maybe three or four minutes. If one of the roosters was clearly dominant the other handler might concede and withdraw his bird before it became badly disabled. Most of the time, however, either because it was too late to save it or because everyone was caught up in the action, you got a fight to the death. The roosters just wouldn't quit pecking and clawing at each other. Soon one was left, the other either dead or mortally wounded. In short order there'd be more fighting, with plenty of other roosters waiting to do battle.

Our being barred from the Hotel Nacional and sent to the villas turned out to be one lucky break for me and some of the other guys. The living was good, but more than that, we found out that rooming next to us in adjoining villas were a bunch of Negro baseball players from the States who were on the rosters of various Cuban teams. These guys were glad to see us and impressed that we were working for the United Nations. Being with them was a thrill for us—they were professional ballplayers, good ones too, some good enough to be playing major league ball.

I became close friends with a few of them, especially with Hank Thompson and Henry Pierson. Many were waiting for their big chance, expected that the major leagues would soon open up to blacks. Watching them on the field with the Cubans I could see how good they were, easily dominating most of the games, despite the fact that they were not, as you shall see, always in "proper" playing condition. "We're going to get our chance." "We're going to go"—you heard that a lot. "The guys up there now are not half as good as we are." "If only we had Spanish names we'd be up there now." They were rooting for each other, hoping that all their efforts, all this waiting would pay off. But below the surface was anger and a sense of frustration. Henry Pierson, a thoughtful guy, talked about this a lot, realized that playing down in Cuba was a waste, that he and the rest of them were losing precious time waiting in the wings, the best years of their playing lives passing them by.

Their playing careers might be leading nowhere, still these guys were having the time of their lives. Day and night, night and day there were parties going on in their villas. Now remember, Cuba was crazy about baseball and these guys were star players.

They were also American, flesh and blood Yankees with all the mystique surrounding those powerful folks up north. And they had money, were willing to spend it, even to give it away. And so the women flocked to them, all sorts of young, attractive women—foreign tourists and local girls as well, all came around, almost all the time.

Whenever I went over, somewhere a party was going on. It would start in one villa, then after a time shift to another and then move on. Now I knew from wild parties. They could get pretty crazy down in the Village, the men and women alike carrying on without much inhibition, but they were all calm and dignified compared to this scene. I mean, these were orgies—no other word I know fits. Everything was going on—music was blasting, food was piled up all over, the booze was flowing, people were smoking grass, guys were gambling, and the women were all over the place in different stages of undress, taking off clothes at every opportunity. If a guy unbuttoned a girl's blouse, she just left it off, same with a skirt. Once a party got underway most of the women would be running around naked and jumping in and out of bed with whoever happened to be around. No, it didn't have to be a bed—a couch, a lounge chair near the pool, the floor—no one was very particular. I had heard the word debauchery before, mostly in church, but I'd had trouble imagining what it might be. Now I knew.

Amazingly these guys could party hour after hour and then get up the next day, stumble out to the ballpark, and play a hell of a game. It was nothing short of a miracle. I'd spot them in the dugout pouring water over their heads, hoping that might wake them up, and then drinking juice to get their systems going. Once on the field, however, the cloud passed and, great athletes that many of them were, they played effortlessly. The games were, so to speak, just the prelude to the day's real sport. Back to the villas they would go, either to rejoin a party still in progress or to begin another night of almost total abandon.

Of all the players, I felt closest to Hank Thompson. I was

"the kid" to him and we hung out some. Talk about a heart of gold. Henry had one. You were in need? No question but that Henry would help out. Many of the local girls, who were real bad off, he'd send home with trays of food from the villas. Not that he didn't take his pleasures. He did, but he understood more than the others and had this sense of obligation. A proud man, he was hurt and angry, scarred I felt by his battles with racism. That had to be one reason he drank so much. Still he clung to the hope of making it to the major leagues.

I stayed in touch with Hank after I returned from Cuba. What a thrill for me when his dream came true and he was eventually signed by the New York Giants. "I made it. I made it"—that's what he shouted to me when I came by the Polo Grounds to see him play, which I did every so often. Still it could not chase away all the previous hurts and disappointments. His anger remained and also his drinking. He'd miss games and the newspapers would hint that it had to do with alcohol. The last time I saw him, he was already fading—"They're juking me, kid," he said, "they're juking me." Just what he meant I wasn't sure, but it was not hard to figure out that his playing days were about over and that this talented black athlete, luckier than most of the others, was still another casualty.

The sexuality of the villa scene featured raw, nonstop action and temptations which none of us could resist. Yet I also took pleasure in another part of Havana where, as a spectator, I watched a series of unusual public courting game rituals. It was on Sunday afternoons that I headed over to the Prado to take in this show. In some ways it was like the strolls we took along Seventh Avenue in Harlem, those leisurely walks after church to show off our fine clothes and to see and be seen. Here in a lovely park setting near the sea wall the emphasis was on flirting and arranging "improper" liaisons. Here the star attractions were the virtuous young women of good family dressed in their best. Promenading in public would have been unacceptable had each not been escorted and shielded by a chaperone. Parading about also were single men of high social status engaged in sizing up the current female crop. They greeted each other formally, then passed on. At the same time though other exchanges were taking place which I came to see only when my cab driver pointed them out.

Shadowing these promenading females were young men of lesser status doing what they could to attract the attention and interest of these "unapproachable" ladies. Well bred women were expected to ignore these vulgar types, and many of course did. But on the other hand some probably hoped for just this sort of release from their strictly supervised lives. These commoners therefore were tempting. The problem (for both) was how to make contact. In time I came to recognize how they managed it, how certain body movements and eye signals told the story. But it was not always subtle. Many of the men took to dropping notes in the path of the oncoming young ladies, hoping they could lead to an introduction. While the women themselves could not be expected to pick them up, their chaperones might. Many to shield and protect "their" ladies, just ignored them. Others played along, maybe following instructions or because of some prearrangement with the "suitor." Once they picked up the notes the courting game might begin.

I found it all real romantic, especially in this setting. Also just adjacent to the parade ground was an area in which men and women were enjoying the afternoon together, the guys looking real sharp in white suits, the women dressed to the hilt. Some were out on boats together, others sat along the water, the men strumming guitars and singing their songs. I'd read about such romantic settings, probably seen them in the movies, but here it was, people actually doing this stuff.

Since we're talking about refinement let me tell you how much more I preferred being seen as a U.N. employee than as an American. Americans were often an embarrassment down there, and and I'm not just talking about your obvious mob types who strutted about town in their immaculate white linen suits and saw themselves as masters of this tropical playground. Too many other "ugly Americans" were around as well, acting like bullies, demanding special treatment. Many were southerners, good ol' boys who treated the locals much as they did Negroes back home. ("Hey, boy!" you'd even hear them shout.) Loud and brash, they looked down on just about anyone who wasn't American, and were always complaining about the service. I remember once overhearing an American asking directions from a member of the national police, who were stationed everywhere to protect and assist tourists. Most all of them spoke English, but somehow this one fellow wasn't providing a satisfactory answer. "What's the matter with you anyway!" The Cuban stiffened but accepted the abuse, figuring the guy might be someone who could throw his weight around. Retaliating against an American could be risky.

Many of the American women were just as clumsy and obvious. Even those looking to have their flings had little finesse, were no match for the brazen and sophisticated German and Swedish women. Even the male prostitutes in Havana, the "beach boys," knew to keep their distance from these Americans. Some got real obnoxious. I saw that side of it back at the villas, where I'd hear them chewing out the maids. Cuba was our playground; Americans were here to have a good time and no one had better interfere with that.

The police and the gun-toting soldiers were not around just to keep the riffraff away and provide directions to tourists. They were what kept Fulgencio Batista in power and protected American interests there. Batista's regime (we had all met the man and shook his hand when we first arrived in Havana) was not seriously threatened while I was there, but trouble was brewing. The Cubans we talked to wouldn't say much about this, but you heard enough to sense a growing unrest. They were more than willing to translate the slogans for us scrawled on walls in and around Havana. These denounced the government, promised liberation or called for revolution. A young rebel, Fidel Castro, some said was among those leading the opposition. Any problems were seen as the work of Castro or his followers.

I myself witnessed two attacks against the government. One day when I entered this train station, I saw it filled with military units together with regular police forces. They were looking over everyone waiting on the platform, seemed to be expecting trouble. In charge was an army colonel dressed in high boots, a saber resting on his side. Suddenly shots rang out. "Get down." "Get down." I and everyone who wasn't a policeman hit the ground, and good thing too because more shots followed. All civilians were quickly hustled out of the station. But as I headed away from the tracks there was the colonel on the ground. He had been struck and killed. Castro himself, it was later said, had been at the railroad station where the shooting and killing took place. Whether he was or not, this opposition was serious, and bold. They were taking their fight against the government right into the capital city.

Then came the second incident. A few of us one day decided to take the trolley into work, something we did now and then. No one was paying much attention as it headed toward the center of town until it came to a sudden halt. (Havana trolleys normally didn't stop. You just ran alongside and got on.) A group of men surrounded the trolley and, speaking in English and Spanish, ordered us off. Then they began rocking the heavy car back and forth. They got it to shake so violently that it left the tracks and tumbled off to the side. This bit of sabotage accomplished, the band took off pronto. The authorities arrived but clearly too late to catch those guys. Such acts of defiance despite tight security in the heart of Havana, the nation's capital, left me with the impression that there was more trouble to come.

Homesickness? No one in our group was in any rush to return to the states, but eventually the trade conference, the reason we were there, ended. For three months, as I think I've made clear, it had been very little work and mostly play for all of us. Giving up this kind of life was not easy, but then we all had fat paychecks waiting for us back in New York. Some deal. Cuba for me had been an eye opener, one incredible foreign adventure. I had seen the world! Not bad for a seventeen-year-old kid.

What I didn't see coming was that my days with the U.N. were numbered. Delegates it seemed were doing more talking than ever, because the work pace really picked up after we returned (or was it because we weren't used to working all that much?). We were doing twelve and fourteen-hour work days under a new boss, a real bastard who insisted that we put in overtime whether we wanted to or not. Production, production, that's all he knew. If this meant guys had to come in on their days off or even on holidays, so be it. Now I got a lot of this secondhand because you'll remember I was working in the press room. I signed in every day at reproduction but then put in my hours over at the press department.

The situation blew early one morning just as the night shift was getting ready to leave. Before they could, word came that the boss needed them, didn't want them going home. They'd have to stay for at least part of the next shift. It had happened before; mostly the guys had grumbled but gone along. This time, they were plain exhausted and just wanted out. They told this to Erickson, the foreman, but he had his instructions. We'd all be fired, he said, if we didn't stay. No bullshit, Erickson added; if we walked, we'd be gone. The guys couldn't believe it. Now I'm taking this all in, real nonchalant like, because I don't see where it applies to me. I'm working the press section; this order was for the reproduction people. I left, ignoring Erickson; so did everyone else.

I wasn't home more than a few hours when this big black limousine pulled up outside, a chauffeur got out, came up to the apartment, and handed me a letter. I didn't have to read it, especially when he told me he had been out delivering the bad news for the last hour or so. What it said was something like: "You are hereby summarily terminated from the employ of United Nations," etc., etc. I stopped reading. I couldn't believe it. I was

22-SKOL

sure they had just been trying to scare us. I called my friend, Benny. He'd already been visited. I won't bore you with the details of what followed. We went back to the place to make our case, we hired a lawyer, we even managed a meeting with the United States Ambassador to the United Nations. No go. Each time it was the same story. What we had done, refusing to stay on the job, had been classified as a strike. And since the rules of the U.N. banned strikes, we were out—no longer U.N. employees. No matter the word "strike" had never been mentioned. No one seemed to care that they had been overworking the guys. The U.N. just washed its hands of us, put up this bureaucratic screen to keep us away, and finally wore us down. After over two years of loyal service, the United Nations of the world had brushed aside our rights, then looked the other way. In the years that followed, the U.N., most folks said, never managed to live up to expectations. If you would have asked me back then in the early days, I might have told you so.

16 | FIT TO PRINT

This time it wasn't back to pounding the pavements and chasing down newspaper leads. I was about to get me some serious training for a real profession. Actually I had already started, working at night, but getting fired really got me moving, thanks to my friend, Stanley Diaz, who as I've already told you, lived with his family in our Queens project. Stanley, almost from the time I moved in, took me under his wing, tried molding me to his ways and beliefs. He was one tough hombre, prepared always to fight the system or actually just about anyone who rubbed him the wrong way. He was a little guy, but boy, was he tough. And radical, probably like I said a communist. A protest march, a demonstration, and you knew he'd be there, along with lots of his friends. Stanley rejected capitalism but then saw no contradiction enjoying its benefits. He had a well paying job as a master lithographer, and with his money became, as I've mentioned, a collector of Cord automobiles. He just loved those slick sports cars with the fancy exposed piping. Each weekend we'd take one of them out for a spin. Even when capitalism crumbled he'd still have his beauties.

Stanley was as dark skinned as I was, but he was classified as Spanish (he was from Puerto Rico) and married to a white Jewish woman. Stanley planned to train me as a printer and then get me into his for-whites-only union. (When I first came to the shop, workers would ask him about me. "Mind your own fucking business" was his most polite answer.) Stanley and some of his printer buddies were known to be "trouble makers," guys looking to shake up the union. The leadership would, he said, not fight him but instead try buying him off. So they might let me in—if I could qualify.

Stanley's company each week prepared the front and back page proofs for Life and Time magazines. It was Stanley's job to do. Considered among the most skilled four-color pressmen in the city, he could handle the pressure. Hell, I was a printer too, fresh off my years as a mimeographer, but I had no clue about lithography. Here was a skill, here was an art, here was a challenge. In time I would learn, but I never came close to matching Stanley. He was and stayed the master.

Most impressive was Stanley's skill at mixing colors and choosing ingredients to match exactly the shadings of the original. Some of these secrets he kept hidden (not wanting me, while I was still learning the basics, to cut corners, use shortcuts as he did). It was his trained eye meeting the challenge of matching the original color. A palette in front of him, he'd be mixing colors, searching for the perfect combination, like a chef—trying for just the right taste. I'd watch him stir, blend, mix, rub his colors together, add a touch of starch here, some sugar, maybe honey, a little turpentine, even urine to the ever changing recipe. He was not easily satisfied.

Four-color printing took total concentration and instant trouble-shooting ability. You never rushed into it. It might take hours of careful prep work first (especially when we had to use silver or gold inks, which were much harder to work with) plus time for test runs. Once the press began rolling pressures increased. Pressmen went in motion to check out all operations and the end product. It was best not to stop the press even when there were problems. The trick was to spot these—the paper feed, the ink flow, tension levels, etc., and correct them while the machine clattered away (and do so rapidly so as not to waste too much paper). It was problem solving on the run. Did it get your juices going? You bet.

In the shop guys also busied themselves with unofficial print jobs. Someone was always running off dirty books on the press, taking orders on these and other print jobs on the side. The bosses, as far as I could figure, either didn't notice or simply ignored it, knowing it meant extra bucks for the guys. Pictures of naked ladies hung all around. And to this day I'm kicking myself that I didn't think to collect those covers we did for *Life* and *Time* magazines. But it's just like printers to ignore what they're working on. Imagine if I had kept copies of these proofs (they were piled all over the place) from the late '40s. The money they'd be worth today! Talking about money, the guys always were making paper currency, not, Stanley said, to circulate, but rather as sort of a challenge, to show off their printing skills, prove how close they could approach the real thing.

Stanley taught me well; he knew he had to. As a black, I would face all kinds of shit from the unions and from fellow printers when I asked to join. That was his plan, that's why he was putting in all this time and energy into training me. He and his fellow Progressives (communists?) were looking to break the stranglehold of the Dutch and German guys who ran the Lithographers' Union. Stanley had nothing but contempt for the union and this big Dutchman, Swaydock, its president. When I first met him I saw why. There was no mistaking his attitude toward me. I didn't belong in "his" union. But Stanley let him know I'd be getting in—whether he wanted me there or not. There might be problems, Swaydock suggested. Stanley's response—"Kiss my ass," at which point Swaydock's face turned deep red. But he quickly steadied himself, prepared for whatever reason, not to challenge Stanley. And so in time I was "accepted" into the union as an apprentice operator. Call me a pioneer. You never saw any of us folks around the shop except for the elevator operators and porters. No one I spoke to could recall any blacks ever being admitted into that union.

As a union man, I'd get a decent job. Still, I never much liked how unions operated. The idea was fine—without them

22-SKOL

employers would step all over you—no question about that. But the unions themselves became the problem thanks to the bullshit politics and widespread nepotism. Exclusive little cliques they were or soon became. "Other" people were to be kept out. An even tighter circle ran the labor organization itself, interested not in the well being of its members, but in filling their own pockets. It was a racket for Swaydock and the shop agents around him. These guys did nothing but handle the monies that flowed into the union treasury and collect fat salaries. Dues were high, you can believe that. Question them at union meetings, mention corruption or wrongdoing, and you'd be asking for trouble. Some gatherings of ours ended with fistfights. Unless you went along, the union might not be a safe place.

The union's knee-jerk reaction to change angered me. Some of it I could understand. It was, after all, there to protect jobs, but that made for problems. Whenever new technology threatened to reduce the numbers of workmen, the union automatically said "no" and defended its special rules and make-work jobs. Planning for changes in the market—not interested. Stick your face in the sand, dig your heels in—that was their way. Incompetence was ignored and seniority worshipped. I hated the old-time pressmen who shuffled around the shop, cigars clamped in their mouths, not doing a damn thing. Nothing could happen to them and they knew it. So they did whatever they pleased (which often meant gathering in the bathroom for crap games). Sure the union protected us, and those with jobs got decent wages, but it could have done so much more.

Stanley's reputation as a master printer led to a most exciting opportunity. The company had just purchased a state-of-the-art four-color press from Germany, a machine way superior to the presses on which we had been working. It became Stanley's machine to master and operate. I was assigned to assist him, along with a paper handler and an oiler. For two days Stanley just looked at this huge press and studied the manual. (The company sent some people from Germany to set it up and assist when we hit snags.) It was a sight, Stanley crawling under and on top of this monster. It was huge—ten feet high at least, its four separate sections filling the entire press room. The press itself made news, became a celebrity, several newspapers covering the story of its arrival in New York City and the preparations for its use. It was state-of-the-art technology that did away with four separate runs through the press for a four-color job. One run now, not four. It was a big deal. No one could touch the machine until Stanley got it figured out and let us in on its secrets. There was a lot of stuff on this baby I had never seen before. It was awesome and once it got going—wow!

We tamed this magnificent mechanism, got it to produce the finest four-color work I'd ever seen. Did I brag about what I did? Sure enough. Now I knew just what my role was and certainly no one needed to remind me Stanley was number one, but still there were those times—sitting in a bar when the talk got around to jobs, that I allowed myself to say—"I print the covers for Time and Life." That I couldn't resist.

17 THIS MAN'S ARMY

It was now June, 1950, my printing career in full swing. Sure I heard South Korea had been invaded, but didn't pay it much attention. Even when President Truman ordered U.S. troops into action against the North Koreans I didn't see how that might affect me. I'd done a stint five years before and hadn't much liked World War II, at least the basic training part. I wasn't interested in getting back into uniform and running off to fight for my country. The old enthusiasm was gone. After my brief and inglorious "service" in World War II, I'd gone home with my uniform and gear, but never did another thing. I was supposedly in the Reserves and scheduled for meetings and weekly training sessions. But the fact is, I received not a single notice and never made the slightest effort to find out why. I had packed my uniform away—that was it.

What a shock then, the telegram ordering me to report for a physical and possible induction into the army. They gave me four days to put my affairs in order! Who needed this just when I finally was getting someplace? The rules said I was entitled to my job when I returned. But I didn't expect my union would give a damn if a black didn't get what he was entitled to. Where the hell was Korea, anyway? What was it any of my business to be fighting over there?

But there I was with all my gear in this great big building on Hudson Street in lower Manhattan, looking for an escape hatch, some angle to get me out of this. It was a bad dream, right? I'd wake up and it would all be okay again. Certainly that seemed less strange than the idea of my going off to war. It was just my luck to be in such good physical shape. The exam was a joke. I was in and out of there in no time—then it was off to Fort Dix. Not again! Memories of the place just five years before were not happy ones. But hey, I was Private First Class now—I had rank. Some of the basic training I could skip; avoid some of the shit jobs. I'd even get to boss people around. It wasn't all bad.

If there was no way out of this "bad joke," why not screw around? I suppose that's how come, when filling out the induction papers, I listed myself as an American Indian. I'd never denied my Indian blood, but on the other hand I'd never made much of it either. Would it make any difference? Meanwhile the Army, I learn, is prepared to offer me my choice of units. Anything to avoid the infantry. So I'm sitting in this auditorium looking for an out when these Airborne guys come on in, flags and all. Wow, I thought. Look at them. Sure as hell weren't your average doughboys. More than sharp, they were the limit. Paratrooper boots shined up like glass, complete with white lacings, white belts, blue scarves—who wouldn't want to look like that? We all knew the reputation of the Airborne. It was one special kickass outfit. Bona fide elite. To these guys Marines were pussycats. Why would I want such an outfit? It's more military than I'd ever want to handle. Still they made quite an impression, knew just what to say. "We're offering you an opportunity." "Join us and you become someone." "It would be the experience of a lifetime." "We're an army within the Army." "We're the first ones in." Yeah, yeah, I'm thinking. Translated it all meant you had to bust your ass, maybe even get yourself killed. I was young but not that innocent. I wasn't going to fall for their pitch.

The presentation over, the lieutenant in charge asks for a show of hands. "Who's interested in Airborne?" he wants to know. No way I'm going. Still my eyes are glued to the stage where the demonstration team has just finished up some really sharp maneuvers and is standing stiffly at attention. I'm thinking "No" but caught up in the moment my hand involuntarily shoots up. Almost before I'm aware of what I'm doing there's this corporal at my side. "What's your name, son?" William Williams, Airborne. Now you know the story.

Not long afterwards I'm on my way to Fort Campbell, Kentucky. From there I'd be shipped off to train with my unit. But as each day passes, guys who I've come down with, along with others who had just arrived, were all heading off for their training. They leave and still I'm sitting around, not hearing a thing. What's going on? Eventually I found out. It was the papers I had filled out back at Fort Dix. "So you're Indian," the sergeant says to me. "Yeah, that's right," I say, all of a sudden remembering how, trying to mess with the army, I had listed myself. "What kind of Indian?" he wants to know. I'm getting a little nervous now. What's the difference to the army, I'm wondering. Is it better to be one kind of Indian rather than another? Who the hell knows! Should I stay with this or is the whole thing going to backfire? I mean are they going to make me a scout or something, put me out front to follow the enemy's trail? I repeat, "I'm Indian," and leave it at that. The guy goes, but now I'm getting anxious, especially as several more days pass and not a word. Still I'm stuck with being an Indian. Can't back off now. Finally it's the sergeant again, this time accompanied by a real live Indian. The army figured, I suppose, it takes one to know one. He was an Indian, I assumed, because he's wearing this pony tail. The army, you can bet, wouldn't let just anyone wear hair like that. "Is this guy an Indian?" the sergeant asks, looking at me. It's at that point that "pony tail" asks me my tribe. "Shinnecock," I tell him. That seems to satisfy him; he doesn't ask me anything more or give any sense that he's heard of the Shinnecocks. "Yeah, he's Indian," he says. The sergeant seems less than convinced, scratches his head and mutters something about how I was a strange looking Indian. He leaves without saying a word to me.

Nothing changes. I'm still waiting around. But now I know the score because hanging out with me are two others in the same boat. Their "problem" also is color. The two are dark, of Portuguese background, from the State of Maine. So where do we belong? The army in 1950 is still a segregated force, with dark-skinned guys like us assigned to all-black units. But then if I'm an Indian and they're Portuguese-Americans and not black, we should all be with white units. The army we figured was having trouble making up its mind, confused by us being off-white. Putting us in a "white" unit might raise some serious questions. But it was the army's problem, not ours. We were enjoying ourselves, free from all discipline, getting our three squares, hanging around, playing cards and lazing about. I took a liking to the two of them, especially to this Gonzalez fellow, who told me all about the Portuguese in Maine. Another three weeks and finally a verdict. I was an Indian, the army at last conceded. Still, it was sending me to an all-black unit! Same for Gonzalez. The other guy, who was noticeably lighter, drew a white outfit. Color controlled. Such was the considered wisdom of the Army. I offered no protest but went off to join my fellow black fighting men, satisfied at least with having created a bit of confusion and killed over a month of army time, doing nothing, avoiding crap. It was, I figured, something of a victory.

I was Airborne, all right; I got that message immediately. Because we were the elite, we would have to be neater, be tougher, and work harder, know more and accept more discipline than anyone else. It was a challenge I welcomed. I had no quarrel with the system. Neat, orderly and strong I already was. Whatever else they would demand of me I could handle.

Neatness knew no bounds. It meant pride, it produced anger, it promoted discipline, and determined status. What it also represented was lots of hard work. Some will say the neatness stuff was all bullshit, but we came to see it another way. It got drilled in so hard that it became us—and what made us special. Why else were guys spending their own money to have uniforms tailored just so, creases sewn into pants, and the trousers tapered for the perfect fit (an obvious difference between us and the other "straight legs" about the camp. For that crisp look we'd put the fatigues and uniforms on top of boards, then under our mattress. They'd be ready to go in the morning, needing just a bit of spray starch and the touch of an iron.) To play safe we all had at least two sets of dress uniforms, some guys even more because people were always stealing them.

Not only were our fatigues starched and ironed, but our boots needed to be shined to perfection. My mother, bless her, had taught me all the tricks of handling an iron. As for the boots, my shoeshining days in Harlem gave me a leg up on everyone else. Then there were our beds—you can't imagine the kind of attention they got. For reasons I never quite understood, beds were the supreme test of the army's neatness crusade. As for Airborne bed standards—they were close to impossible. Talk about bed training—we got an earful of it. And plenty of practice—the requirement was three bedding changes a week, enforced by periodic "sneak" inspections (usually once a week). The sheets had to be folded under just so and the pillows fluffed up to a point where all creases disappeared. And the demands were for tightness, always more tightness. Airborne beds had to be done up tighter than anyone else's—by a mile! Forget the usual methods. One sheet would never do. The solution—double-sheet the beds. Even then it might not be tight enough, so many of us invented hooks to grip and pull the ends, and tried pins stuck through the sheets to keep the tension. The supreme challenge, the one nearly all inspectors used, was the much dreaded quarter test. The flight of that coin determined the success or failure of all our efforts. To pass, the twenty-five-cent piece had to bounce and bounce high enough off the bed top once struck: if it moved just slightly or didn't clear the bed after impact, you failed. It was then that the staff sergeant made his hateful move. He ripped the blanket and sheets clear off the bed and chewed us out as if we had just betrayed our country. And you could never tell about that coin: beds once tight loosened up; quarters dropped from an insufficient height would not bounce the "necessary" distance.

Humiliation, pride, discipline, order, obedience—all that was wrapped up in those bedsheets.

And foot lockers were not far behind. What they wanted were not lockers but display cases, all your clothes and personal items arranged in perfect order without looking the least bit sloppy or cluttered. Impossible. There was too much stuff to store; not all of it folded up neatly. Most of us relied on an extra cache of personal items which we hid outside the barracks. Only then might our foot lockers pass inspection. Not necessarily though, since we were subjected to a series of inspections—master sergeants, then first and second lieutenants. All of them wore white gloves! Getting past one meant little. For sure the others would find fault, trip you up, do what they could to humiliate you in public.

If it wasn't uniforms, beds or foot lockers, then it was butts, bathrooms and kitchen patrol. Whether or not it was real work was less important than that it be done in a certain way, the army way, and no other way. The grounds around the barracks had to be spotless, everyone expected to pick up the smallest scrap of paper plus every single cigarette butt. Those of us who drew bathroom duty, whether out of punishment or as a regular shift, had to do it down on our knees, cleaning every tile, every toilet bowl, every latrine with precision, using nothing more than a toothbrush, bleach and sand as an abrasive. Inspections, of course, were frequent and demanding. K.P. was a living hell, as bad as everyone has always said it was. All those potatoes had to be peeled—by hand, all the pots cleaned and dried, and the floors kept spotless and polished. It was probably no more difficult facing incoming enemy soldiers than dealing with these endless rounds of bullshit housekeeping chores. And that was probably the point of it all. The idea was to harass you, anger you, reduce you, whoever you were, to a bundle of fury. Out of this would come, they thought, better soldiers, obedient, precise, filled with a pent-up rage and frustration easily turned toward any enemy.

We Airborne never walked; we trotted or we ran. It wasn't our idea. They demanded it, wanted us moving all the time, let us know when our pace fell below the "Airborne Shuffle." Never did a group of guys get into shape so quickly. We'd be up at 5:00 a.m. and right after would come our first run of the day, a three to five-mile trot with 50 to 75-pound packs on our backs. There'd be a colonel running right along with us in the dark. There he was, carrying the unit's flag, the guys behind him running in their starched fatigues and tee shirts in step, in cadence, singing as we went. As the darkness turned to light it was a beautiful sight, seeing our unit moving along rapidly in tight formation, our voices shouting out in clipped vigor. Here was a unit in the making, guys who knew that even when fatigue set in they would keep on going if on nothing more than pride. After breakfast we'd all do it once more. Then later on in the day would come our third go at it. In between, when moving from one place to another we'd proceed at a brisk trot. If we slowed down and were spotted by an officer, punishment was certain, generally pushups—right on the spot.

Neatness and physical fitness were just preparation for the serious training in basic combat and survival skills. We learned for example what to do when poison gas drifted across a battlefield. We were taught how to maneuver through open fields under gunfire. There was no cutting corners when it came to maintaining the weapons and equipment we'd be carrying. You were expected to master them. Take it apart, put it back together again. Break it down, reassemble it. Guys would practice this all the time. Then came the supreme test—doing it blindfolded and in a matter of minutes! I got to know my pistol and my rifle . . . intimately.

In the army there's no confusion where you stand, who you gotta take shit from and who you in turn can dump on. If, in civilian life, the pecking order gets fuzzy because of random mixing and talk of equality, there's no such uncertainty in the army. It's all spelled out. Rank determines and explains most all behavior. Forget about equality. Don't expect your "rights". Individualism? No way. The army considered personality a distraction. It ranked everyone and expected automatic conformity to one's place in the hierarchy. The whole damn system depended on the acceptance of rank, the assertion of rank, enforcement of rank. And I must say it worked pretty well. For those who couldn't handle it, who tried to fight the system—that was the sign the army looked for. These were the misfits who it moved to control, isolate or remove.

Rank decided who you hung out with, who your buddies were, who you could count on, drink with, and tell it like it was to. First and second lieutenants hung together, master sergeants and sergeant majors as well, as did captains and majors and light colonels and colonels. But then there were other circles of influence which extended outward through the ranks to complicate the official pecking order. You might for example outrank a particular warrant officer, but you would never, never want to mess with him. He handled all the supplies, knew exactly where everything was. He could screw you royally. So everyone catered to them. Everyone knew how important the NCOs were. These guys had the experience, the know-how, the ability to get things done. An officer knew that with a good NCO things would run smoothly even when he himself was unaware of what was going on. A captain, for example, could strut around looking impressive so long as his first sergeant had things under control, which he usually did. The West Point types I found the hardest to stomach. Spit and polish all the way, they expected the same from everyone else. The special skills officers—the engineers, the lawyers, the doctors, were far more flexible and understanding. So in general were northern officers, as opposed to their southern fellows who generally were in for the long haul and were quick to let you know it. Their way was the only way.

Keeping this order, at least at the lower ranks, were the MPs. They might be decent guys but they were totally devoted to maintaining the system. Kept separate from the rest of us, this I imagine made them a breed apart, tough suckers who you'd best not cross. Challenging them made little sense; the army would, everyone knew, always back them up. MPs seemed to enjoy their authority. (Many of them became cops back in civilian life.) And whether on the base or in town they did their job.

I "joined" the Airborne because the guys were sharp, because they were tough. And what could be more glamorous than jumping out of planes? So early on it was off to jump school (at Fort Benning, Georgia), scared, I must admit, but also anxious to prove that I could do it. Lots of guys I heard washed out here; I didn't want to be one of them. They gave you every reason to throw in the towel. They treated you like you were lower than shit. They demeaned you at every turn—you were nothing, you were pathetic, you didn't belong with the rest of them! "When will you become a man?"—"We'll tell you." Berating us all were career soldiers, many of them still wearing their World War II gear and helmets. Who could live up to their expectations? They were in your face all the time—swearing, cursing, belittling you, getting physical without the slightest hesitation. If you fought back in the least, why he'd arrange to meet you off duty and settle the score (or get someone to do it for him). You were never right. You couldn't even breathe right. The only way to limit the abuse and reduce the pressure was to do exactly what you were told without a moment's hesitation. I did—most of the time. Only on one occasion did I strike back, telling this here colonel to kiss my ass, which led to a fight. I had, I realized, played right into their hands. Resist and they can go about beating you down further. Having figured this out I no longer fought them. Actually I came to appreciate their manipulations, even found satisfaction in following orders. (That's when you know they've gotten you. Sure, you can fake it, snap to and pretend to be with the system—but you know what?—that's when they got you, too!)

They wanted to break you down, and then they wanted to build you up, instill commitment and a sense of pride. Sure it didn't work with everyone—no way that it could. But the army wasn't into individualizing its methods. These had come about over the years, were time tested and largely successful. The army was about tradition; it was not about to change its ways.

You don't start on a plane. You begin on top of a tower 50 feet up (just like the parachute jump at Coney Island, I thought). You hook onto a rope and you slide down into a sandpit. Up on the tower with you is a sergeant telling you what to do. Down at the bottom are two corporals and a sergeant watching your every move and letting you know what you didn't do, chewing you out every chance they got. What you're working on here is how to hit and roll along the ground. You bet it's scary up on that tower. Now I had spent plenty of time up on the roofs during my younger days in Harlem and never much minded it. But this was different. They were expecting you to jump off again and again. If at the beginning you hesitated they just pushed you off. If after some time you still were afraid to jump off on your own, you were finished, washed up. The Airborne wasn't interested in forcing you to do it. Guys who needed that sort of "encouragement" all the time would only be trouble later on. If their pride and appeals to manhood were not enough to get them leaping off that tower, the Airborne was prepared to ship them back to ordinary Infantry units.

By the time you get to the 75-foot and the 100-foot towers, it feels like you're on a plane. In fact I later realized that being up at, say, 5,000 feet aboard a plane was not nearly as frightening as staring off the 100-foot tower. But do it time after time and there is less fear. You learn to use your knees as springs, to roll at just the right time to minimize the impact. Adding gear doesn't much change things.

Next you meet your parachute. It's yours in the sense that you are the one who has to fold it carefully and pack it. Right off the chute looks complicated, unwieldy, a maze of cords running about. How in the world, you wonder, is it ever going to fit into the bag? The packing is done in a large shed lined with long tables on top of which you roll out the parachutes. It all goes by the numbers, each associated with a particular fold of the chute.

(If you just stuffed the chute into the bag, would it work? I never asked. I certainly wasn't about to try it.) In many ways it was like folding a handkerchief, which most men in my day wore in their jackets. All folds had to be tight and flat. If when you finished it didn't fit into the bag—you had screwed up. Two, three hours a day we kept at it, folding our parachutes, closely supervised by riggers and the jump master. Here's one system we had no thought of challenging. We folded our parachutes their way—willingly. We'd always be jumping with two chutes (the second a smaller one), but we prayed we'd never need that back up!

Once I got the hang of packing a chute properly, it took about forty-five minutes to an hour. My name was on the chute; my life, I figured, was in my own hands. Not so, I then found out. When we were ready for airplane jumps we would wear parachutes prepared not by us, but by a special Airborne unit whose job it was to pack the chutes. (In fact I made only a single jump in a chute I had packed.) They wanted us to know how to do it, but they didn't want us worrying about whether we did it right. The guys who actually did the packing signed off on each chute; if it didn't open they'd know who to go after. These guys were also responsible for all parachute repairs. None of us questioned the competence of those professional packers. The army puts a lot of emphasis on trust. We trusted them.

After about three weeks of tower jumping and parachute folding we were ready for the wild blue yonder. At least that's what they told us. Very few were all that eager to get into those planes. You figured the good athletic types who made all the right moves naturally could handle it. But how would they react from three to five thousand feet above the ground? The macho types who kept telling you how they couldn't wait to leap from the plane were a good bet. But who really knew? For everyone the first time up would be a challenge: we hoped we'd be up to it.

I didn't know it then but later learned that the jump master already had sized up the guys, and those he knew would jump without hesitation, he placed up front. Those about whom he had doubts were seated toward the back on both sides of the plane. The reasoning was that once the first couple of guys stepped off, the rest would find it easier to follow. All of us are hooked to a rope set high along each side of the plane. Once we jump it's that hook that will yank open our chutes. They couldn't risk having guys panic or blank out and forget to pull their rip cords. Later on we'd be allowed to jump free and clear and decide for ourselves when to pull our cords.

As the plane heads to the target area for our first jump, a few guys look eager, are full of wisecracks, but mostly there is an anxious silence. You know lots of your buddies are pissing and shitting in their pants. It's a bad time. We'd been told that when the pilot cuts the engines, that'll be the signal to go (you don't jump with the engines on or you risk hitting the tail after you've exited. With the props cut you head straight down after leaving the side door).

Sure I was scared, like the rest, my heart pounding away, but once the engines stopped we were rushed along and out. The door shot open and the jump master literally started kicking guys off. Bam—slap—out the door they hurtled. Some shouted, probably to boost their courage, others left jaws set, eyes fixed straight down. In less than a minute the plane had emptied. Snap—snap—pop—snap—pop—the chutes opened. Everyone was floating down, a few chutes real close to each other, some drifting off to one side or the other. I can't tell you what a relief it is to see your chute fully extended high above you. Now came the easy part, maybe two or three minutes of heading down at a comfortable speed before the ground rose up. Time then to concentrate, to think of what we had been taught and practiced repeatedly, about how to yank the riser cords and release them just before we expected impact, and then to roll. By God, it worked! All of us had survived. What followed was plenty of laughing, shouting, hugging, with some trying to cover up wet pants as we gathered our chutes together and headed off to the assembly point. We were Airborne now, by Jesus. We were kings of the hill!

After about a half dozen drops I was ready for the ultimate jump experience—free falling. Instead of yanking the rip cord you head straight down through space, the wind whipping past you. The speed alone takes your breath away, until you hit a rising column of air and slow down considerably, even appear to be floating on a cushion. Whether you're more thrilled or scared it's hard to know. Finally you break out the chute, and brace for one heck of a jolt. (I still have burn marks on my legs where the harness straps took some part of the shock.) Time now for a pleasant descent and an opportunity to relax, to enjoy the scene, check out your fellow parachutists, do all sorts of silly things and try to pinpoint your drop target. I volunteered for additional jumps, pocketed the fifty dollars extra a month as my Airborne bonus, and considered myself as having made the grade (although strangely when I returned to civilian life I became afraid of heights. Anywhere above the seventh floor of an apartment house made me dizzy.)

Those who finished jump school successfully believed more than ever that we Airborne Paratroopers were the sharpest, toughest, meanest hombres in Uncle Sam's army, the equal of any three American soldiers. And prove it they did each and every time they left base for the neighboring town. That meant they had to tear up the place and fight everyone in sight. On the other hand the "straight legs" often were out there gunning for us, resenting our superior manner, looking to make their mark by getting the best of one of us. (Rangers and Marines were also subject to these kinds of "make your reputation" assaults.) Didn't even matter if these soldiers won; that they had come forth to challenge the army's elite was enough. Being Airborne made you both an aggressor and a target.

My first assignment with the Airborne was with a tank unit, but I didn't much take to these metal monsters. Now some guys adored them, worked over them lovingly, were really gung ho about tanks and bragged how in battle they'd be charging into the thick of things, but none of that stuff excited me. I didn't like being inside; I felt claustrophobic, also terribly hot. I wasn't going to be a tanker if I could help it. But how to get out? That's when I discovered how my being in those shaky, terribly noisy, oversized cans had brought on headaches. This, I figured, just might be my out.

The headache pain, I told my superior officer, was severe. He actually believed me, even suggested I might develop a chronic condition. See a doctor, he recommended. Here's where I got to thank my lucky stars. The guy turned out to be Dr. William Kilpatrick, who I had already met in jump school. Now I knew Kilpatrick from back in Harlem where he practiced, had seen him professionally once or twice about a medical problem, and had bumped into him socially at some of the local bars and jazz clubs. Now when black guys are down south and run into someone from back north, the bonding is almost automatic. In fact Captain Kilpatrick and I hit it off at once. Before long the two of us were hanging out off base in Nashville, doing some drinking while reminiscing about life back up in Harlem. As for my headaches—"They might even get you out of the service," Kilpatrick thought, adding, "but I don't want you leaving me here." If I couldn't get out of the army, the headaches might, I figured, get me out of those damn tanks. What about my becoming a medic? "What experience do you have?" he asked. "I once worked for several weeks as a cleaning man in a hospital." Three weeks later my transfer to the medics came through.

What did I know about being a medic? Well, the army's also a school, prepared to teach you all sorts of subjects. So I learned about barracks sanitation, personal hygiene, medications and wounds, that kind of stuff. There were all those army texts which spelled things out so that anyone could understand. I devoured these manuals. And then Kilpatrick was teaching me all the time, showing me what to do. So also did the other guys in the unit. After the basics they sent me to Fort Sam Houston in Texas for additional training. I took to it all pretty well, became an Army medic, even a competent one!

If ever a unit took itself seriously it was ours. Collins, the chief medical officer, saw to that. Maybe he wasn't a fanatic; let's just say he had a certain passion for sanitation. It was not appreciated. Maybe he reminded the guys of their mothers, especially when lecturing them on how to take care of themselves and what not to do. (Signs and slogans were posted all over our quarters about the virtues of cleanliness.) Even worse, he inspected them closely and frequently. And he worked them hard, insisting for example that they scrub down the showers with Lysol and ordering them, when on maneuvers, to build extra deep trenches for outdoor latrines.

Simply mention "short arm inspection" and most every former soldier, no matter how long he's been out, will cringe. Collins' were notorious. Picture this scene, the guys all standing there in the buff lined up next to their bunks. That in itself was a sight, especially given the observable variations in human anatomy. With each guy the procedure was the same. With everyone watching and some joking, but most shuddering because their turn would soon come, Collins began his top-to-bottom inspection. He first searched for hair lice, then shoved two gloved fingers into the asshole (with all his concern about hygiene he never changed the glove, simply dipped his fingers into alcohol as he moved from one guy to the next!), then checked the mouth and afterwards looked closely at the penis and surrounding area, checking for crabs and gonorrhea. After that he directed that the barracks, especially the latrine, be sprayed all around including underneath the structure. Before we'd leave there'd be a lecture about not contracting V.D. and a warning that many of the town women, the "conquests" about which they bragged continually, were often infectious. We'd then hand out safety kits which included condoms, distribute the de-licing powder, and urge them to come see us if they developed strange symptoms. Their faces told you that's the last thing they'd likely do. The minute we were out the door they'd be cursing up and down, denouncing our intrusions into their bodies and into their personal lives. Still most all of us in the medics—I soon felt committed to the cause, you see—believed in our work and understood the hostility (some of it coming because we lived in separate barracks). Had positions been reversed we would not have been any different.

Yes, circumcision and inoculation both were services we provided. All men should be circumcised. That was Kilpatrick's firm belief. It was a matter, he said, simply of cleanliness and preventing disease. Remove that flap of skin, he preached, and you save yourself lots of trouble. He sounded convincing, and as a result a pretty steady stream of customers came by our office wanting to get the job done. Kilpatrick would do it and have us watch while he first injected a local anesthetic and then turned to the cutting itself. Our job would then be to trim the foreskin, stitch things up, and apply a large bandage. (The procedure generally meant soldiers were excused from duty for a day, perhaps two.) As long as I was there Kilpatrick continued to preach circumcision. His concern for the welfare of soldiers knew no bounds.

The army is forever giving shots to anyone in sight; we did a land office business. Usually it was routine stuff, but some customers required special attention and service. Take the wives of the soldiers for example. It was absolutely comical. The problem was how we guys (mostly black) could inject them in their rear ends without compromising their modesty or violating the South's racial arrangements. Blindfolding wouldn't work, nor would looking the other way. The solution—raise a large sheet across the area! So we'd be sitting on stools on one side, the women passing by on the other side of the sheet. That way we couldn't see who they were. What about the shots? Brilliant solution—give them through a hole cut out of the sheet. They would, at our directions, place their fannies next to the hole and we'd do the shooting. Theoretically all we would observe was a small patch of anatomically neutral skin. But boys being boys, some of us worked out ways to cheat. Some created larger than necessary holes in the sheet and simply peeked through. But most considered that a "crude" solution. The preferred strategy was mirrors placed on the floor that allowed us medics to view the scene on the opposite side of the sheet. It was all very funny, and once the women left you can imagine just how often the matter of comparative anatomies came up for discussion.

The other special group of "inoculees" were officers and certain notorious loudmouths on the base. No one had to say anything. Our goal here was to do nothing to reduce the discomfort of these injections. No problem. We knew we had succeeded just from listening to the guys muttering and complaining after we'd finished with them. The shots would be painless, they had been told. And so they might have been.

For sure my proudest moment as a medic came strangely enough in connection with a very unusual "search and retrieve" mission that I was sent on. It would take me into a world I might have imagined but certainly one I would never otherwise have entered. It all had to do with Billy, this young soldier from Kentucky, from a place not very far from Fort Campbell. It was right down the road, you might even say. There had been trouble ever since he had come on base. He had never before been away from home, and although an Airborne volunteer, he soon realized that he just didn't fit in. Sent to the medics, our records showed that we'd been unable to do much for him. Lonely and homesick, picked on by the guys, that was his problem. The Medical Corps didn't have shots for that. He had gone AWOL once and had been brought back by MPs, and along the way treated rather roughly, I understand. Now he had done it again. Clearly he would never fit in; he'd be of no use to anyone. But of course the army just couldn't ignore him or allow him to run off. If it did, it might as well close the base, for it would be deserted within twenty-four hours. No, he had to be brought back and "disciplined" in some way, and then discharged from the army.

Finding him, most everyone thought, would not be difficult. He had in very likely gone back home. Convincing him to come back—that was the problem. He was, I found out, from a close knit little community up in the hills somewhere. Would they try to hide him? Might they join him in resisting? Very possible. Certainly if MPs were sent up there to fetch him there could well be trouble, remembering what happened the first time. No, the decision on high was that the mission be low key and non-threatening, and that's why it was handed over to the medics. A medic might go where an MP might not without immediately arousing suspicion, without provoking a confrontation. So the job was turned over to Kilpatrick, who asked for volunteers, knowing full well he wanted me to do it. I don't quite recall why I agreed—maybe I appreciated the opportunity to get off the base for a day by myself.

Only as I was preparing to leave did I realize what I might be getting into. Here a black man in the segregationist, nigger-hating South was being asked to travel alone into the backwoods and bring out a white guy who clearly had no interest in coming back and would have other whites around to back him up on this. Could this be a suicide mission?

My destination was about 175 miles from the base. Had to be a real small place because I couldn't find it on the map I was using. Knowing the general vicinity, I figured I'd ask the locals for specifics once I got to the area. I didn't bring much with me in the Jeep. My medic insignia I counted on to get me through and keep things cool. But I did bring an MP's armband if it turned out that a stronger show of authority was needed. Also a pistol.

Driving through the rural south hour after hour was an eye opener for me, a city boy. There just wasn't much of anything around, and the roads were barely that. I passed a few folks here and there who didn't seem to pay me much attention, but I expected they took a very good look back once I passed them. I figured that somehow they were signaling ahead to alert the countryside that a stranger, a black man, an army man, a government man, was heading their way. I couldn't imagine anyone up here who'd be happy to see me.

Having arrived, according to my map, in the "general vicinity"

I now needed specific directions. I caught a break when I met up with someone who actually knew the guy I was looking for. He'd say nothing, however, until I explained why I was there. In a most matter-of-fact way I told him about Billy's leaving the base and how the army had decided to discharge him but only if he would return so that it could be done according to established procedures. Sure it was strange explaining what was, after all, army business to a civilian in such detail. But I knew the army didn't mean much up in these hills. Unless I appeared to want to help Billy I'd never find him. He bought my story and, as only a country person could, directed me back further into the hills with a series of turns at trees, forks in the roads, piles of rocks and at least one bridge. Road signs were out of the question here. Fortunately I was driving a Jeep which, if you forget the bucking and bumping, could handle the terrain. These were the backwoods, a house here and there set back from the road, a church or two, a modest schoolhouse, but otherwise nothing. While I didn't see anyone I couldn't help but feel I was being watched and that those doing the watching were also waiting to see if I was alone or whether I had come with backup. Would they be hostile? Who knew? Would my military uniform offer protection? Maybe not, especially if these people knew what had happened to Billy, how badly he had been treated by his army "buddies." And then I was black, probably the only one for 50 miles around here. Had folks up here ever seen one?

In a clearing just off the road there were the four houses I had been told to look for, and sure enough, there was one with a porch, which was where Billy supposedly lived. Now I knew why Kilpatrick laughed when I suggested we call first. "What if he wasn't there?" I had said. One look at the houses and you knew there'd be no phones. I saw no power lines either. Let's face it, they were little more than shacks patched up here and there, roofs that were sagging, some windows boarded up and piles of wood stacked up against the side. Around them were rusty car hulks suspended on cinder blocks, chickens and a few other mangy animals roaming about. These folks were living in what had to be some of the most miserable shitholes I had ever laid eyes on. These white folks were worse off than any of the blacks living near the base, actually worse than any blacks I had ever seen.

It was about the middle of the afternoon when I stepped onto the porch and knocked on the door. I was going to be as gentle as possible and very understanding. I wanted a chance to explain the situation and an opportunity to speak with Billy and assure him all would be worked out once he returned with me. First a woman, thin and pale, trailed by two kids hanging on to her, came to the door. Introducing myself, I immediately began my story. She listened, said not a word nor gave any indication whether he was there or not. Then an old man joined her. Seeing him and figuring he might be someone with greater authority, I began all over again. I'm pretty certain they were expecting someone from the army to show up, because without any hesitation, without checking with anyone, he answered. "He doesn't want to go back." "You mean he's here?" "Yes, he's here with us." "Well, I have to take him back with me," I said without trying in the least to challenge him. "You can't take him back. He'll go back only if he wants to." There was no mistaking his meaning. I had no standing here as far as he was concerned. What I had to do meant nothing until Billy decided what he wanted to do. "Can I talk to him?" "I suppose you'll be able to, sometime after dinner," he answered.

Pretty good progress to this point. I had located him. I had not been shot at or otherwise attacked. Being black didn't seem to be a problem. And I was going to get a chance to speak with Billy. I supposed they had put me off so that they could all talk and decide what should be done. So I went back to the Jeep, tried to make myself as comfortable as I could in the front seat, and waited. A number of people, some adults and a few kids, appeared, but they just stared at me from a distance. I waved at some of the younger kids who seemed to want to come closer, but they were held back. Dinnertime was coming on. Would I be offered any food? I had brought along my canteen and some rations, but little in the way of a meal. But no one came over with anything; no one came over at all. Instead all sorts of people began arriving at the cabin. I spotted a minister walk in, a guy carrying a guitar, and quite a few others. All stared at me before disappearing inside, but that was it.

Dusk gave way to darkness; I began to grow a little uneasy. Maybe the whole thing was a trick. Maybe Billy had slipped out of the back of the house and was, at this very point, making good his escape. They were just stalling me so as to give him a good head start. Maybe he hadn't been in there in the first place. Keeping me out there was a form of humiliation, revenge for the abuse he had received back at the base. I was tempted to go back up to the door and be a little more forceful this time, but that I figured could be risky. They knew I was out there; they'd get back to me only when they were ready. Maybe I should leave and come back the next morning. But where the hell would I stay? Blacks just didn't go around these parts, especially after dark, asking for accommodations!

There'd be no dinner invitations that night. I broke open the rations, unscrewed my canteen, and dined alone. I was going to wait it out. Needing to take a leak, I spotted what was obviously an outhouse, but decided it was best not to use it. Having walked the streets of Nashville as well as Hoptown and Clarkstown, located just outside Fort Campbell, I knew southerners didn't fancy us blacks relieving ourselves in the same places they did. With no "black only" outhouse out here, I decided to hit the bushes. It must have been 8:00 or 9:00 p.m. when the people left the cabin and, paying me no attention, headed off to wherever it was they lived. Then the lights began to go out in the shacks, and in no time it was dark. There I was in the Jeep, maybe thirty feet from the porch. I'd remain there all night. It was chilly, all right. (Fortunately, it was an ambulance Jeep. It carried a blanket and I was able to set up a cot in the back of the vehicle.)

Not until the sun came up the next morning did I stop shivering. Some merciful soul finally took pity on me. A little boy approached the Jeep and handed me a glass of milk and two hot biscuits. I guess they knew I was still there. I wet my handkerchief with water from the canteen and washed myself as best I could. I was in an endurance contest with these people. Spending the night out in the Jeep, I hoped, would give them the message that I would not give up easily, that I was taking my duty seriously. The next move would be up to them.

About noon it came. It was Billy himself, tall, thin, frail looking, who came out of the shack and walked ever so slowly toward me. Before I could say any more than hello and give my name, he let me know where things stood. "I don't want to go back." I understood how he felt, I said, and told him I knew about the rough times he had had. Next came my now familiar pitch about how he'd be discharged soon after he got back and how my being sent, not the MPs, showed that the army understood his situation. The kid listened, but whether I had any effect on him I couldn't tell. I began to think that a final decision was not something he was prepared to make, that others would decide. When the old man (who obviously had some connection to Billy) joined us, I sensed that he might be the one. He was noticeably warmer to me today (maybe even impressed that I had survived the night in the Jeep), in fact brought some chicken out for me. I took advantage of this gesture and asked if I could use the outhouse. "Nobody's stopping you," he said. "I just wanted to be respectful and get your permission first," I replied. "That's good," he answered.

I was now invited onto the porch and asked to explain my mission to a group of people, including a minister who had come around. How many times would I have to repeat the story? I had perfected it. It sounded, I thought, rather convincing by now. I began to realize that Billy had been something of a hero in these parts for having volunteered for the Airborne, and that they were upset and hurt because it had turned out so badly. These people spoke real slow like, and were going to reach whatever conclusion they would at their own deliberate pace. While the older folks were talking to me and among themselves, a number of teenage girls had come around and were standing real close by, laughing, kidding with me, enjoying themselves. This was crazy, I thought. Here are these white girls being so friendly to a black man right out in public. Were the same thing to have taken place in Nashville, there'd be hell to pay. Somehow up here all those rules, that viciousness, melted away.

They were close to a decision, the minister clearly now in charge of the proceedings. "Will you swear," he said, coming right up in front of me, "that if this boy goes back he won't be hurt?" That provided me with yet another opportunity to repeat my lines about how he'll be in the safekeeping of the medics until discharged. "Will you swear to this on a Bible?" he asked. I said yes, and in an instant there was a Bible and there was me with my hand on top swearing once again that he'd have nothing to fear. The fact that I was wearing a cross easily seen around my neck, I think, assured them I could be trusted. Certainly the minister seemed pleased when to his question I told him I was a good Christian and a Baptist. I must have at this point gotten carried away by the growing sense of mutual trust, because I guaranteed them that Billy would be home within two months. How the hell could I guarantee anything, I thought. Who was I to give them such assurances? The army could do with him whatever it damn pleased. I'm sure it was my own doubts that led me to blurt out that if he was not back in two months, I would return myself and explain to them what had happened. I meant it, not thinking how they'd react if the army didn't deliver on "my" promise.

With this show of sincerity and reassurance the standoff ended and the atmosphere turned festive. Out came food and drink aplenty. There was to be a farewell party. I was now a popular guy, a center of attention. My spiffy uniform (despite the creases that came from sleeping in the Jeep) certainly was one reason for this, and so I imagine was the fact that I was from up north, spoke differently, and was more worldly than most anyone else they had met. Teenage girls and several others older than that gathered around, talking and joking, even wanting to touch my uniform. I was amazed at their directness, their playfulness, and that they considered it not at all strange or "dangerous" to be flirting with a black man right out in the open. Scenes such as this were hardly typical of the South I had come to know.

As Billy got into the Jeep I could not help but feel triumphant. I had gone alone into the backwoods, played my hand right, and come out with my man. The army hadn't trained me to do this sort of thing, so I had improvised, and in the end accomplished the mission. That's what counted. But the two of us didn't just drive off. They insisted on escorting us out of the area until the main road. Was it simply a friendly gesture and a way of hanging on to Billy a bit longer? Then one of them mentioned that they sure as hell didn't want anything happening to me. Now I understood. These were isolated people, who didn't cotton much to strangers. I was an outsider. To prevent any mischief they'd provide safe passage down and out of the hills.

The story does have a happy ending. I turned Billy over to Kilpatrick upon my return. Judging from the looks I got I think a lot of the guys were surprised I had made it back okay, especially since I was overdue by a day when I pulled up in my Jeep. That Billy had agreed to come back with me was not how most figured this would turn out. While accepting congratulations I knew the story still needed a final chapter. Would the army keep its "word" and discharge him or would it reconsider and decide morale would be undermined if guys like Billy just took off and got away with it? And if he was not discharged but instead transferred to another unit and even to Korea where "trouble makers" often got sent, then I knew what I had to do. I had given my word. They had trusted me. I would have to go back and tell them why he had not returned. Talk about a tough mission. A month and a half went by and no word. Then one day Kilpatrick let me know that Billy had been discharged and was heading home. What a relief. The army had kept "my" promise. I can't say that Billy really belonged up in those hills, but certainly he didn't fit in back here with us. The army by discharging him as much as admitted it had made a mistake. Billy would have to find some other way to grow up and become a man.

Not long after this I too went AWOL, or something very close to it. It all began with a telegram I received from the Alexanders, friends from back in Queens. My mother, it said, was ill and had been hospitalized. A goiter in her throat was making it very difficult for her to eat or drink. I could not remember my mother ever being sick, let alone being in a hospital. The fact that they had telegrammed (I had never before received one) convinced me that this was something serious and I had better get on home. Unlike Billy, I was a "good" soldier, not given to just taking off on my own. I would ask permission, which I figured would be granted. I did, but it wasn't. The whole unit, I learned, was on standby, with orders expected momentarily regarding assignment to Korea. Under these circumstances there could be no leaves. But nearly everyone I went to said the same thing—"If it was my mother, I would just go and explain things later." One of my superiors, however, offered even better advice. Take off, he said, but before visiting my mother get over to the army base at Staten Island and explain why you're in town and get their "permission." That way you'll be covered, sort of, he hinted. That made sense to me as I prepared to "disappear" from Fort Campbell.

Leaving the base without papers I knew was risky, but doable. As a sergeant I could take off without arousing suspicion. There would be MPs at the train stations, but a smile, a wave, and the fact that I was an NCO would probably get me through. I got to New York without a hitch, went immediately to Fort Totten on Staten Island to "check in," then headed over to Jamaica Hospital to see my mother. She had recently been operated on and it had gone well, she told me. Out of danger now she was, she assured me, receiving good care and constant attention. (She worked in that hospital.) Besides which the Alexanders were visiting almost daily, providing her with whatever she needed. I was greatly relieved. I spent two days with her and then prepared to go back to Kentucky and face the music. First, though, I headed over to Fort Totten, where the base commander was most obliging and wrote a letter for me to the authorities at Fort Campbell. Back at the base my "escape," I learned, had not caused any undue concern. Most understood my reasons. Still this was the army, and a mild dressing down from the commanding officer followed. "Now you can forget about it," he said. "Of course you understand you're busted for this." (Minus a stripe, I slipped down a notch on the old pecking order from sergeant first class to staff sergeant.)

But about a month later another telegram arrived, this time from the hospital. My mother, it said, was in serious condition,—return at once. I had no difficulty getting permission. The train trip back seemed endless. What had gone wrong, I wondered. Why was she back in the hospital? I would stay with her until she recovered completely, even if it cost me another demotion. From the train I rushed over to the hospital. Everyone seemed to know the news, but no one could explain why. My mother had died! I had arrived too late—by one day. "Complications associated with the surgery"—that was the explanation.

Devastated, I just cried and cried. How could I not have been with my mother when she needed me? Always she'd been there for me. Friends and some hospital staff hinted that someone had blundered, that my mother had died needlessly. I listened but was so overcome with grief that I made no inquiry of my own. What's the difference; she's gone.

My mother, my "father," my friend, my teacher, my companion, she'd been all of these to me. I had been a good son, but I had wanted to do so much more for her. I wanted her to see that all the effort and energy, all the sacrifices she had made for me, were worth while—that I would become someone, make her proud. Now she would never know. This beautiful, noble, loving, wise, warm woman, cut off in her thirty-sixth year of life—much,

much too early. Who could have been more deserving than Estelle? What was the justice of it? What sense did it make? She had so much more to give, so much more to enjoy.

As methodical as ever, my mother had left instructions in the event of her death. Among other requests she wished to be cremated. I didn't recall ever discussing this with her, so I found her choice strange, she being a religious person. But then my mother had always been an independent type. She'd reason something out and then make up her mind and stick to it, do as she saw fit. I picked up the urn containing her ashes from the funeral parlor, carried it onto the subway, and headed toward South Ferry and New York Bay. Sitting there I imagined everyone staring at me and my package. I had, however, covered it up. Who could have guessed its contents? Leaving the subway I boarded the ferry and prepared to say goodbye to my mother.

It was a clear October day, the sun still warm, but the air noticeably cool out on the water in New York Harbor. There were few passengers on board this midday trip as the ferry left its slip and headed over to Staten Island. In uniform I stood by myself on the stern, holding the urn. In front of me were the massive towers and dramatic structures of lower Manhattan. I would wait, I decided, till the boat was well offshore somewhere in the middle of the bay. Meanwhile I kept thinking about my mother. In a few moments even her remains would be gone. It would be painful, but I could go on without her. That was part of her doing. She had loved me and kept me close to her but also knew that I needed to become my own person, independent and self-sufficient. That had happened.

The ferry was now cruising at full speed. I opened the urn and looked down at the boiling waters below. I said a prayer, my lips moving but with hardly any sound coming out. I turned the urn over slowly and the ashes flowed out, carried quickly by the breeze over a wide stretch of water. I would have liked to see them settle on the surface, see where they in fact had landed, but instead they mixed instantly and were carried off by the force of the ship's propeller. I doubt if anyone saw me do it. I can't remember now whether I tossed the urn into the harbor or not, but no matter. My mother I would never forget. I never have. She deserved no less from me.

I spent the next few days feeling terribly sad and busied myself putting my mother's possessions in storage. The apartment into which she had poured her love, her energy and her boundless creative talents would be vacated. I would never again live in a place that she created, that she fashioned for the both of us. Among her instructions was the request that in the event of her death, her brother be informed. Now I knew she had a brother living in New Jersey, but it had been years since she had ever mentioned him to me. Whether she had been in touch with him at all in the period I had no way of knowing. Still I thought it important that he know. And with my mother gone and in the absence of other relatives I felt the need for "family" contact. He lived, according to my mother's note, in Montclair, New Jersey; it would be simple enough getting there.

I found the address. Was there some mistake? My mother had told me he was light-skinned, but never mentioned the fact that he was well off or lived in a swanky neighborhood. This certainly was the white section of town. Dr. Foy—his name was on the door. When I rang the bell a maid answered. Behind her were two young children, fair skinned, with blond hair. Now I hesitated. Could these children actually be my cousins? "Is this the Foy residence?" "Yes, it is; what can I do for you?" she replied. I still hadn't quite gotten my bearings and was not sure what to do or say next. Fortunately he now came to the door, wanting to know what was going on. Foy was darker than those children, but certainly not recognizably black. I introduced myself and told him I'd traveled out to his house to let him know that my mother, his sister, Estelle, had died. His face remained expressionless. "I don't have a sister," he said. "You must have the wrong person." With that he guided the children away and closed the door. It took me a while to sort out what had just happened, but however sad, it was not all that mysterious. Foy had married white and had chosen to live his life as white. He had passed over to the other side, quite successfully, it seemed. I had threatened his world, so much that even in death he chose not to acknowledge a blood relative, not recognize his sister.

It was good that I was returning to the base. I could more easily live with the pain here where the daily grind of army routine could fill the emptiness, could serve as a needed distraction. I had by now taken well to army life, learned my job, figured out how the system worked and how to play the game well enough (even to the point of not bitching about the food since there was plenty of it, much of which I enjoyed.) At twenty-three I was no kid anymore—hadn't been for some time.

I should also explain that I had developed a lucrative side business on the base—lending money to soldiers. Guys were paid once a month and most, soon as that money hit their hands, were off to town to blow it on booze, on girls, or watch it disappear playing cards. That's where I came in—tiding them over between paychecks. Two dollars on ten for two weeks—that was my price. My reputation was good; the flow of customers steady. The tough part was screening those who came around. And limiting the amount I would loan to any one soldier. Typically the sum was anywhere from five to twenty-five dollars. Even then, a few deadbeats and you could find yourself out of business. As a medic I had access to certain useful "business" information. I knew, for example, which guys were about to be transferred from Fort Campbell. No way would they get another "loan." When the guys got paid I made it my business to be there in the room. Miss them then and you could forget about your money for another four weeks. If a guy needed more time I preferred that he ask for it rather than avoid me and make up stupid ass excuses. Sure I got beat from time to time, but I never used enforcers. This was a business based on trust.

I built my business up to a point where I had about $2,000 out circulating as loans. I dared not put the money in the base bank; that would have aroused suspicions. Instead I kept the cash on me at all times in a money belt which I never took off (even in the shower). For protection I had earlier bought a two-shot Derringer pistol (which I originally planned to use in case of a run-in with the Klan). Now as a businessman it was a comfort to have this ace in the hole close by. They never tell you about business opportunities in the armed forces. (I was, after all, small time. There were other guys I knew who were into the stolen property business.) Maybe they should. They might even attract would be entrepreneurs.

What made these army years much easier and more pleasant than they might otherwise have been was my relationship with William Kilpatrick. Our previous acquaintanceship drew us together despite differences in age (he was in his thirties) and the fact that he was an officer. Kilpatrick was a good-looking guy, fair-skinned with red hair and freckles. Back in New York he had hung out at many of the same places I had, the bars and jazz clubs up in Harlem as well as the Village. A man of sophistication, he felt quite isolated down here in hillbilly country. Barred from the white officers' club on the base, he found that as a northerner and a professional he had little in common with most of the other black officers around. I filled a need for him and he was helping me get through my army service. He had arranged my transfer to the Medical Corps and had taught me the ropes. It was Kilpatrick, I hoped, who would continue to insist I was indispensable around the base and so keep me from being shipped off to Korea. Sure we were using each other, but the relationship was real. On the base, given the differences in rank, socializing was a problem, but in Nashville and with both of us in civvies, it was a different story. There we hung out, strolled about, drank together and laughed ourselves silly about the South and its absurdities.

Now for a surprise. Would you believe that I was about to be married! I had run into Gloria Powell when I was on furlough back in Queens. We had met at a party and right off I was enchanted. We struck up a correspondence when I went back to

Kentucky. And when I wasn't writing to her I was making these records on base which carried my words by mail directly to her. This courtship at a distance seemed to be working. It was a match that made sense to me but not to any of my friends. They were not shy about emphasizing the negatives. She was about eight years older than I was. Sure, she was a "looker," but was it love they asked or just infatuation? How did I know I could get my old printing job back after my army days were over? Their objections I just brushed off. It was my life.

Why I was so eager to get married I can't say. Maybe being away in the army had something to do with it. More likely it was connected to my mother's death. I was now alone and vulnerable. We got married over my next furlough in a lawn ceremony up in the Bronx at her brother's house. Whatever their misgivings, my friends all showed up to wish us well. After a brief weekend honeymoon I packed my bags to return to Fort Campbell and she remained on in her Bronx apartment. I was due to be discharged within the year. Then we could begin married life together.

Life on the base continued as before except that the Korean War began to get closer. More and more men were being shipped over there from Fort Campbell to fill in for guys coming home and for others wounded or killed. From what I saw and what I heard from soldiers who had returned, I wanted no part of Korea. I wasn't afraid of being in combat or even being shot at. No, what scared the shit out of me was the idea of having to fight in the freezing weather. I hated the cold. Guys were telling me how happy they were to have been shot so that they could get out of there, get someplace that was warm. Many of the wounded we were treating, were also suffering from frostbite and exposure. Seeing these men, so many in terrible shape and listening to their ghastly combat stories made me want to stay far away from this war. Had other soldiers at Fort Campbell seen what we saw you would have had a hard time shipping them off to the Far East. As for me, I was prepared to do just about anything to stay in good old comfy Fort Campbell, Kentucky.

Unlike many of the other guys I wasn't that eager to leave the base for either of the two small towns located practically outside the gates of Fort Campbell or for a visit to Nashville, Tennessee, about a half-hour drive away. These places lived off the soldiers but the people there didn't much like us. Some of the reasons were obvious. "Hoptown" (Hopkinsville) and Clarksville were your typical small southern towns which reacted in horror to the swarm of soldiers, many of them northerners and westerners, who at times practically overran the place. What were these guys looking to do? Chase after girls, drink and fight, activities not likely to endear them to the locals. Of course the whoring and the drinking, but what about the fighting? Guys fought to unwind, they battled because they were drunk and they challenged one another to "decide" which service or unit was the meanest and the toughest. Whatever the reason nearly every soldier was regarded as a troublemaker. But the local sheriff and his many deputies could be as tough and as mean as the orneriest soldiers—and get away with it. They could rough up and lock up guys whenever they pleased, or so it seemed, and sentence them to several days in the local jail for disorderly conduct. Worse, they could force them into work details to clean the town. Here were U.S. soldiers led out onto the streets and obliged to perform common labor in their army uniforms. Why the army allowed these men to be treated in such a humiliating way I never understood. It was I guess committed to respecting local ways, but wasn't this going too far?

For blacks leaving the base meant facing up to the strict racial segregation on the outside. It was the law here, so no matter where we came from we had to accept it. Fort Campbell itself maintained distinct white and black units, but the segregation on base was nowhere near that on the outside. The nonsense started right on the bus leaving from the base to the nearby towns with blacks obliged to sit in the back. More outrageous, when only blacks were on a bus the drivers, all local residents, refused to let the guys sit in the section usually reserved for whites. No matter there was not a single white guy around! What they'd have to do is sit only in the rear seats. When it was only white guys crowded onto the bus the driver said nothing and let them go anywhere, including the section in the back "reserved" for blacks.

Whatever the town, Hoptown, Clarksville, or Nashville, each made clear where blacks and where whites could go, and at least the white residents saw to it that these regulations were strictly enforced. Separate facilities or sections were everywhere, one for blacks, one for whites only. Signs usually eliminated all guesswork. Sometimes it was obvious, as with a white drinking bowl alongside one that was metal. Should you make an error and use the wrong facilities or enter the wrong section, some white person would likely set you straight. Some black guys from the North found this hard to take. At times they'd challenge the system, refusing to sit in the back of the bus or deliberately using a white facility. It had to feel good doing it, but it didn't get them very far. The cops would arrive and arrest them. On occasion black soldiers fought back, battling with the police, sometimes alongside white soldiers (usually northerners) who also took exception to the system. It was a no-win situation, especially when the MPs showed up to support the police. Black and white soldiers would all be jailed and soon put to work in uniform out on the streets. By and large the older black veterans back at the base took little interest in such confrontations. It wasn't their way, and besides, where would it lead? (Officers at the base had little sympathy for such racial protests, figured the guys who broke the law in town might just as easily challenge military authority.)

As much as I avoided crossing the line and challenging southern ways, one incident got me right smack in the middle of it. It would have been funny had it not been so damn sad. It came about when Kilpatrick's wife and mine decided to come down south and spend a few days with us. That might seem simple enough, but that's only if you were white. For blacks the simplest things often became real complicated. Kilpatrick's wife was white; Kilpatrick, of course, was black. Such racial intermingling was taboo in the South and also illegal. The potential for trouble was obvious. Gloria, though black, was very fair skinned. She was married to me and there was no mistaking the fact that I was a Negro.

Their trip down to Kentucky was uneventful. No one questioned their presence in the white portion of the train. We had arranged to meet them at Brown's Hotel in the black section of Nashville and, without thinking, had simply told them to take a cab over there. That's when the first problem arose. Getting a white cab was simple, but then the driver heard them say Brown's Hotel. This threw him. "You must be mistaken," he told them. "You can't go there. That's a Negro hotel in the Negro part of town." They were not white, they informed him, but black, and Brown's Hotel was where they wanted to go. He'd have nothing of it. "If you're black, you're not black now," he said. "You're white. What's more I'm not gonna take you to a black hotel." Realizing they would get nowhere with this guy they got out and managed to find a black cab. But now the black cab driver figures he has a problem. Here were two "white" girls asking to be taken to a hotel in a black part of town. That could spell real trouble for him. Eventually they convinced him that they were black and, after a delay, he finally got them over there. But that's when their troubles really began. The first cab driver it seems, suspicious of the whole deal, had informed the sheriff's office that two white girls were on their way to Brown's. To the cops this must have seemed like a promising situation so that they were on hand when Gloria and Patricia pulled up. Evidently the cops were not satisfied by what they heard, so the two were taken in for proper identification and further investigation.

Down at the police station the two women are not having much success convincing the cops that they are black. (I had insisted that Gloria bring her birth certificate with her which "proved" she was black. The police, however, questioned its authenticity.) They're not buying it, or at least they don't want to. It clearly upset them that these two seemingly white women were traveling to join two black men. (If they're so white, why in the world are they insisting that they're black? "There's no reason for you to be black!")

Kilpatrick and I had one hell of a time finding out what had happened to the two of them. Once we did, we high-tailed it over to the sheriff's office, hoping to untangle matters, but when we got there, it only got worse. After Kilpatrick identified himself as a captain, and a doctor no less, the police had a fit. How does a nigger get to become that? They didn't have to say it. It was written all over their faces. Why, I asked, did a soldier in the U.S. Army, someone prepared to die for his country, have to face this kind of crap? Neither of us made the slightest impression on them. Instead we were thrown into jail along with the two women. They agreed, however, to call our colonel. Let him sort things out for them. I suspect they accepted our story but saw the opportunity to teach us a lesson in racial etiquette.

Four or five hours must have passed before he showed up. The colonel was not a happy guy, angry, no doubt, that he had been forced to leave the base and drive over to Nashville and upset at Kilpatrick for having gotten into this mess and for thinking he could get away with this kind of stuff in the South. (Kilpatrick knew it was a risky thing to do, but he was that kind of guy, willing to take chances and challenge the system. I suspected also that the colonel himself might have been offended by the sight of the two "white" girls with us black guys.) Still his appearance saved the day; we were all released.

The incident proved so upsetting to all of us that we scrapped most of our plans to travel about and take in the sights. And when we did leave the hotel, almost always there was a sheriff's car waiting outside to "observe" and tail us. How could it be that "white" girls preferred to be black and hang out with black guys? There had to be something wrong here. In that way and in so many others does racism mess with their minds and worse, with our lives.

I received another bitter taste of southern hospitality when, toward the end of my three-year army hitch I went on special assignment. I was then a staff sergeant and my orders were to guard (along with four other soldiers, three blacks and one white) about a dozen German "prisoners" and transport them from our base to Washington, D.C. Here we are fighting the Korean War, yet these guys were Germans. So what were they doing here after all those years? I never did find out. But then my job was to follow instructions, not ask such questions.

Still their presence was not altogether surprising. Most everyone suspected there was some secret stuff going on. What aroused our suspicions was this large section of the base (Fort Campbell covered many square miles) that was off limits, fenced off from the main area. None of us had access to this portion of the base. And why was it that Marines, not army personnel, guarded all entrances and exitways? Plus all activity in this "off-limits" area took place underground. What was going on there? We speculated plenty but none of us had the faintest idea. So when we arrived to take charge of these dozen guys and discovered they were Germans it was not that much of a shock. Dressed fairly well in European styled clothes, they all carried suitcases, but whether they were scientists or spies or workers or prisoners of war, no one knew. And no one asked. (They spoke German among themselves and we exchanged few if any words with them).

The orders seemed simple enough. We were to take them first by bus, then by train to Washington, D.C., where we would hand them over to others. Trouble was not expected, but my instructions read that in the event of problems we were authorized to shackle them together. How they ended up in chains is what I must tell you.

Nothing unusual happened until the train pulled into Bowling Green, Kentucky, where, we were told, our railroad car would be uncoupled then attached to a train heading into Washington. With time to kill we decided to escort our prisoners to a nearby eatery. It's when we entered the place that trouble began. The woman inside, whether she was the waitress or the manager I couldn't tell, immediately approached, obviously uneasy about something. Now remember, there are five of us in army uniforms, and the twelve civilians. But that's not what she saw. What set her off was the fact that four people in the restaurant were black. "We can't serve you," she said. I knew at once what she meant. The Germans were not the problem, we were.

It was an old story. Making a fuss about this would get us nowhere. Still we black guys were steaming. My decision was to send the one white guy in with the Germans and to have the other three blacks go round to the back of the restaurant, where they would be served. I would wait out in front. Nothing more probably would have happened; it would have been just another concession to southern ways had the Germans not made light of our situation. Whether they understood what the woman had said, I can't say, but clearly they had witnessed our "retreat." We were the soldiers, they the civilians, yet nearly all of us had been forced to leave. We were Americans, they were foreign-speaking Germans, yet they were served at the regular counters while we suffered the indignity of going to the back. The tables had been turned, that they could see, and it struck them all as very funny. So they started laughing while pointing at me standing outside the front door. The sons of bitches were throwing it in our faces. Well, they'd see who had the last laugh. They'd pay, I decided. As the first German came out the door I hit him one and he went down. Right away the smiles disappeared from the faces of the others. I then directed that all of them be chained together. I was within my authority; they had given me "trouble." During the rest of the trip we didn't much bother with them. For the sins of the South these "innocent" Germans suffered.

Blacks might catch hell in the army but they weren't alone. West Pointers looked down on and berated all non-West Pointers; southerners considered the army their personal domain and so put down everyone else, and it was always open season on Italians. Sometimes referred to as "black niggers," Italians more than any other group were scapegoated, made the butt of jokes. Guys called them "chicken," refused to serve in the same units with them, did all they could to get transferred out. Homosexuals were also targeted, made the butt of jokes. The "fags" according to the boys were all over but you would have been hard pressed to identify most of them. Supposedly they were concentrated among the cooks, medics and typists. Speaking for the medics, there was some truth to this. I had less firsthand evidence about the other two groups. Gays, I thought, went out of their way to be tougher than most other soldiers, overcompensating, I suppose, for their supposedly effeminate mannerisms. This was certainly the case with our colonel who, try as he would, apparently could not help walking with a certain swish and talking with a distinct lisp. The whole company understood he was gay but they also knew he was not the kind of guy you'd ever want to mess with. He was a soldier's soldier, all right, up at 5:00 a.m. to run miles with his troops, carrying on his back exactly what they packed, subjecting himself to the same conditions to which his men were exposed. Gay or not, this was one guy we would follow into hell.

In the barracks we had two sergeants and a corporal who most of us suspected were fags but who were tough hombres quick to kick our butts if we got out of line. If there was another side to their lives we hadn't seen it. But one day that all changed. I was sitting in the day room adjacent to the barracks sleeping quarters when I heard this terrific commotion. Now I didn't see exactly what happened, but the story in full detail spread like wildfire. It started when a group of officers entered the barracks unexpectedly in the course of inspecting the structure itself. What caught their attention was this guy at the other end of the room bending over, his back to a wall, pants down, and wiggling away. So preoccupied was he that they got up real close before he realized who was there. Once he does he jumps up, startled, pulls his pants up and backs away from the wall. But that exposes the large hole in the wall against which he had placed his butt. Past the wall was a room, and in it, also caught in the act, was this master sergeant humping a field sergeant. It had, it seemed, been quite a workable arrangement for the threesome, two in the room and the third on the other side of the wall. But they were promptly carted off, tried and convicted and sent to federal prison. Word of the incident spread across the base and remained a never ending source of wisecracks for weeks. No one doubted the presence of gays at Fort Campbell, but few were prepared to accept or defend such behavior. To be a "fag" was to be a failure and a victim, and also a threat.

But some things were changing in this man's army. It was about to get desegregated. President Truman had wanted it done and it had even become the official policy of the army, but what really got it moving was the need to train soldiers fast and get them off to Korea and elsewhere to fill in for undermanned and banged-up units. Under such pressures you just couldn't continue a segregated army with all the idiotic inefficiencies and time consuming duplication that it involved, plus the racial tensions that went with it, especially here in the segregated South. Most had occurred before I arrived at Fort Campbell, but many spoke as if it had just happened that the 710th Tank Battalion (an all black unit) had come close to rolling out of camp to shoot up the town because of certain racial provocations there. (The army covered up this stuff, but word had it such outbreaks had taken place at other bases around the country.) Aside from the racial incidents I myself encountered, there was no ignoring the general climate of prejudice all about. Everyone knew that black soldiers in town had it far worse than the whites. If, as I've mentioned, they were found in the "white" section after dark they were certain to catch hell from the sheriff and his deputies. In disproportionate numbers blacks were arrested for disorderly conduct or some such offense by the local authorities. Many a time I saw guys returning to base at night, but waiting for them at the gates was the sheriff and his men, snatching guys clearly drunk or who were alleged to have committed some offense while in town. Not surprisingly, more blacks than whites were hauled off.

On base, as I've said, the PXs were segregated, as were the officers' clubs. Kilpatrick, I know, never went inside these clubs. A smooth, sophisticated northerner, he would have nothing of such restrictions. Rather he headed off to the base hospital, whose lounges and whose wards were desegregated. There he felt comfortable. It sure was strange and often confusing—segregated PXs and a desegregated hospital on base, a desegregating army and a legally established segregated society just outside of the base. We blacks had to figure all this out, make sense of it all, or pay the price. Of course it made no sense and the price was much too high.

The local bus drivers who drove us from the base into town clearly objected to the new arrangements. For years they strictly enforced "blacks-to-the-back-of-the-bus," no exceptions. But now the unthinkable had happened—the helter-skelter mixing of black and white soldiers on the bus. You could see them seething when blacks, for example, seated themselves directly behind the driver—unimaginable in the "good old days." Still and all desegregation came to Fort Campbell, and by and large it arrived and settled in without much incident. Desegregation generally went smoothly because at least at our base it involved a gradual infiltration process, blacks and whites mixing more and more as men shifted in and were transferred out of different units. My group started out as all black but by the time I left it was an entirely integrated outfit, half blacks, half whites. Without drama we adjusted to the day-to-day necessities of keeping an army going.

For a personal encounter with military desegregation consider my final tour of duty at the out-processing center on base. Now the army is famous for getting you to bust your tail but it's also notorious for allowing folks to do absolutely nothing but mark time. You will I'm sure recall my lazing about for weeks while the army figured out what to do with me when I first arrived. Here it was three years later, and once more the brass is content to have me sit around for weeks on end just waiting to be discharged.

Did I mind? Not one bit, especially when the rest of my outfit was about to be shipped to Asia. Had my time not been up I'd have been with them, off to God knows what in the "Korean Conflict." But I wasn't home free. Unexpectedly I stirred up a real hornet's nest at the processing center.

The sergeant in charge there had a real sweet deal. When I arrived about fifty guys were scurrying about doing his bidding and competing for his favor. All of them were southerners, so just imagine their reactions when I arrived on the scene. As a staff sergeant, I'm now the ranking soldier there. "Why the fuck do we have a nigger here?" Talk about the potential for conflict. Desegregation is one thing, but not when it means having a black guy over you and all your good buddies. Then, too, I was Airborne, slick-looking, real sharp, and these guys mostly a bunch of undisciplined slobs. Sure I could have pulled rank and really dished it out to this bunch. Believe me, it was tempting. I had, after all, been on the receiving end on more than a few occasions. But I didn't have the stomach for it. I'd be out soon; why make waves? But I kept the group guessing at first, left the sergeant wondering whether I would relieve him of authority, put an end to the cozy little shakedown system he was operating. My presence you could see made everyone uneasy. Why on earth did they have to stick us with a black guy?

Once I had my "fun" I let it be known that I would not pull rank. Officially I would be in charge but I would, I assured them, not mess with whatever they had going. The sergeant would remain "the man." That did it. You would have thought I was the Messiah. Everyone relaxed; the hostility evaporated. They would not have to take orders from a black guy after all. "Hey, Sarge, you're all right." I heard that a lot now. Desegregation, if this is what it was going to mean, stood a chance of working!

So I gave three years of my life to my country. I went along and largely got along. I was no hero, was not even an especially efficient or loyal soldier, but did what was expected of me—I got the job done. No, the army didn't make a man out of me; I came in already independent and self-sufficient, certainly as someone mature beyond my years. Still the person who came out was not the same one who entered. I could now jump out of an airplane, enjoy the ride and not give it a thought. I could set up and operate a field medical unit with the best of them and administer inoculations generally on target and without causing excess pain. I knew my weapons inside and out, could make a bed as tight as a drum and polish a boot to dazzling brilliance and take forced marches in stride. When I left the army I was in the best shape of my life. Order and discipline for me had now become second nature. Looking at me you had to know I was Airborne. I came out respecting the army, not for what it stood for but because of how it operated. It took you apart, then put you back together again, squeezed out personality and individual preference and created a working machine of interchangeable interdependent parts. The results could be impressive. I never had to fight, but I knew for sure that I could. That I had become a soldier I did not doubt.

22-SKOL

18 | HOME SWEET HOME?

My return to civilian life would, I imagined, not be difficult. I couldn't wait to get back to New York; I had had enough of the South. My printing job, I hoped, would be waiting for me, as would my new wife. Married life, put on hold by army service, might now begin. But what happened to me upon my return made me wish for a time I had never left Fort Campbell. Gloria was waiting to help me move from Queens to her apartment up in the Bronx. She was still working at Radio City Music Hall (as a seamstress) and so we had some money coming in. The problem was my job. I had expected to be back producing Time and Life cover proofs with Stanley. Nothing doing. The union had in my absence shifted other guys in there. I'd have to wait, they told me, until something else turned up. Hell, that wasn't the way it was supposed to be. Here I had "wasted" three years of my life, been the good citizen, and now I couldn't even get my old job back! I stormed into the union president's office; Swaydock was not happy to see me. "What are you raising hell for, nigger?" he said, words still chilling to recall. "You should be happy you're in the union." Being in the union now meant that I was on a "waiting list." I was now forced each day to head down to the union hall and hope I'd be assigned to a job. So each day I went there and each day I came back—empty-handed. Welcome home, soldier!

Meanwhile it was not all lovey-dovey back at home. Sure, Gloria and I were married, but we were, after all, still strangers. I hardly knew her. It might in time work out just fine but it didn't help that I was not working. Instead I stayed home most days (after returning from the union hall), did the housework, cooked, and waited for her to finish work. I even made dinner for her friends, one in particular. She knew this guy, a police detective who on several occasions she invited to eat with us. I didn't pay it much attention, although it was a bit odd, I thought, because this fellow was married, and yet she never asked his wife to join us. Then one day late afternoon I was sitting at home staring out the window as this cab pulled up to the curb alongside the building entrance. I could make out a woman inside. I noticed that as she opened the rear door she apparently was being pulled back by someone inside. Several seconds elapsed and then she got out. It was Gloria! What was she doing in a cab? She always took the train, then a bus. Who else had been in the cab? What exactly had happened? I decided to act as if I had seen nothing. "How was it getting home today?" I asked. "Just trouble," she replied. Simple words but they cut right through me. Or was I reading too much into this? What could I accuse her of? I'd wait and see.

A week later it happened again. Soon after the cab pulled away she was at the door. "You must have had a rough time on the subway?" (It had been a particularly hot day.) "A real killer today." That's all she said. Could there be any doubt now? Something real strange was going on. But I had to catch her in the act, whatever it was. So on the same day the following week I headed to her place of work. Once she left the office I planned to follow her.

I spot her leaving the building and watch as she heads right past the subway entrance. Sure enough he's there, that son of a bitch detective, the same guy I had cooked meals for. She gets into his cab and off they go. I'm in a rage. I could have torn both of them apart. Instead I dashed into the subway, hoping to get to the apartment before her. I made it back in time, then watched a repeat of the now familiar scene. There are the two of them kissing, this time in plain sight, kissing right in front of our apartment house. Can you believe it? That was it for me. I would not, I said to myself, get violent. I was young and real strong. Who knows what might have happened? No. I just wanted out.

"How was everything today?" It sounded casual, I thought. "The subway was just as bad as usual." My next words were said as deliberately and calmly as I could manage—"Monday of next week, everything you think I own in here put in the middle of the floor. I'll be back to pick it all up. Just give me whatever is mine. We're going to bring this to an end." Hearing this she got real scared. What had happened? What was going on? I told her, let her know that she had been caught in the act. I was leaving. That was that. That following Monday I came to pick up my things. "I don't want to hear from you," I told her. "Don't you ever bother me for anything." With my stuff packed in a car I left the Bronx, headed for Queens. Ten years would pass before I'd see Gloria again. The marriage, or what there was of it, had lasted all of six months. Earlier I had said I was a man. At that point I was not quite so sure.

Some better news on the job front. Throughout this period I am taking every civil service test in sight—Fire Department, Sanitation, Sheriff's Department, Police, Transit Police, Corrections—you name it. I'm doing well on all of them, consistently scoring in the 90th percentile. As for the physical tests—I smashed 'em. Few people were in as good a shape then. Given the overall scores I put up it was, I figured, only a matter of time before I'd land a City job. Meanwhile dragging myself down to the Printing Union shape-up hall finally paid off (after weeks of watching other (white) guys get jobs while I just sat there). I had gotten my old job back.

Why they put me back with the sophisticated four-color press and with Stanley soon became clear enough. Not long after I returned Stanley, to my great regret, left for another job. Now I was really stuck. Most of the other guys didn't know shit about four-color work. I was expected to operate the machine and teach them at the same time. Plus I wasn't exactly popular. The old timers resented me because I was black, probably because I was young and most certainly because I knew much more than they did. Stanley you know had taught me well. But no matter how unpleasant things were I just couldn't leave; I wasn't a free man. Working out my indenture in the Printers Union meant I had to accept whatever assignment they offered me. The union called all the shots, completely controlled these matters. By taking a black guy in, the union had done me the greatest favor in the world. They wouldn't let me forget this. So I was back with the four-color presses. The challenge was as thrilling as ever. In no time I had that machine humming. The only mistake I probably made was teaching the older pressmen. It was not that long before they began to get the hang of it.

Even while I'm teaching the press to the older guys I'm being treated like an outsider and frozen out. Come lunch time I'd be by myself, the guys heading off. But that wasn't the worst of it. They began sabotaging my press and my work. They could, they figured, now handle the machinery themselves; they didn't need me any longer. They wanted me out. I'd come back from lunch and notice things weren't as I had left them. I couldn't start up the machine again. The ink fountain and the water fountain no longer were in sync. They had been tampered with. Spitballs were turning up in the press, some of them lodging between the rollers and the blanket. That could really mess things up. When I complained to the boss he'd hear none of it. I was, he said, just trying to cover up for my poor work. I knew if I went to the union and complained they would side with my boss. Besides they'd take great pleasure in hearing that I had screwed up. I didn't belong in the Printers Union in the first place; this proved it!

Call it a miracle, but I was just about at my wits' end when this letter arrives from the Sanitation Department. There is a job opening and, based on my scores, I had the position if I wanted it. What a question! I couldn't have taken another day in the pressroom. Actually I wanted just one more to do a little mischief on my own, to turn the tables on the bastards. I'd give them a lesson or two in sabotage. I spent most of my last day on the job doing my best to disrupt the operation (without anyone suspecting what I was up to). I changed tensions, messed with the inks, placed pennies here and there near the gears and reset gauges. I can't say how badly things got fouled up, but I gotta believe these were the makings of a major snafu. Then too confronting the shop boss and getting in the last barrage of foul words sure felt good. You dream about doing such things; here I got the chance. In this way did my career in printing come to an abrupt and inglorious end.

19 | GARBAGE MAN

As a kid who ever dreamed of becoming a sanitation man? But why not; the job sounded just fine. Hell, it was a City job; that's all you had to know. For the longest of times blacks had no chance at all at these positions. It was honorable work, steady work, for a decent wage. It was a job that meant you could raise a family, pay the rent, have food on the table and earn some self-respect. I had no trouble with the Sanitation Department. So what if we were called garbage men? It was a job that had to be done and we sure worked hard doing it. I was assigned to a district in Harlem on 135th Street and Fifth Avenue. For me it was a homecoming. It had been almost ten years since I had left for Queens, so it was nice getting back to visit the places and neighborhoods I had known as a young boy.

My first job, of course, was to learn how to do the job. Sure, it's mostly about dumping garbage into a truck, but it's also about becoming familiar with all the work related equipment. That meant hanging around the Sanitation Garage and watching the mechanics get the machinery into working order and learning how to attach various pieces of apparatus to the vehicles, such as the plows to the water trucks or the snow chains to the wheels. We had to figure out how to drive all the different trucks we put out on the streets. Some were monsters which still called for delicate handling, especially the fine art of shifting gears. Then there were the mechanical sweepers, giant brooms able to dart into the narrowest spaces, spin on a dime, leave the gutter clean and the nearby cars untouched (most of the time anyway). And always your basic oversized hand brooms where not much skill, but devotion to duty counted.

At first we learned by watching, but all too soon it became on-the-job training out on the streets, collecting the garbage that waited for us each day. Picking it up—that could be a problem. Many of the cans, particularly when jammed up with ashes, were darn heavy, some weighing in close to 200 pounds. There was a right way to lift them and there were other ways which increased the risk of your getting hurt. You were best off following old timers here, watching them position their backs and use their legs, and noticing that they wore belts and even back braces. I wore my army belt that was it, but real tight. I approached the cans like a weight lifter and was not careful as I should have been. Luckily, I escaped injury. Others didn't. (Accident rates and injuries among sanitationmen, when I was with the department, were much higher than that of cops or firemen. Plenty of guys stayed out or were put on light duty because of injuries.) Think of it: one awkward lift out of the dozens and dozens we did each day might lead to a lifetime of pain. Guys' backs were forever giving out; hand injuries and hernias were always a problem. You also risked getting hurt putting those big chains on tires or when attaching heavy plows to the trucks. Of course you could be hit by cars or slip on the snow or drop a can on your foot. This was heavy duty work, and risky business.

The Sanitation Department was organized, like the military. We wore uniforms (green with red striping and green hats). At least we were supposed to. The foreman in our garage was an Italian, a real nice fellow, while the assistant foreman, William Hart, a black guy, was one hell of a fine person. The men were mostly Italian, Irish and black, a mix that worked out just fine. Sure there'd be some good natured kidding plus the usual ethnic putdowns, but almost always as a joke, never to give offense. (Hart, the foreman, was quick to transfer trouble makers, guys who simply couldn't or wouldn't get along with the others, out of the district.)

We were a close knit group. I for one couldn't wait to get to work in the morning; I really enjoyed being with the guys. Many of us would eat lunch in the garage and shower together at the end of the day. Somebody's wife would always be sending in soup—enough for all the men. We had a fund put aside to buy presents for guys celebrating special events and helped out when they were sick or injured. I was particularly close with two Irish fellows, and after hours we would cross over the nearby East River Bridge and go drinking together in the Bronx in a neighborhood Irish bar.

The work day began at 7:00 a.m. and ended at 3:00 p.m. Our three-man crews operated so well that most could finish their routes by about 1:00 or 1:30 in the afternoon. Many times we knocked off then. But when we suspected an inspector might be around we put in full days, as we did when we'd help a nearby crew which had run into trouble or had fallen behind schedule. You had "good" routes where the loads were not especially heavy and those that were more demanding, especially the ones that included the projects, or the schools with their backbreaking barrels of ashes. The driver ran the crew, leaving the other two guys to handle the brunt of the work. Sure there were drivers who sat in their cabs smoking a pipe or a cigar and didn't move a muscle, but most would get down to help out with the cans and bags. Drivers had also to deal with the cars which backed up behind the truck as we worked our way down a narrow side street. No, we didn't enjoy blocking their way or slowing them down. Of course if some guy kept blasting his horn we might take our time; normally we hustled when cars were waiting. You'd even see a driver go around the block when there was a backup and then come around for a pickup. Or he would pull all the way over, even get up on the curb to let cars pass. Most folks recognized we had a job to do and stayed cool behind us as we lumbered down the street.

22-SKOL

To do our job right we needed the cooperation of the building superintendents. If they were nice guys the cans would be standing right near the curb (or in the winter on top of the snow banks next to the street), the garbage and the ashes in separate barrels, the big bulging burlap bags piled up alongside them. Those who were indifferent, or who were overworked and couldn't keep up with things made our work harder. We'd have to carry the cans longer distances, the bags would be torn, the stuff spilling out all over the street (which we were then obliged to pick up—not the case today) and the ashes and garbage mixed together. Some, once we told them, became more careful. Others simply didn't give a shit. But we could retaliate. We wouldn't empty some of the cans or would simply drive off and take their torn burlap bags. In the winter we'd leave the cans scattered about on the far side of the snow pile, forcing them to walk over these mounds to retrieve them. If this didn't work we'd send in the Sanitation cops, who had the power to issue summonses for violations. These fines usually brought about a change in behavior if not in attitude.

Once the truck was full the driver would bring it up to the Bronx dump for disposal. He was supposed to go by himself, but sometimes, when he wasn't feeling well or simply wanted company, one of the guys would ride along. Trouble was, he wasn't allowed to bring anyone, so this guy would be forced to hide on the floor of the cab when the truck passed the inspector waiting at the dump entrance. They wanted him going alone so that the rest of the truck crew could spend that time out on the street with a broom and shovel, getting in between the cars and cleaning up near the corners. But no one liked doing this; it was considered demeaning, unglamorous work. I mean everyone enjoyed driving those monster trucks around whose noise everyone noticed. Maneuvering the heavy cans, then tossing the garbage into the hopper in a regular rhythm was something a man could really dig. Everyone got a real kick directing the mechanical brushes in and out of tight spots or letting torrents of water come rushing out of the water trucks, but pushing a broom—that was something else. I felt the same way. I knew it was important because it often was the only way to get between tightly packed cars and, the only way to keep corner sewer grills free of clog and debris. And I also realized the public wanted to see this. Just as they liked to see the cop on the beat they wanted us guys out there with the brooms doing the "dirty work" in the gutters, not off in a corner having a smoke or sitting high above street level in some fancy-assed machine enjoying himself while keeping his hands clean. But a black man pushing a broom just reminded me too much of what we'd always done in America, what people figured was all we could do. I pushed the broom some, but I couldn't wait to get back into the mechanical sweeper, pretend I was a pilot in complete control, cut the corners as sharply as possible, be the dashing figure that I imagined myself to be.

When they talk about a garbage collector most folks don't give much thought to the "collection" part of it. Even though my district was hardly a swanky one there was always stuff being thrown out that could be put to use or that could be sold. As we made our way down the street we were always looking for items for our "treasure box." There was one on every truck. You weren't supposed to do that, but everyone did. Bed springs, suitcases, furniture, old refrigerators, toys, ironing boards, wood and metal—we looked for stuff like this and held on to it. Today some of this might even qualify as "antiques." But, it was mostly junk and there were junk shops all along our route where we could sell some of it and make additional money. We did, but we also fixed up old toys and handed them out on Christmas and donated all kinds of items to the Red Cross. We were, after all, community minded.

Some items left on the street, if properly harvested, could yield sizable dividends. Take the case of Bill Hart, the black foreman in our garage. We loved the guy, would do just about anything for him. Actually he was rather specific about what he wanted. He owned property in Sag Harbor, way out on Long Island, and planned to build himself a house there. He figured he could squirrel away enough material picked up off the city streets to save himself a bushel of money. We were his scouts, instructed to look for various items that he needed. Little by little what we accumulated would go to build Hart's "dream house." Lumber—sinks—refrigerators—metal piping—each time we spotted something he'd send out the "house truck" to pick it up. All of it would be stored in a corner of our garage. Soon there was some pile there.

One day word went around that the borough inspector would soon be making his rounds. All that crap had to be carted off before questions were asked. Hart pressed us into action. Would we, he wondered, be willing to pile everything into the house truck and drive it out to Sag Harbor? Me, Smithie and Louie were the guys he asked for this favor. We weren't crazy about the idea. The three of us after all would be driving a New York City Sanitation Department truck well beyond the borders of the city. Just how would we explain it if we were stopped? What the hell was a New York City garbage truck doing on eastern Long Island anyway? The thought did occur to us that our jobs could be on the line. But Hart was a good guy; he'd cover for us some way or other. Of course we could not implicate him in any way. Louie, taking no chances, put together some boards to cover the lettering on the truck, and put tape over the license plate. It would now not be so easily recognizable as a city vehicle. Some collection. It took five guys to load it up.

The three of us set out on a Friday afternoon, worrying all the way about the truck breaking down or our being stopped for one reason or another. But the trip came off without a hitch. It was a long drive, and by the time we got to Sag Harbor and tracked down his property, it was dark. We unloaded and left everything at a spot Hart had described. In the headlights we could see a foundation for a house and the framework for the ground level. We drove back to the city and parked the truck outside my place in Queens, where it remained until early Monday morning when I drove it back to the garage. Hart's reward to us—a fifth of whiskey for each man. Sure enough the borough inspector showed up and was mighty pleased with conditions at our garage. The area where Hart had stored his stuff was of course perfectly clear.

I understand Louie later made some other runs out to Sag Harbor for Hart. All the effort was worth it. Afterwards, Hart threw a party out at his Long Island "estate" to which the guys were invited. It was absolutely ingenious the way he had transformed the castoff debris of Harlem into his new house, built mostly with his own hands, assisted by some of his neighbors out there. It was a beautiful setting, the house resting on a large tract of land overlooking an inlet. Here was Hart, a black guy, living in a way that I thought was possible only for whites. It felt good being in some way responsible for helping make it happen.

In fairness I should also mention there was a less uplifting side to this tendency to help ourselves. Some of the guys I know made their own arrangements with store owners and commercial facilities to pick up their garbage rather than have the private carters do it. They were paid for this and naturally pocketed the money, though they were working on city time with city equipment. Obviously we all covered this up, considered it one of the perks that came along with the territory. It was the same attitude that encouraged some of the guys to divert gasoline supposed to be for the garbage trucks to the tanks of their own private cars. They would bring gasoline cans to the depot where the trucks gassed up, and have their cans filled. Or they would, during the run, skim off gasoline directly from the tanks of their trucks. They were a great bunch of guys but no, they weren't angels.

And some clearly were goof-offs. I'm speaking here mostly of those on light duty (due to some injury or illness) who were given brooms and put out on the streets. A lot of these guys were hanging on just to get their twenty years in before starting to collect their full pensions. I'll let you guess at their level of efficiency. After a few feeble pushes with their brooms these guys were likely to disappear. They knew which schoolyards they could hang out in and where else they could go without being seen. Their best days as sanitation workers were long behind them.

We picked up the garbage, but along the way we were also collecting acquaintances. It was among the nicest features of the work. You got to know a whole lot of people, most all of whom were real nice to us and appreciated what we did to maintain the area. Want to really know about a neighborhood: who should you ask? If you said the cops, you'd be wrong. When they walk around, if they do at all, it's with an attitude and a feeling of superiority, even contempt for civilians. No wonder they're not on top of all that's going on. People don't usually talk to them and, with certain exceptions, the cops prefer keeping to themselves. The same holds true for firemen. Now they are respected, that's for certain. Unlike the cops, the folks in Harlem understood that when it came down to it, a fireman would risk his life, would go into a burning building if he thought someone was inside. No, the firemen were all right people. Their "problem" was that they didn't leave the firehouse, didn't circulate much on the outside and were not "street smart". So who was? Try your local mail carriers and us sanitationmen. Both had a feel for things along their routes, probably we more than postmen, given the larger territory we covered. Because we also saw ourselves as tough guys, we might even take on added responsibilities might, if we came across a robbery or some other mischief swing into action. On every truck there were baseball bats and other makeshift weapons. And most guys knew what to do with them. Put a uniform on a person and don't be surprised how quick some are to throw their weight around.

This neighborhood connection was never more obvious than in the summertime. That is when people are out on the streets feeling comfortable and usually not in such a big hurry. In summertime, kids gathered to watch us go through our paces, and we obliged them by maneuvering the heavy cans with a special flair we had developed. In warm weather local storekeepers saw to it that we got a beer or a soda as we went by.

Then of course there were the girls. Many of the guys were young like me and eager to get to know the local talent. What better time to make their acquaintance than in the summer. Because it was comfortable outside we were in less of a rush to get through our rounds. Because it could get real hot at times we had the excuse we needed (despite regulations) to take our hats and shirts off and let everyone see our manly physiques. I wouldn't say the girls swarmed over us garbage men, but many a relationship did begin with some idle chatter, well directed whistles or with certain less polite advances from some of the guys. Our supervisor knew all about this stuff and warned against it. "Don't put your hands on anyone"—"Don't form serious relations along the route," he told us. That could only interfere with the job. Of course we ignored him. If opportunities arose, we went for them.

Most everyone in the garage enjoyed working the streets as I did, but not always. A truck would break down from time to time, forcing us to hang around waiting for it to be towed away and another one brought in. Fortunately this didn't happen very often. Each crew took out the same vehicle each day and tried as best they could to maintain it. The more reliable the truck, and the fewer breakdowns, the easier our days. However smoothly trucks operated, they never ran noiselessly. Some racket they made. Sure you grew accustomed to the noise (many of us wore ear plugs), but it was never pleasant.

Just as unpleasant were the smells and the grime that was our stock in trade. Let's face it, ours was a dirty, smelly business—there was no escaping that fact. Some odors would stay in your nostrils all day and into the night. No matter what you did you couldn't get rid of them. You even dreamed smells! And at the end of the day you were filthy and sweaty and dirty and grungy. Thank God for the showers in the garage. Everybody took one each day. The place quickly became a steam room but all that hot water did the job. Not likely you'd see a sharper, cleaner bunch of guys coming home from work than us garbagemen.

Some of the stuff we picked up not only was heavy, it might

also be dangerous. Broken glass, sharp objects of all kinds, bottles of acid, chemicals, oil, fecal matter, you had always to be careful. (That's why we wore big thick gloves most of the time.) If it was something we were reluctant to handle we called in to the garage and a special truck came to pick it up. In the brief time I worked for Sanitation (just about two years) we ran into several body parts as well and at least two dead babies wrapped up in rugs. You never really knew what to expect. Gruesome surprises such as these were always possible.

The worst part of the job came during winter. First off, you reported to work in the dark, and if it was particularly cold, no one was in any rush to get out there and begin the route. Believe me, the cans seemed heavier in the winter, and probably were because more of them were filled with ashes than during the warm months. If snow had been piled up along the curb we'd have one hell of a time getting the cans up and over these icy mounds. And during those bone-chilling cold spells, as often as not the heaters in the cabs did not work. Just about every crew brought a bottle of brandy along to get them through such days. When we were referred to as "brandy boys" you now know why. Our goal was to get through the day as fast as we could. Cold weather meant little socializing; few people stopped to talk to us.

Clearing the snow was a major nuisance. Sure seemed like we had more of the white stuff back then. Many mornings instead of collecting the garbage we'd be hooking up the plows to water trucks partially filled (to provide weight) and putting snow chains on the tires before heading out to do battle with the snow, ice and slush. (How much better it was operating those water trucks in the summertime when we flushed down the streets and incidentally attracted mobs of kids who followed us down the block, cooling themselves off in the spray.)

Snow removal had its kicks. If it was light and you were moving along at a fast pace, the snow flying off the plow, you felt you were hot stuff, putting the snow in its place. But when it was heavy and wet and deep, it was tough going. Obstructions were a pain, especially parked cars that kept you from doing the job right. And if their owners were around when I came through with the plow, you'd hear them cursing me up and down the street. Hey my job was to open the thoroughfare. That meant pushing the snow to one side or the other—up against the cars. I had no choice but to block many of them in. Please accept my apologies.

For real danger it'd be hard to beat the times we'd be driving those heavy trucks with the plows attached up and down some of Harlem's steeper streets. Making it worse was when there were layers of ice and your brakes wouldn't grip. To this day it still gives me the chills. I was driving a snow plow east on 145th Street. It is not a street to go down when your brakes aren't gripping because for four or five blocks, it falls off steeply as it heads toward the Harlem River. So here I am starting from almost its highest point, picking up speed, as I head down the hill. I had the presence of mind to lower the plow in front of the truck, hoping to get it to scrape along the roadway, but with ice and snow on the street that accomplishes very little. Going even faster now, I start blowing my horn again and again, trying to warn people, let them know a runaway plow was coming. Those who got the message quickly scattered. I see the traffic light on Eighth Avenue is against me but I go right through it, just missing some cars in the intersection. You bet I'm scared to death, but it never crosses my mind to jump from the truck. That's because I kept thinking if you can believe it, of all the paper work I'd have to fill out if I did. That nightmare probably kept me from trying to crash into some parked cars as a way of stopping.

I can steer up to a point and so I'm able to avoid cars double-parked on the street. Otherwise I just keep blowing the horn, applying the brakes and hoping I wouldn't hit anything and that the truck would slow down. I was now passing Fifth Avenue where 145th Street begins to level off. Maybe the brakes finally took hold or could be the level street brought the truck to a stop; anyway I had survived. Only then did I begin pissing in my pants. The story of the runaway snow plow—or the four-block long skid—quickly made its way through the garage. It was nothing new, the veterans assured me; many had been through such scares. No question it was the worst experience of my brief career as a sanitationman.

Our crews worked hard and cared about getting the job done in our district. But in the year or two that I was there I saw that we were not able to do all that might be done, that the situation was beginning to get out of control. The problem is complicated and one I've already mentioned. Sanitation would obviously suffer because too many people were now living in the district, and fewer and fewer people were providing necessary services. Harlem, which during my childhood days never seemed dirty was now heading downhill. It made me sad to see this, but such problems were beyond what me and the boys could do out there on the streets each day. We were fighting the good fight, but we were losing.

Maybe it was just as well that I didn't stick around to watch as the buildings burned and the garbage piled up in Harlem. It would have been hard to be on those streets each day and be unable to do much about it. After a little over two years as a garbage man I decided to move on. Not that I had any problems with the Sanitation job. I was enjoying most of what I did each day, and getting along great with the guys. It's just that I had never considered it as a career, as something I'd do until the day I retired. It wasn't just me. Guys were always moving around from city job to city job, looking for higher pay, better working conditions, fatter pensions or more chances to get themselves promoted. In my department, for example, a lot of the Italian guys were just waiting to get out, hoping, many of them, to work at street paving in the Highway Department. Quite a few moved over there when I worked the streets. Remember that I had taken all those Civil Service tests, and it just happened that Sanitation came through first. But now word came that, based on those test results, I had been selected for the Transit Police. Now being a policeman was something I had thought about from the time I was a kid. Most young boys, I suppose, felt the same way. So when word of the opening arrived, I went for it.

20 UNDERGROUND COP

What I knew about the Transit Police was that it was a relatively new and small force about to expand big time. That sounded good to me. Promotions, I figured, might not be that hard to come by. And like Sanitation, it was a city job, secure, steady, and, I had to admit, with a little more dash to it than cleaning the streets. I soon discovered just how many Korean War veterans like me, especially blacks, were looking for those same jobs. Most of these veterans were quality guys, mature, capable, conscientious fellows, the kind who could put this department on the map. And at least in the beginning, the Civil Service tests were run honestly. With no one manipulating the results, without much nepotism screwing things up, lots of us blacks made the force. It was, I recall, about fifty-fifty in my graduating class at the Academy.

Most guys found the time at the Academy, where we trained alongside the regular cops, not all that tough. We got pretty much the same instruction, although for us they cut out classes in traffic control and spent lots of time on the rules and regulations of the subway system. We worked our way through the Penal Code, the Criminal Code of Procedure, and a mess of chicken-shit rules like about how and when to call in ("three minutes after the hour") and how to keep your memo book and record every goddam time you breathed. The physical part of the training was very much like the army, so for me and many of the guys it was a piece of cake. We had, for example, to put a 50-pound bag of sand on our backs and run around a course. Thanks to Airborne jump school this had become almost second nature to me. So was broad jumping and climbing over walls. Tougher to take, though, was the attitude of the regular cops training with us. No way did they consider us their equals. We were a new and relatively small unit, had none of their specialized services—plus no pride, no tradition. Besides, what we would face was nothing compared to what they would deal with—that's how they saw it. Were they wrong. Our job, it turned out, was in many ways far tougher and more hazardous than what these jokers normally had to contend with.

Even before my training period was over I got a taste of how hard and harrowing it could be. Before you go out there on your own you're considered an instructional patrolman and assigned as sidekick to a regular officer. There we were working the Jamaica lines (in Queens) not very far from where I lived. So I felt comfortable, especially since they put me with an old-timer anxious to teach me the ropes.

We were on our lunch break when it happened. There I am up at street level, right alongside the "El" line. I'm gulping down a hot dog when I hear the awful screech of train brakes above me. I don't pay it too much attention especially as part of the sound was drowned out by the traffic noise at this very busy intersection. I didn't see it hurtle down, but out of the corner of my eye I spotted something hit a car which was waiting at the light, a woman behind the wheel. When I saw what it was I turned sick instantly. It was the lower half of a human torso, sitting there right on the hood, blood all over the windshield. Rushing over we could hear the woman screaming hysterically. I looked up but all I saw were more drops of blood coming down from the tracks, then splattering the car. The other half of the body I figured might come down any second, but just the dripping continued.

My partner's disgusted, not so much by what happened—as an old timer he had seen everything—but because of the time and trouble this was about to cause both of us. "Oh shit, oh shit, why does this have to happen on my tour?"—pretty much summed up his attitude. I'm nauseated—a typical rookie reaction, and about to throw up. "You go upstairs and take charge there," he ordered. "I'll cover things down here." Naturally , most of the problems were certain to be up there on the tracks and platform; not on the street. But then I was supposed to be gaining experience. (I didn't remember learning anything about bodies cut in half at the Academy.) Besides, I'd just as soon not deal with the hysterical woman, who showed no signs of calming down. Scrambling up the steps of the El to the platform I'm thinking I'd better call this in, and get them to turn the power off. We didn't need anyone frying. I'm telling them suicide, but I'm wondering how I could be so sure. True, everyone's shouting "Suicide, suicide," and it was as good a guess as any—but who knew. Maybe the guy was drunk? Maybe he had just been trying to cross the tracks. Could he have been pushed? Murdered? Or just slipped? Suicide simplified things, though.

At that point it didn't matter a damn. What did was evacuating the passengers from the train that had cut our friend in two. Everyone rushed off the platform once word spread about the body. Fortunately it was someone else's job to remove it or what remained of it from the track. I just wasn't ready for that much "reality" yet. As they were backing up the train to let the emergency crew get in I remembered I was supposed to be recording all this. I didn't trust myself to do it right the first time, so I wrote it down on the back of my record book, figuring I'd transfer it all later—the line, location, motorman's name and number, the name of the emergency unit. I then headed back to the street to check with my partner. Not much change there. The torso had not yet been removed from the car and blood was still dripping down from the elevated tracks. The woman was in terrible shape. Whatever consoling my partner had tried seemed to have had little effect. Crowds had gathered and the traffic was just about at gridlock. Fortunately regular cops soon arrived and took control of the situation. I had seen more than enough for one day.

Not long after that I was sworn in as a regular member of the Transit Police. It was then that I began to see more clearly why we represented a force for change in the department. My class was the first sizable group of new, young recruits to enter in some time. We would bring new energy and a sense of commitment which, if it had ever existed among the transit cops, had long since disappeared. Many of the old timers had moved into Transit from other agencies. Rigorous training they never received. At best they were subway guards. That's probably all officials thought was needed at the time. For years trouble down there had been taken care of by the motormen and conductors. They had kept order in the subway. But after several of them were hit by lawsuits they stopped getting involved, it seems, and special Transit cops were assigned to handle such problems. Looking at some of these guys it's hard to imagine they could have improved the situation much. So many were sloppy looking and fat, with sizable beer bellies indicating how much of their time was spent. Few of the change booth clerks I talked to had a kind word for them. What I heard was that most did very little patrolling or actually much of anything. Instead they'd go to sleep, be out of circulation most of their shifts. They'd pull up a milk crate in a booth, unbutton their uniforms, and off they'd go. Transit cops, I soon learned, needed to rely heavily on these subway clerks. How to convince them that we were a different breed from the old guard—that was our challenge.

The Transit Authority was trying to make up for lost time. Overnight they were attempting to overhaul the security force and introduce professional standards. That meant plenty of pressure on us as they tried to undo the past and raise the reputation of the Force. They wanted us out on patrol—all the time. They expected us to be visible—in all parts of every station all along the line. They wanted arrests, lots of them, and they wanted us to hand out all kinds of summonses. A tall order.

Then there was record keeping—that was the killer. Every move we made, every observation, every action taken, all of this had to be written down in proper form in our memo books. For anyone out there on their beats it was just impossible, too much to ask. You see, these folks were civilians. Effective policing, the proper organization of forces—it's not something they knew much about. Their main concern—keep those trains moving, get people where they wanted to go. They were train people, track people, folks concerned with revenues and fares and capital improvements. Sure, police were needed; obviously the public had to feel safe underground and be assured that its letters of complaint (they came in continuously) were not ignored, so let's put a few more guys in uniforms on the platforms and trains, let them keep detailed records so we'll know what they've been up to, and we can defend ourselves better in the case of lawsuits. That should do the trick. Not a bad move, but they didn't get it right.

The problems of policing the 320-mile subway system were huge and not automatically solved overnight with young recruits pressured to produce and to write down everything they did. First off, if you ask me, they put us in the wrong type of uniforms—stiff, heavy, impossible to keep clean, unsuited to conditions in the subway. Consider the hat we had to wear—oversized, restrictive, with a stiff, curvy, wide brim in front. It was, I know, part of a uniform that said we were important, that would command respect from the public, but it didn't work well down there. Dirt sank in easily; steel slivers from the tracks worked their way through the fibers. Just try keeping uniforms clean while working in filthy subway cars. (Then there were the white gloves we were ordered to wear. Imagine what they looked like at the end of a shift!) Fatigues and a baseball cap are what we should have been issued. Such outfits would have sent a clear message—we meant business.

Our guns were also a problem. If you fired and missed your target, the bullet became an absolute menace to everyone in the station. Steel-jacketed, they would ricochet off the solid walls of the subway tunnels. The shooter stood almost as much chance of being hit by the bullet as the intended target. Several years after I joined the Force the Department shifted over to soft lead bullets. These simply gouged a hole in the wall or the platform, were less of a threat to innocent bystanders.

Communications were crude. Talk about the second-class status of the Transit Police. It was real hard keeping in touch with each other. Sure we had special problems—being in underground tunnels and surrounded by high noise levels—still, without portable communication devices we were out of touch lots of the time. Now that was a problem with us patrolling a huge system divided into dozens and dozens of stations and hundreds of separate platforms and mezzanine areas. And we were doing it alone. When regular cops put us down they ignored the fact that unlike those guys, we patrolled by ourselves—no partners—no immediate backup—no one to jump in and save our asses. That was the frightening fact we faced as we walked the long, deserted platforms, checked out the bathrooms and staircases and tried pushing our way through packed subway cars. No wonder some of the guys developed into brutes. Out there alone the choice often came down to busting someone up or taking a licking yourself. Help, when it arrived, usually came from the regular cops on the street. When they got calls for assistance, they came a-runnin'. That I have to admit. On more than one occasion they saved my ass (though they were quick to take over and to grab the credit for any arrests that followed).

I didn't mind working alone. Hell, I was Airborne. I was tough, in terrific shape—I could, if I had to, take on the world. Besides, I had, much of my life, done things by myself. Take a break when I wanted, go for a smoke, talk to people on my beat—being on my own had its benefits. Plus there was another advantage. I was free to take chances without worrying about putting someone else at risk. I would, as you will see, make some pretty stupid moves; others could have gotten hurt. Walking the beat was man's work. Those who joined the Force with me changed quickly; matured fast.

We recruits had another problem with the old timers. They could be helpful, breaking us in, teaching us the ropes and showing us about how to cut corners and survive. But they sure didn't appreciate our being there. My class literally flooded the ranks of the Department. There were about 350 of us who entered in 1953—that doubled the Force overnight. Next year over 400 graduated and joined us. For these holdovers the handwriting was on the wall. The new bloods would shape the future, and their professionalism or at least energy would expose the old timers for the slobs and bumblers most of them were. Not surprisingly their advice to us was to slack off, not get too involved, avoid becoming gung ho. Do your time—stay out of trouble, don't expect rewards for your efforts, and wait, just wait for that pension. That made no sense to me, at least not during my early years in the Department. I was into it. I read the Criminal Code, memorized the subway rules—reviewed all the regulations. I was a reader, you know. That's how, years before, I had become a medic. I wanted to be a good cop, and I figured knowing the law in all its details would get me there—know it, and then enforce it.

For old timers the rule was to let things slide. Not me. I tried patrolling every inch of my beat. Of course, it was impossible, but I tried—day after day. Everything went into my memo book (actually I recorded it once informally and then rewrote it to get it just right. I listed columns of frequently used words in my book so I would not misspell them and expose my fatal flaw.) I tried to enforce as many of the regulations as I could. To me, it wasn't petty shit. Spitting, littering, smoking, fare beating—I didn't look the other way on any of this stuff. I confronted the offenders, told them to fess up, issued summonses when they didn't, and if their attitude offended me, I hauled them into the local police station and booked them. Chalk some of this up to youthful enthusiasm and a belief in playing it straight, going by the book. But remember too that I was a black cop. Hadn't we always backed down, certainly before white people? But now this black man didn't have to; he had a uniform, a gun and a shield. He represented authority; he was in charge. I had the law behind me—some people had better look out.

Enter the subway system and you were in another world. It could be mighty unpleasant, uncomfortable, certainly dangerous, but also exciting, bustling, and unpredictable. Passengers, perverts, pickpockets, policemen, prostitutes, bums, robbers and gamblers—all of them were going about their business in these dim subterranean caverns. Each station had its separate community and cast of characters and for enforcement every one presented a separate challenge. Before a cop left for his rounds he checked what were called condition cards which told him what he might expect at every location. Fare beaters, gamblers, pickpockets, rowdies, flashers, illegal salesmen—all had their favorite hangouts.

To know the subway was to appreciate its various moods and rhythms. Terrible noise, unbearable crowds, could, in no time, give way to empty spaces and periods of silence. New York's subways weren't clean then—probably never have been, but they were decently maintained. Porters worked hard to sweep away the daily debris. Work crews came through every three days to wash down the walls and flush the platforms, and cops like me rode herd on passengers. Dumping garbage onto the tracks, spitting in all directions, tossing away cigars, cigarette butts, or folded newspapers—I wouldn't put up with any of that. Remember, the graffiti artists had not yet invaded the subways so I wasn't busy chasing after them. Even the rat population was kept under control then. You'd spot them down on the tracks and racing across a platform, but mostly they stayed out of sight. Now I hear they've practically taken over down there.

For eight hours every day I lived in this underground world. I enjoyed it—the activity, the action, and yes, a lot of the people. I became friends with many of the token clerks. I made most of my hourly call-ins from their booths. That way they'd see for themselves just how conscientious I was. The trainmen, the porters, some of the newsstand operators—all became familiar faces on my beat. Same with many of the passengers. "Hi, Officer." "Hi, Earl." "Good morning." "How ya doing today?"—it felt good when they greeted me.

Community patrolling is all the rage today, right? Weren't we doing just that back then? Covering the territory on foot, mingling, talking to people, trying to be helpful—that's how we went about the job. I sure did. Can't tell you how many times each day I stopped to give directions. That was my strength. I knew the system cold—every BMT, IRT and IND station and the E, the GG, the D, and whatever other trains there were. I could tell you every stop they all made and each transfer point. I went out of my way to help blind people. It was amazing to me how they made their way into and out of trains and up and down the stairs. For women in the subway, I was a godsend. No matter that I was black. With me around, they felt more secure and relaxed. Even to the point of striking up a conversation. You'd be surprised how eager they were to talk while they waited for trains, to reveal problems, personal stuff they probably wouldn't mention to others. When they missed me, a few days running, I'd hear about it. "I've been looking for you." "Haven't seen you in days." These were "my" people. They counted on me.

One day while patrolling at 74th Street and Roosevelt Avenue in Queens I spot a young black woman in her twenties. She's putting toilet paper under her dress between her legs. Practically hemorrhaging, she was trying to stop the flow of blood as best she could. You can imagine how embarrassed she was. I quickly escorted her back to the ladies' bathroom and blocked it off with a garbage can. I then called for an ambulance. As a former Army medic I could handle bleeding. By the time the ambulance workers arrived, it was under control. She refused a stretcher and walked out with them. Stuff like this happened nearly every day, was part of the job. Several weeks later, she spotted me on the platform and came right over, greeting me warmly by name.

"I got your name from the clerk," she says. "I've been looking for you. I want to give you something." Hoping to run into me, she must have brought this package with her each day. It was a large, expensive box of Barricini chocolates. I accepted the gift, and for months afterwards we exchanged greetings nearly every day.

But happy endings were not guaranteed; the system sometimes got in your way. Walking along the platform at a Queens station I'm approached by an airline stewardess in uniform. "A guy has been following me since I got on at 34th Street," she says. "Look over my shoulder at the staircase and you'll spot him." Keep going, I tell her; I'll circle around and check it out. Sure enough there's someone walking right behind her, matching her step for step up the staircase. As she nears the top, he reaches out for her, figuring, I guess, that no one else was around. "Hey, Buddy," I shout and he turns, a shocked look on his face. I'm standing there, my gun out, pointed right at his midsection.

The stewardess does not want to miss her flight. But she promised she would be back the next day to file a complaint. But what am I supposed to do with this guy? I hadn't seen him do much, plus the "victim" is leaving the scene. I still want to book him for harassment. But it's not quite so simple. We used regular cops to process our cases. That meant we had to bring the "perpetrator" outside and locate the precinct nearest the scene of the crime. Then we had to battle with the desk sergeant. Remember now, these cops had little regard for us, considered us an annoyance. Many of our arrests they regarded as little more than chicken shit cases. You heard this all of the time when you walked in. "All this paper work, all this bother. For what?" Only if it was possible to jack up the charges, make them into more serious offenses, did they show any interest. This made dealing with these blowhards a real pain in the ass. That is what they wanted—to make you think twice before hauling someone in front of them.

As expected, the sergeant wasn't happy when I brought in

our stalker. The guy, meanwhile, had not said a word since I interrupted whatever mischief he had planned. As I'm booking him, his record comes through. Sure enough, assaulting women seemed to have been his M.O. Still the precinct lieutenant is not pleased. "Without a complaint you're wasting your time," he tells me. "Well, then, I'll charge him," I shouted back. "You charge him and the case will be thrown out faster than lightning down a pole." "That," I tell him, "is my business." But I see he ain't moving on this, so I call my boss and explain. "You're right," he tells me," but there's nothing you can do." So the guy walks.

Comes the next day and our stewardess is back as promised, ready to press charges. I can't wait to get her over to the precinct. The same son of a bitch who let the stalker go the day before is on duty. "Well, you wanted a complainant; here she is." Our boy behind the desk is squirming plenty. "Tell the lady why the guy isn't here." The stewardess, a well mannered, sophisticated woman, is obviously agitated. "I was told he would be held," she says. "Well, you weren't here and we had no idea whether you were coming back." Does she let him have it with a tirade that just warmed my heart. But there is, strangely enough, a "happy ending" to this tale. The guy, I found out, was locked up shortly after "our" incident. He had been picked up by another Transit cop at a Queens station for doing exactly the same thing. I contacted the stewardess who was anxious to cooperate. Our testimony helped convict the guy. Sometimes, only sometimes, you do get a second chance.

Helping people was one thing. Quite another matter was dealing with those eager to help us. For me that was a problem. Mostly, it involved free meals while on the job. I preferred paying for mine, didn't want to be obligated to anyone. But I assure you, I was not typical. Most of the cops ate on the cuff, didn't expect to pay, and weren't asked to. They were "guests" of management. (Some owners would invite guys to eat in the back, where they could take off their uniforms and guns and relax a little. Most cops preferred such arrangements.) Restaurants liked having us around. Once a place became known as a cop hangout, it kept troublemakers away. So it was a good deal—the police got their meals, and proprietors their peace of mind. But this led to awkward situations when owners refused to accept my money. I felt uncomfortable and they were insulted. I had rejected their hospitality (and delivered a message about my fellow officers.)

Some of our guys were real pigs, always looking for handouts. For a freebie, these "scrounge bastards" would go clear across town, drop into a place not even on their beat. No, it wasn't extortion, but it came close. It had to cause some resentment. I picked this up when, for a time in Queens, precinct brass sent me to this one bakery for several dozen bagels. Each time, the owner grumbled about having to "cooperate." But did he have a choice? What if he said the bagels were not "on the house." Wouldn't he expect there'd be "consequences"? (I felt he probably took revenge on us and that all the bagels he "contributed" had at some point fallen on the dirty floor or been spoiled in some way.)

Listen, I was no angel either. Early on, I was one of the cockiest guys around. I was determined to be a cowboy, one tough hombre. I swaggered, I strutted, to the max. I assumed the cowboy "look", got myself fancy pearl-handled guns and changed the standard issue holster issued by the Department. The official one rode up high on your body and made quick draws difficult. I took the holster, loosened it up, moved it lower, right at arm's length. My belt sagged, looked a bit sloppy, I admit, but my draw—it was fast. Yup—there I am walking down Main Street ready for a shootout. At home I'd stand in front of a mirror and practice drawing my gun again and again—as for the bad guys, forget about it. I was the law, so you'd better watch out. Here was one black man who was not going to back away from anyone.

Eventually this look, this attitude, passed. Were some of the guys laughing? Maybe. When I saw other patrolmen acting this way I realized the cowboy had to go. Maybe I just grew up and became more confident of my ability, didn't need to swagger or pretend to be someone else. So the pearl handles went, same with the low-slung holster. And what bluster remained did not survive the following incident.

There I was, still the "cowboy" riding the local train, heading south from 125th Street station. Sitting in a nearby seat was this little white boy, maybe three or four years old. I'm smiling at this kid and figuring that to him I must seem an incredible hero. Then in a clear voice others in the car could hear, he says, "Is that a nigger cop?" Talk about a body blow. The mother was speechless. In that instant a simple, "innocent" question took me down "several notches" stripped away all the swagger. I couldn't let this go. When the mother said nothing, I spoke up. "Yes, sonny, I'm a nigger cop," all the time looking at her, my raised voice filling an otherwise silent car. "See where this shit comes from?" I said to her as I left the train at 96th Street. The blow had hit home. In the eyes of others I was no cowboy, but just a "nigger cop."

On most days patrolling followed a familiar routine. At our district office, I would first check the latest station condition reports to find out what problems had been reported or might be expected along the route. Then I'd catch a train and begin walking through the cars. At each station I'd get off, check out the platform, walk the stairs to the mezzanine and then cross over to the other side where trains ran in the opposite direction. (At some stations getting to the other side meant exiting the subway, crossing the street, and re-entering the station now on the opposite platform.) Always there were bathrooms to look in on which, as you will see, could be trouble spots. Closed entranceways or exits had also to be checked. I'd then head over to the token booths, chew the fat with the clerks and, spend a few moments checking out their coins. (I was, you see, a coin collector. So many different coins came through the subway system on any given day. In little time I had myself a fine collection.)

Clerks liked having us around; we were their main protectors. I was at risk out there on patrol alone, but the token clerks were far more vulnerable. Cooped up in a small booths, they were sitting ducks. I could move about, hide behind the subway pillars, even run if need be. But a clerk was a stationary target. And the bad guys knew this. Token booth holdups happened all the time. Robbers used bullets, fires, stink bombs—any way they could get at that money inside the booth. If it meant killing or disabling the clerk in the process, so be it. No wonder they were happy to see me hanging around.

To satisfy the brass much of my time was wasted filling up my memo book. Let me get this off my chest. It was a bitch, especially for me who never could write worth a damn and certainly couldn't spell. I'd almost rather be in a shootout with a crazed dope fiend than write up a fare beater. But the job demanded it and I wanted to keep the job. They expected entries in your memo book based not upon recollection at the end of your shift, but as you were on the go. "Checked stairs 8:10," "crossed platform 8:18," "inspected bathroom 8:22." Hey, if we were this methodical I guess they figured the job was getting done. Guys cheated of course, let their imaginations do the walking. Remember though, your memo book could save your ass.. If you're playing it straight and a guy is killed on the stairway at 8:10 and I was there at 7:45, recorded it and went someplace else at 8:10, well, then, I'm off the hook, not responsible. But I'm out of a job if he dies at 8:10 and my book says I was there at 8:20 and records "all normal." Trouble baby. I played their game. If they wanted a full memo book, they usually got it from me, mostly non-fiction.

Even with precise entries in a memo book, something was missing. I was a good cop trying to do a conscientious job but there was no way I could cover the territory and give all places the kind of close attention expected. I'd stick my head out the door of a train and survey a platform, but that would be it. The doors would close and I'd be on to the next station, already behind in my schedule. I'd check out a mezzanine area or enclosed stairwell but would be gone in a matter of seconds. Only by chance would I run smack into a situation where I'd go into action.

Sure, my being there made a difference, would discourage criminal activity, but once I passed through a station all hell could break out and I'd just plain miss it, or, if I got word of trouble I'd have to wait for a train going back that way. I couldn't be everywhere—I understood that, but that didn't make me feel any better about it.

Sometimes you didn't miss it. One day on 168th Street and Broadway I ran smack into three guys shooting craps right there on the platform. Break it up and leave the station. That's all I planned to say. They had other ideas. Ignoring my order, they jumped me and began forcing me toward the edge of the platform. I struggled with them, shouting at the same time in the direction of a subway porter. While one of them has his arms wrapped around me, the other two are hard at work trying to get to my service revolver. Fortunately, our holsters were built to discourage this sort of thing. The gun would not come out unless you push and pull in a certain way, so their tugging and pulling got them nowhere. But it gave me time to get one of my arms loose and to reach for my second gun, one I wore in a shoulder holster. I drew that gun and broke away. The game was over for them.

I guess I should explain this second gun. I know the public has its own ideas about why we carry another weapon. Everyone "knows" we have it to leave on the scene alongside a shooting victim to prove that "he" was armed when cops shot him. It's happened that way, of course. But that second gun is mostly there to save our skins. I can't tell you how many guys have gone after a cop's service revolver. While they're grabbing for the gun, we can't get to it. So it's the other gun that saves the day. Once we draw it—whether it's from a shoulder holster or strapped to a leg, these guys got to give it up—they've lost. One other thing. Off duty we're still supposed to go armed. Lots of guys hate lugging their heavy service revolvers around. The second gun, smaller and concealed, is much more comfortable. So there you have it—another police mystery solved!

Catching a criminal in the act does not necessarily mean you can stop it. That's certainly the case when dealing with pickpockets. These guys loved the subways. With its packed crowds and constant jostling, they were in their element. Even I had to admit the real pros were artists at work. Give them a sharp razor and it became a piece of cake, cutting through pockets and removing all valuables. Carrying newspapers or umbrellas they knew how to hide the loot there until they'd left the scene. These guys usually worked in teams, one or two creating the diversion, the other in charge of lifting the goods. Chances were the person targeted would have no idea anything was happening. Only afterwards he'd discover his pants pockets had been cut away or a pocketbook emptied. That was the problem for law enforcement. The victims were gone before they realized they were victims.

Pickpockets were not only skilled but downright clever. Keeping up with their cat and mouse games was not easy. Just when we thought we had figured out their modus operandi, what places they were hitting and when, they'd change patterns. Just when we had put the puzzle together and figured out which guys were working the trains together in teams, they'd switch around, bring in new faces. Even when I'd spot the pickpocket I might have no idea who he was working with. Sure I could grab him, but he'd have nothing on him, having transferred his razor and his loot to an accomplice who had already left the train. Talk about balls. They'd be going about their business in a subway car with me right there!

I might be there, but they knew I couldn't or wouldn't move. I'd spot the crime but, jammed in by the crowds, I couldn't make my way over to them. Even if I could I might not do anything because of all the passengers. There was no telling how a pickpocket would react or who might get hurt. What you'd hope for is that the perp stayed on along with the unwitting victim(s) while the train emptied out. Then I could make my move, collar the suspects and have a witness right there. Guess how often that happened? Like I said, these guys were craftsmen, you couldn't help but admire their technique. We'd catch up to them every so often, grab them with the goods and have ourselves a conviction. They'd get a six-week sentence, be out in two to three weeks, and would be back on the trains. They had their job to do; we had ours.

Then there were also the novice pickpockets, guys who would themselves pretend to be homeless or drunk and then would steal from drunks, slit open the pocket of a guy asleep in the cars, or grab a business briefcase, cut it and dump it in the garbage, sometimes two stations away. (There were ways to detect guys who were faking inebriation in order to get into position for their dirty work. I'd check fingernails and shoes. If they were cared for and neat I'd get suspicious. A guy wearing cologne or with his fly not open put me on alert.) If these pickpockets were caught in the act they could get violent and end up attacking the victim. Such lowlifes we despised. When we caught them we'd rough them up, no questions asked.

We all drew the "bum squad" once in a while. Drunks, down and out guys (also quite a few women), the homeless, all found their way into the subways and rode the cars up and down the lines. They could sleep, it was warm and it was cheap. But our job was to stop them from sleeping there through the night. The trains had to be emptied. Work crews needed to move in and clean them up, get them ready for the morning rush hour.

Some of these folks were trouble and took out their anger against us once we came in to remove them. Some cops roughed them up, treated them real bad. I could never do that. I felt for those guys. So what if they cursed us, it didn't mean a thing. It was all they had left. True, I kept my mouth shut, did nothing about what I saw. You just didn't. That was the system. You cover up for each other; you don't antagonize fellow cops. Why? Because you never knew when you're going to need this other guy.

After waking up, those able to leave took off. Some begged to be locked up and threatened to smash a car window or do other damage unless we took them down to the station. Often in no shape to go under their own power, we carried them out. I wrote up these guys all the same. "I put John Doe out at 2:15 a.m., 179th Street—intoxicated, incapable of going on his own." Outside a van waited to deliver them to the precinct house. They'd take a shower, get some fresh clothes and a bed for the night. And they'd be safe. It was, I felt, the right thing to do for them. I know today they've got their rights and you can't corral them the way we once did. They're on their own now and mostly, I think, the worse for it. In these "good old days" we had more authority, and greater control. We could remove panhandlers, chase prostitutes; we could control unruly youngsters with loitering statutes—our hands weren't tied. Agreed, there's good reason to restrict cops, but consider also what's been lost.

Bathrooms were trouble. Pay them special attention, we were told (one reason why we were sometimes referred to as "shithouse inspectors"). I did, both the men's and the women's (where I knocked first). Nothing that went on there surprised me. (Back then you should know these public toilets were usually well maintained, a porter in charge of the facilities in one or two stations. They did a good job, and believe me the public appreciated it. Later on, crime and costs forced most all of them to be shut. Try finding a usable public bathroom in New York City today!)

You always had to be cautious walking into a bathroom. This one time, for example, on 23rd Street and Ely Avenue in Queens I knew there'd be trouble. A Post Condition Card listed the bathroom as a hangout for gamblers, and when I got to the station the clerk confirmed the fact that non-stop action was going on. At first the door of the men's room wouldn't budge, even when I put my full weight against it. But I knew it wasn't locked, so I tried pushing it again. All of a sudden it gives way and in I stumble. It was standing room only with maybe eight or nine guys playing craps. In one of the stalls I spotted some heavy "queer" action.

At first everyone ignored me. Then one or two looked up but went right on playing. Why you wonder. Other cops on the beat

22-SKOL

they knew let them be or were paid off to look the other way. They figured I was in on it. Smashing my nightstick against the sink, I hoped might give them another idea. It made a deafening sound but that's all. "All right, guys, break it up—go on home." I was really angry now. That did get a reaction. What the hell was I doing there, one fellow wanted to know. Another wondered why I wouldn't just take a few bucks and leave! Break up the game and get the hell out of there, I repeated. No one budged.

I grabbed the dice; I was serious. But so were they. Three guys jumped me, dragged me to the floor, with one of them deciding to sit on top of me. Meanwhile they continue to roll the dice. This is crazy. Lucky for me the station attendant who had heard me talk about checking out one of the bathrooms peeks in at this point. I shout for help and off he runs to get some—I hoped. I'm fighting and kicking but I'm still down on the floor. One guy in particular is taking special pleasure in kicking me from time to time. No one, fortunately, is going for my gun.

It was some rescue. Talk about the cavalry showing up! They came, and they came in force, led by this old-fashioned cracker type sergeant who probably hated "niggers" but would be damned if he would let any civilian put a hand on a guy in uniform. His men, seeing me there on the floor, went beserk, swinging their nightsticks in every direction. In no time there was blood and real serious damage. It didn't matter that these guys were pleading for the police to stop. For the three who jumped me the sergeant reserved special treatment. "I'm gonna teach these bastards that when they put a hand on a cop they're all gonna catch hell." "Do you understand that, boy?" he said, turning to me. He then ordered me out of the bathroom. I couldn't see what happened next, but I knew—it was brutal. All three had to be removed on stretchers. No, it didn't really bother me, probably because I was nursing a large swelling over my right eye. These guys had hit me plenty hard. Would the sergeant and his men be held accountable for excessive force? Not this time. They were after all defending a fellow officer; there'd be no questions asked.

I'd been on the job long enough to understand that the police, in upholding law and order, put a lot more emphasis on order. It was expected of them. And in the name of order they would not always need be too scrupulous about the law. The guys shooting crap had defied the law and then became disorderly, striking out against those representing it. For this they would pay.

I had expected to find a crap game in that Queens bathroom, but "men's" rooms could, I knew, often hold other surprises. Consider the time I was patrolling the BMT line at the Bowling Green station near City Hall and headed over to inspect the men's bathroom. Now there's a technique to checking out a toilet. Given the narrowness of the place you run the risk of being jumped. So what you do is walk with your back against the walls and bend over to check out the scene in each stall. Well, I started doing this, then stopped short. Looking underneath I spotted a pair of feet facing away from me toward the opposite wall, which might not by itself have caused me to take notice had I not also caught sight of a face bobbing up and down above the panel of the stall. What's this? Pushing the door in I immediately had my answer: there was a guy, his pants down, standing atop the toilet seat, getting a blow job from another guy whose feet I had already noticed. The one with his back to me was going about his business with enthusiasm and total commitment, completely unaware of my presence. But the guy on top of the seat looked horrified. If he could have flushed himself down the toilet, he would have. He tried nudging the one below, attempting to get his attention, but got no reaction. Both of them were well dressed, one apparently a businessman judging from the expensive attaché case resting on the floor of the stall. Perspiring heavily, he finally managed to pull the guy off of him, then pointed to me standing there. Turning around, this fellow sees me and nearly collapses on the spot.

I was no innocent, but this time, for whatever reason, I'm revolted. Could have been I'd had a bad day. When there are no witnesses what we usually do is break it up and chase them. Anything else and you're asking for trouble. You've got a weak case, and you may even end up being sued for false arrest. I knew all this, yet this time I just can't let it slide. I grabbed them both and cuffed them to each other.

They're embarrassed as hell, that's plain enough. Then one of them became sick. At the stationhouse I get the usual crap from the sergeant, "Get rid of this shit—who needs it?" But I've gone this far—I'm not backing down. I wasn't even thinking about who these jokers might be. (It turned out one was a lawyer, the other worked for a stock brokerage house.) Cops do worry about these things. If we think a guy's got a "rabbi," has some pull and could make trouble for us, we're not anxious to push a case. It is called saving our own skins and not making waves. I called in to my command and got the same response. "Let it go; we don't need these headaches." But I'm real stubborn. Besides, no one has the authority of talking you out of making a legitimate arrest. I'm sworn to uphold the law, am fully empowered to go ahead no matter what the advice of others. "Do what you want to do," the captain says, "but once you're done, you bring your ass down here." It will cost me. He's gonna chew my butt off.

Meanwhile the two guys are scared to death. They never dreamed, I'm sure, they'd be hauled into a police station for their "private" behavior and charged with sodomy. They keep telling me how sorry they are. But the case is already moving through the system. They are booked and taken to a holding pen, and I'm on my way to Centre Street for the arraignment. (That's one reason why the brass doesn't go for your making petty arrests. It takes you off the beat; your post goes uncovered.) Down there, what I have to do is relate the story to the arraignment clerks, who type it up and "correct" the situation, make it suitable for court presentation. The guy I tell the story to doesn't even blink when I relate the particulars. He's heard it all. But he is impressed with all the detail I'm able to recall. After he finished with it the story seems airtight, the case made.

I'm worried, though. My bosses are pissed at me for pushing this over their strong objections. What if these two decide to make a case of it and concoct some bullshit about me trying to shake them down after catching them in the bathroom? It could get sticky. Because one of them is a lawyer I could find myself in deep shit. In court the judge, after hearing the charge, asks me whether the two had resisted arrest or shown me any disrespect. "No, they did not, your Honor." (So now we're probably just talking misdemeanor.) Then comes the crucial question—"How do you plead?" If they answer "not guilty," we got ourselves a problem. But to the great relief of the judge and the D.A. and of course yours truly, both say, "Guilty." This means the case can be wrapped up neatly and quietly. A fine, they're out, and nobody has to know. Now I'm hearing I did a "great job," "good work," "congratulations on the guilty plea." But there's a warning too from the higher-ups. I'd better not ignore their instructions next time or they'll be hell to pay. I came out a winner, but it was a close call.

Matters of sexual activity clearly outnumbered incidents of criminality in the years I worked the subway. Most but not all was of the sex-for-pay kind. Prostitutes like working the subways. There were lots of potential johns around and all sorts of concealed areas. You'd be amazed where I found some of them servicing customers. Maybe you've seen those very narrow spaces between the back portion of the token booths and the adjoining station walls. Well sure enough I'd catch a prostitute now and then doing their quickie numbers there. Our policy with prostitutes was simple—clear them out, keep them moving, and hope they end up someplace else, and don't bother bringing them in.

But it wasn't always commercial sex that I came across. Consider the time I'm riding to the end of one of the lines late at night. I'm by myself, about in the middle of the train. It's coming to the last stop when I detect some moaning and groaning. But where in the world is it coming from? I'm moving in the direction of the sounds when I suddenly realize they're coming from the motorman's cab in the front of the subway car. They're supposed to be locked. How the hell did anyone get in there? Sure enough, it seems locked. But then I twist the latch again and it opens. There's hardly any space inside, but you have never seen a man and a woman in the kind of position I saw these two in. He was screwing her, there could be no mistaking that. Her dress was up to her head, her panties off, and his pants at his shoes. Caught in the act! I had myself a rapist. I grabbed him with both hands and yanked him from the cab. Out came the handcuffs. This guy is mine! But why is the woman screaming at me to let him go? Screaming, I tell you. "What are you doing to him? That's my husband!!" She shows me they're wearing matching rings. The guy, meanwhile, is totally dazed. No way had he expected to be caught in the act. "What are you doing to me?" he mumbles. Jesus, they are husband and wife! There had to be some charge I could bring. "You're trespassing. You can't be in here." They were not impressed. "We do it in here all the time. We like it," the husband insisted.

The train has stopped by now and the doors flung open. The two stagger out. He's still pulling up his pants and zipping his fly; she's trying but making little progress in straightening out her dress. Meanwhile the porters and cleaning men waiting on the platform to get in to clean the train can't get over the two of them, and are laughing their heads off. What a sight. Now I know married people are supposed not to let their sex lives become humdrum, but I gotta believe this couple was over the edge.

Was that perversion? Maybe not, but I'll leave that to others more expert in the field. Clearly abnormal was the action I ran into at 50th Street and Rockefeller Center one day. I'm riding up the very steep escalator there when I notice that this guy ahead of me is leaning back in a strange way. In front of him is a woman but he doesn't appear to be bothering her. My curiosity aroused, I move closer. When I spotted it I had to do a double take. Sure was something I'd never laid eyes on. Taped or maybe strapped to his foot was a mirror. And his foot was positioned in such a way that let him look up her dress. He had been leaning back so as to be at the right angle for peeping. How much could he actually see? I guess guys like this don't need much. The sight of her calf or knees—that was enough of a thrill. Should I arrest this creep? Who would believe it? Better to harass him. I chewed him out real good, threatened to lock him up. A family man, he became really scared. He wasn't likely to continue his weird hobby, at least not for a while. And if he did, he'd need to get himself another mirror; I took his. In fact I took it home and tried it out. Very disappointing. There's just not much you can see, I decided. Later when I mentioned this to the plainclothes guys they barely reacted. It was old hat to them. In truth they saw much more than I ever did. In uniform my presence tended to put a lid on wrongdoing and strange behavior. The plainclothes squad, on the other hand, could move around anonymously and catch many in the act. I discouraged; they apprehended. We both had our different jobs to do.

One type of pervert who seemed to enjoy the subway lines was your garden variety flasher, the guy who loved exposing himself to women. Of the many I ran into the following character stands out. It happened at the 23rd and Ely station, the last stop in Queens before Manhattan. It's usually a pretty quiet place, not much doing here. Except we were getting station condition cards indicating that a flasher had been seen working the place. He was reportedly a guy about 30 years of age, good looking and well dressed. And yes, he wore a trench coat, believe it or not.

Working the station one day I noticed this guy on the opposite platform acting a bit strangely. And sure enough, he's in a trench coat. I'm not going to take my eyes off him. Unfortunately working the subway is a bitch because there are obstacles all over, especially when moving trains come along and block your view. Try looking through the windows of a passing train! The guy doesn't get on the train; he stays on the platform, which already tells me something. I take off my wide hat and squeeze behind one of the pillars on the platform. Peeking out, I see that he's into his act. As the train pulls out of the station, there he is opening his trench coat and exposing himself to those passengers inside sitting by the windows. He's got a big erection. And he's smiling, obviously enjoying himself.

Sure I could arrest him, but to make the charge stick it's best to have a civilian complainant. My patience paid off because as I'm watching, a woman who had exited the train begins walking along the platform. Sure enough he notices and follows after her. Suddenly he coughs, a strategy expected, I imagine, to get her attention. It works because she does turn to see who's behind her. That's his opportunity. Wide open goes his coat. Does she let out a scream! All the pieces are in place but now I've got to catch this guy. That means running up the stairs, crossing over to the other side, then dashing down the stairs to the platform level. I rush past her, shouting that she stay put until I get back. He's taken off and I'm giving chase, no easy matter because of the gear I'm carrying, maybe 40 pounds worth, most all of it shaking like crazy. But I'm young and quick, and I catch him heading up the staircase. "You're under arrest." "For what, Officer," he replies, unexpectedly calm. "I just got off the train; I didn't do anything." "Come with me," and I take him back to where I hope the woman is standing. Thank goodness she is, but then she says she's not interested in making a complaint. "I gotta get to work. I don't need this headache." I can't blow a collar like this. I've got to persuade her. "Lady, if we let him go he'll just do it again. We gotta get this guy off the street." I promise to phone her job and explain. Finally she agrees. I call for a wagon, cuff the guy, then search him. You wouldn't believe his outfit. Under the raincoat he's wearing a shirt and a tie, with his pants cut out in front and held up in the rear. With his raincoat closed he would appear fully dressed, but once open, his genital area is fully exposed. Pretty imaginative styling, I thought.

This really good-looking Italian guy turns out to be a professional hairdresser. Once he is cuffed and hears the woman agree to press charges against him, he starts to cry. Couldn't I just charge him with something else, he keeps asking on the way to the stationhouse. He's married, I find out when he pulls out a picture of his wife, an absolutely gorgeous woman. I can't believe it. A handsome guy, a great-looking wife, living together in Forest Hills, a real nice neighborhood, and working the subways, flashing away!

He asks me to call her and when we get to the precinct, I do. I can tell from her voice she's not that surprised or especially upset. Still she shows up at the station, accompanied by this dude who she says will be representing her husband. She was a knockout, most likely you'd figure her to be a showgirl. Then I began to get the picture. She's suspected her husband for some time, she tells me. "I was going to leave this shithead anyway. He's the sickest bastard I've ever known. Even around our apartment house he was doing some strange things. Now I've got my reason. If you need my testimony just let me know."

The trial became a circus with daily newspaper coverage. It had it all—a good-looking young guy, his gorgeous wife, and the titillating accounts of his subway escapades. What the public didn't know was that the lawyer his wife hired to represent the husband was her lover. How I found out was simple: she told me. "I'm gonna divorce him. You know the lawyer, that's my boyfriend. You don't think he can beat this case, do you?" This threw me; I hadn't expected this twist. I had in fact come to like the "flasher." He was a real sweet guy. Sick, of course, but nice. At the trial everyone was lapping up the details. You could even tell from the judge's detailed questions that he was not eager to wrap it up. The testimony of psychiatrists and so-called experts added considerably to the show when they discussed his perversion and the various forms it assumed. I had to be at the trial each day, a paid holiday, to be sure. After three days of hearings, our flasher, for whatever reason, had had it. "I'm guilty," he declared, just like that. A happier ending there couldn't be. The wife had her grounds for divorce, the lawyer had his fee and, I presume, the wife, and the flasher had his problem out in the open, felt relieved because of that. And me, I got some rest plus a conviction.

-II-

There was a wonderful feeling of togetherness when my class graduated from the Academy and joined the Transit Police. Given our numbers we would, we realized, soon become a force in the Department and that as it grew we would advance quickly. We were not the first black transit officers, indeed several already occupied upper level positions, but their overall numbers were small. That all changed with my class. Not only were we there now, but many were like myself, army veterans, conscientious guys committed to the job, to each other and to a future as cops. It didn't take very long, however, for this sense of unity to slip away.

Politics, preferential treatment, promotions, all worked to separate us, to pit us against one another. Some guys soon got ahead because they were able somehow to pad their records and attract attention to themselves. Others found themselves "rabbis," guys who looked out for them, who were in a position to reward them, to speed their way up the ladder. Togetherness gradually gave way to divisions based on race, ethnic background, or religion. Exclusive societies were organized within the Force: Hibernians for the Irish, then the Guardians for blacks, Holy Name for Irish Catholics, St. George for Protestants, Shomrim for Jews, Columbians for Italians and Catholics—organizations specifically formed to look out for their members, to make sure they got their share and were not overlooked or shortchanged. What this did was to make for a whole new set of loyalties and payoffs. Each group protected its own and were jealous of the others. The perspective of most every cop as a result narrowed. He was forced to become a member of one of the societies and support it at all times. I joined the Guardians, hung out with some of these guys and attended a number of their functions, but I never was one to play their games or to use the organization to get ahead. I just wasn't cut out that way. Nor did I wish to limit my after hours socializing to black guys. I had white friends and had always felt comfortable with them. But most guys in the Guardians couldn't accept that. When they saw me with or heard that I'd been drinking with white cops, there was grumbling. It was not the way you played the game. You were letting your own "kind" down.

My approach was not one that was appreciated by any of the groups. I found that out quite painfully, I should add, with Joe Lefume, a fellow cop. I considered him one of my best friends on the Force. I'm pretty sure he regarded me in the same way. For a time we were practically inseparable.. He invited me to his house, where I met his wife and his father, who took great pleasure in the homemade wine he produced. "Guinea Red," he called it. Joe was an honest, sincere guy, but opinionated and closely identified with the Columbian Society in the Department. Ambitious and energetic, Joe was looking to get ahead, and saw clearly what it would take to scramble up that departmental ladder. And as he began to make his move we saw less of each other. Always there were excuses when I asked Joe about getting together. What was happening I couldn't understand. I had, I was sure, done nothing to anger him. One day I simply asked for an explanation and he flat out told me. His people [the Columbian Society] were giving him a fit, he said, for hanging out with that "nigger." He wanted to move up in the Force and in the PBA [Patrolmen's Benevolent Association], and hanging out with me was not the way to do it. I had become an obstacle. He made his choice.

It was like solitary confinement in the Department for a man in the middle, for a guy opposed to or uninterested in joining one of the organizations and playing the game. I had my Irish associates, my Italian buddies, my German acquaintances, as well as my black friends. It was an anomaly; I fit no accepted category. (Friendships were probably not as intense among the Transit Police as they were with regular cops. We worked alone, as I've said, while the policemen were on duty together with partners. That could cement relationships for obvious reasons.) I wanted to move up, that's for sure. I would have loved to have found myself a "rabbi" and used his pull to get promoted, but sucking up to anyone, doing favors, showing up on all the right occasions, buying all the raffle tickets or going to all the social functions—that wasn't my style. Moreover, while I was a good cop, a loyal cop, I never swallowed the line about how we were a different breed, superior to civilians, and how that meant we should keep separate and associate only with other cops. It led in the wrong direction, made us reluctant to admit that cops make mistakes, or believe that civilians could be trusted or could understand police matters. I also had my differences with the PBA and its approach. Defend any and every cop no matter what he did. The PBA never deviated from that position, standing up for and protecting any number of rotten cops when it would have been wiser to back off and let those guys get what they deserved. But the PBA knows just one way—"defend our own, always"—and usually angered the public every time it did.

As a black cop I tried to be fair—to both blacks and whites. Every cop I know feels a sense of power out there in uniform with his gun. He's the law, he represents authority, folks had better listen up. As a black cop I know I felt this way and even more so. I wouldn't have to take shit from anyone. Man, I could hand it out and "they" would back me up. Sure I was a bit cocky; we all were. Only later would I come to see cops in a different way, as an occupying force, as an instrument to maintain the pecking order and to keep lesser folks like blacks in their place. Actually it was not the Transit Police but the regular cops who did this. Not that we acted in a fair-handed manner, we didn't; it's just that we were new and unlike the police, we weren't in a position to hold the lid down on people in a particular neighborhood. So we weren't exactly the bad guys.

We were no different, however, when it came to handling black offenders or "troublemakers". Take the kids who used to tear up the trains on their way back from school. The whites were probably more aggressively malicious than the blacks, but who do you think were hit with youth cards (a form of warning)? Naturally the black kids—though not from me. I resented this unequal treatment. If you look at my record, I went the other way, handing more of them out to whites than blacks. That was my way of trying to even things out. But don't think that I went lightly with blacks who crossed my path. (Most black cops didn't either, that's a fact. If anything, to prove their commitment to "the system" they generally were tougher with them. We all got the "how about a break, brother?" shit, but most of us didn't buy it.) Locking up a white guy gave me no particular satisfaction. I was prepared to arrest anyone who violated the law, white or black. I felt no more sympathy for black offenders than white. However, I did go out of my way to treat blacks properly, to address them courteously. That I felt was important because it mostly didn't happen—especially from white cops. I talked to them, tried as best I could to be helpful.

What troubled me greatly was the fact that even though blacks and whites had joined the Force in almost equal numbers, the whites were, we were told, passing the tests in greater numbers and were, as a result, being promoted. Now that was mighty peculiar. Remember all those intelligent, experienced black fellows who came in with me, guys whose smarts easily matched any of the whites? But somehow the test "results" were saying something else; too many of these guys were being overlooked. It happened to me as well. Call it sour grapes if you want but I tell you those scores were rigged. I had, after all, taken plenty of Civil Service exams in previous years for all kinds of jobs. Each and every time I scored near the top. Why not this time? Some of the guys I know were getting coached, but it shouldn't have made that much of a difference. The answer had to do with politics, power and prejudice. We're talking quotas. We would not be allowed to run the Transit Police. I think what they did was to check the scores (they knew who the black and white test takers were) and once they saw too many blacks with high scores they changed the "key," regraded the tests, and reduced the numbers

2-SKOL

of black achievers! In time word circulated that blacks can't pass these tests. Some blacks even bought this shit and demanded they be given special tests. What crap! We were had; they didn't play fair with us. And when later we asked for affirmative action, the answer came back-no special treatment. Well hell, we were getting special mistreatment all those years. What is wrong with admitting it and doing something about it? Quite a few black guys I knew left the Force over the years, discouraged because they had been passed over for promotion. Not only did they seem unable to "pass" the tests but there was also the message, pretty obvious to me, that they were not welcome in the Department.

Sure I got along fine with lots of white cops; still I couldn't avoid having my race become an issue. That would have been asking too much. Take my relationship with Mike Daly. He was already there when I was reassigned from Manhattan to a cushy post in Queens. (While I didn't get my promotions I was not treated badly by the Transit Department. I had well placed friends, did my job, kept complete memo books, didn't fight the system, and so I generally got the shifts and posts that I wanted.) Daly clearly belonged to that breed of "crazy cop." Either he was nuts or he saw it to his advantage to act crazy a lot of the time. He would, for example, get drunk and shoot his gun off in a locker room. Off duty he'd be in a bar and go berserk and tear the place up. Talk about being a powder keg, Daly was explosive, and he got away with it. Another thing about Daly, he just hated "niggers." As crazy as he was, he was even crazier on this subject. He saw himself, moreover, as the self-appointed "mentor" of all blacks in his district. He would tell them exactly what they could and could not do. Soon after coming to Queens I met this son of a bitch.

Now for the shocker. He and I became close friends. Believe me when I tell you, he took to me and I to him almost from the start. Go figure. He had me to his house all the time and his wife cooked for the two of us. "Take care of Mike," she would say to me, knowing full well how volatile he was. I promised I would.

Ingrained as his prejudice against blacks was, for reasons I never figured out he saw it not in the least strange that we were friends. He'd get violent if anyone ever called me a "nigger" in his presence. Even so, he kept on hating blacks.

One day this strange paradox blew up in our faces. We're sitting in the precinct locker room when he turns to me and out of the blue says, "Niggers are giving me a fit. Never trust them niggers!" "Mike, what did you say?"—"I'm talking about that nigger." (He apparently had had a run-in with another black cop.) "Mike, how did you mean that?" I say angrily. "Just like I said," he shot back defiantly. "Are you offended by it?" "Yeah, I am." To which he replied, "That's right, you're a niggah." By that point it all boiled over. I leaped on top of him and we started clawing at each other and wrestling in a serious way. The other guys around us made no effort to break it up. I was a wrestler, and easily got the upper hand. And he was bleeding, having at some point banged into a locker. "You quit?" I asked him. "I can either let you go or hurt you. It's your choice." I loosened my choke hold on him so he could answer. "All right, let me up." He looked at me for the longest time, then said what I never expected to hear. "I'm sorry." Our friendship would never again be tested.

And it would be needed. Not long after I was posted in Forest Hills I ran into a problem. Someone was looking to break into my locker where I kept my uniforms and my service revolver. One day they got inside and using a razor slashed my dress uniform and all the tailored shirts I kept there. I immediately reported the incident to Captain Taks, who would, I knew, back me up. Mike, when I told him, went berserk; he'd kill the bastards who did it. Race, I was sure, was a factor, but maybe also the fact that I had recently been assigned to Roosevelt Avenue and 74th Street, considered the choicest post on the line. I was a target both because I was black and a privileged newcomer to Queens. The old guard was not pleased. Both Taks and Daly had their suspicions. I was to do nothing, however. They would handle it.

Then came the second incident. Opening up my locker one

day I spot a brown bag I knew wasn't mine resting on the bottom. Inside was a stinking pile of dog shit. Sure it threw me. Who knew what would be next? It wasn't long before I found out. The warning came from my friend, Walter Hass. "Watch your ass on post," he says to me. "Someone may be cooking up a scheme against you." Taks too somehow learned the pot was aboiling. "I'm gonna let it happen," he tells me, "then I'm gonna bust them." That's all well and good, I'm thinking, but not very reassuring. Who? Where? When? Everyone seemed plugged into this network of conspiracy except me!

Caution became the watchword. I was afraid of doing anything on the job that might in some way compromise my performance and justify a transfer, or worse, a demotion. I kept away from the clerk's booth so I could not be accused of goofing off. I covered the post like a blanket, walking every foot of the place, observing everything. Prostitutes always were working the stations, but why was this one girl so obvious about it? And why was she watching me, giving me the eye? That was unusual, because prostitutes almost always scattered when cops came by. We weren't exactly good for business. (I was always polite to them—"I think you've been here too long" was usually how I put it.) When I passed by she began speaking to me. "I haven't seen you before," which of course couldn't be true because I was here all the time. She was, I had no doubt, coming on to me, but why? This was just the beginning.

The next day and the one after that she "bumped" into me and we chatted. I reported this to Captain Taks, figuring that this "relationship" was strange, certainly suspicious. Taks apparently thought so. If it happened again, I was to call him immediately, he said. Sure enough the following evening she's there again at the station. This time, however, she complains about being very dizzy. Could I get her to a place where she could lay down until it passed? There was a private room in the station where some of the guys went to have a smoke or catch a few winks. I take her in there and then excuse myself. It was time, I said, for me to ring in on the hour. As instructed I call Taks. "Stall her," he says. "I'm on my way." Before returning I let the clerk know where I've taken the woman. She is not feeling well, I tell him, but he winks at me.

But when I get to the room she's recovered or so she announces and then puts on a more serious expression. "You think I've been hanging around here," she says, "just to do tricks? That's not it. I'm interested in you." Ordinarily I would want to believe her. She's cute, about twenty-five years old and still fresh, not the hardened streetwalker I was accustomed to. At this point she begins to open her blouse. Where the hell is Taks? (His post was just two train stations away.) "Let's get it on right now," she says. "Hey, I brought you here to relax, not for sex" is my noble answer. "Don't do that," I tell her (as she's about to remove her blouse), "or I'm going to have to leave you." It's at this point that I've got the whole thing figured out. She was playing her part well, but it was a setup—it had to be. She'd strip down in my presence, then make a scene by running out of the room and claiming she was being assaulted. They'd find me in there and I'd be in for shit. Try explaining why you were in a room with a partially dressed prostitute while on duty.

Taks, though, saved my ass, walking in just as her bra was about to come off. He confronts her immediately. "Who put you up to this?" The directness of the question threw her. She'd figured it would all go according to plan. Now that it didn't, she was flustered, vulnerable. "You're going to jail for this," he tells her. With everything coming apart and plus the threat of jail, she cracks. Some officers, she admits, had arranged for her to set me up and then claim "rape." "Who got you to do this?" She named the ringleader, but insisted she did not know the other two officers. She is trembling, scared to death as she tells this to Taks. Meanwhile he's not even looking at her but instead is writing it all down. When he's finished he orders her out, then he turns to me. "Don't you say a word about this to anyone. I will handle it in my own way." Ever thorough, Taks reminds me to tell the token clerk on my way out that everything's back to normal.

I said not a word about it—not to Mike or Hass or anyone. But the locker tampering stopped; there was no more harassment. Several weeks later I heard about these three guys who were transferred out of the district. Taks had handled it his way.

Another openly racial incident involved a case of mistaken identity. Or was it? It happened one night after I had finished the 4 to 12 tour. Instead of going home I decided to drop into a few bars, see who was around and unwind a bit. I was driving a brand new Chevy that I had recently bought. I was one proud dude behind the wheel as I drove along Merrick Avenue in Queens. I stopped first at Eddie's Bar but nothing much was going on, so it was back into the car and on to Post's. Same story here. I wasn't ready to give up yet, not that eager to go back to my apartment. So I decide to try the Shangri-La Bar. A lucky choice, I say to myself, because there's a parking place right in front. But then even before I can get out of the car, two white guys grab me, bang me against the car and start cuffing me. "What the hell is going on here?" "Keep your goddam mouth shut," one of them says, very unfriendly-like. Meanwhile the two of them are going through my pockets. I spot a third guy just sitting there in the front seat of a car double-parked ahead of us. "What the fuck is this?" one of them says as he gets to my service revolver. "We got ourselves something. Where did you steal this from?"—"Go through my pockets and you'll find something else," I growl. I'm trying to keep calm but with these guys all over me it's not easy.

Why hasn't someone come out of the bar, someone who could tell them who I am? But the door stays shut. Finally one of the guys came across my shield. "Oh, my God," he says. "Why didn't you tell us you were a cop?" "Who the hell are you guys?" I burst out. "We're police officers." "What was I supposed to have done?" "We were thinking you might be a holdup man once we spotted you moving in and out of several bars along the strip here." We're talking this way but meanwhile he still hasn't taken the cuffs off. At this point the guy sitting in the car gets out. "What's going on," he wants to know. "He's a cop," they tell him. "That nigger can't be no cop" he mutters. At this point this black guy exits the bar. Thank God! It's Billy Brown, a detective. "Mind your damn business," they tell him when he comes over. "This is my business," he says brusquely. "Meanwhile, who in the world are you guys?"

Now the three start backing off. They've made a mistake, they realize, and do not want to make it any worse. The guy who was in the car even mumbles an apology and motions to one of the others to get my cuffs off. But Brown's not willing to let them off the hook that easy. "You know people are getting sick and tired of this shit you guys are pulling." By this time other black guys, including some cops attracted by the crowd outside, have left the bar. "What command you guys out of?" Brown wants to know. "103rd Special Unit." "Well, I'm going up there right now. You can either ride there with me or follow along. I don't give a shit what you do." And motioning to me, "Earl, you take down their numbers," at which point some of the other cops joined in, "Yeah, get their numbers." Now the three white cops are shitting in their pants. Not only might they be in real trouble, but they're wondering if these black guys are going to get rough, give them a taste of their own medicine.

I'm angry, hurting and in no mood to let things drop. No way these guys are getting off the hook. They let me have it; why not a little heat on them? So it's off to the precinct house to report the incident. I figured I'd have a hard time with the desk sergeant, and I was right. Here's the exchange: "I'm Patrolman Williams. I've just been accosted by two men who claim they're police officers. I have their shield numbers. They said they were out of 103rd. Do they work here?"—"What do you mean, 'accosted'?" the sergeant said in a tone unmistakably sarcastic. "Well, two guys who said they were cops jumped me for no reason, in front of witnesses. I'd like to know if they're police officers." "If you didn't think they were police officers why didn't you bring them in with you," he said, figuring he had exposed the flaws in my whole case. "Come on, would you bring three guys in with guns if they tell you they're police officers—and show you their shields?" I say, with obvious impatience. "I don't want to talk to you. I want to see the captain." "What do you mean? I'm in charge of this desk." "Yeah, I know, but you're not in charge of the precinct."

I probably wouldn't have gotten anywhere at this point had not Brown and two other black cops arrived. Brown knew this precinct. Besides he's cocky enough and angry enough to bulldoze his way through all obstacles. "Let's go upstairs and see the captain," he says. The sergeant protests, insists that we wait until permission is granted. Brown will have none of this. "We got his permission," he snaps, and with that the three of us bound up the stairs, followed in short order by the sergeant and some other guys. Meanwhile the three characters who started this thing haven't arrived yet. They were, I was pretty sure, out there somewhere concocting their story. Once they had it down they'd show.

The captain lets us in. I tell the story, leaving out nothing. I can sense that he's prepared to back up his guys. Sure enough, once I'm finished he launches into an explanation of how these things "happen." These guys were maybe overanxious, he admits, but they were just doing their jobs. I don't buy it, I tell him. "You read about too much of this shit in the newspapers. They saw a black guy and they started imagining things. If I was acting suspicious they should have kept on following me. They were out to kick ass, that's how it was." Just about this time the three guys show up and head up the stairs. The captain meanwhile is hemming and hawing. "It's hard to get it straight. After all, I wasn't there." Brown wouldn't let this go. "You don't have to be there. I was there, plus a whole bar full of people." Brown has worked himself up to the point where he's as angry as I am. "We ain't gettin' any satisfaction here," he says. "Earl," he says, turning to me, "call your command and get one of your captains over here. That's the only way to get it done." The idea was enough to get the captain thinking a bit harder now. "Just wait, let me talk to these guys." It's obvious they're not eager to talk with him but he manages to herd them into an adjoining room.

After a few minutes the captain's back with us but nothing's changed. It's the same shit we heard before, like how these were "family men" and how they were "just trying to do their job." Naturally he hit us with "they could lose their jobs over this," which only prompts Brown to ask the captain, "Would you stand up for me if I got into trouble the way you're standing up for these guys?" To this the captain had an answer. "I'm just looking out for one cop against another cop." I had been thinking along the same lines, and the minute he put it that way I knew there was a way to resolve this matter. "I was waiting to hear you say that, 'one cop to another cop,' because I think that's how we can settle this. I'd like to go into the back room with these guys one at a time," I tell him. "I'd like to understand them better. I want them to tell me why they did this."

With these words the room became quiet. Not everyone got it, but a few guys, including Brown, did. He knew what I was talking about. So did the captain. "If they want to do it, it's all right with me. I think it's best you settle it amongst yourselves." (Thinking, I imagine, that I would ask each for a personal apology.) I entered the adjoining room by myself and waited for the first cop to come in. As soon as he comes through the door I smack him, then hit him again. He's got tears in his eyes and blood running out of his nose. Still I'm sure he's figuring this is a better way to end it than going through all the bullshit paper work. I let him leave, which he does, but not without threatening me. "I'll get you, I'll kill you." The second guy is not coming in so fast. "Where's your buddy," I shout. The captain appears at the doorway, his face beet red. "I don't want no violence here." "There's no violence here," I answer. "The door just hit him in the nose." The guy who walks in now is the one who had been in the car. "You want to talk to me?" he says, at which point he throws a punch, but it misses. I grab him, get on top of him, and jam his face into a nearby desk. The captain's not having any more of this, comes running in and pulls me off him.

And that's how it ended. Well, actually, not before I announced that I was "totally satisfied" and called upon everyone to "act like it never happened, right, Captain?" And turning to my three assailants, "You guys agree?" A barely audible "Yeah" came from one of them. "We'll remember you," one of them says, a feeble gesture of defiance. I never again saw any of them.

-III-

I could have avoided all this crap, you might say, had I not been bar hopping that night. But don't forget, I was a single guy looking to have a good time, and the bars in Queens were usually the place to be for such socializing. I led the single life for many of the years that I was on the Force. What that meant, of course, was that off the job my interests tended to concentrate on clothes, playing cards with the guys, and on girls. We blacks were good dressers then. Actually it had been that way a long time. We are naturally actors, we want to be seen, to make an impression. That's why we've always been drawn to fashion, why we've often set the fashions. From top to bottom, from the fancy expressive shoes to the flamboyant hats we often favored. Many of the guys I hung out with were really into dressing. A lot of it rubbed off on me. Not necessarily the custom made shirts and suits, but the big-collared open shirts, the large cufflinks worn two inches below the sleeve, the fancy folded handkerchiefs in the lapel, a choice of colognes worn on different occasions. These guys knew the kind of attention good dressers attracted. Don't forget, it was the white population that in the late '50s and '60s lowered the standards in clothing, with their jeans and sandals and casual, even sloppy look. Don't blame us.

Much of my social life as I've said revolved around a string of bars along Merrick Avenue in Queens. When those cops beat me up in front of the Shangri-La I was doing something I often did—checking out the action. Each bar had its own style, pace, and clientele. Where you stopped depended on what and who you were in the mood for. The Shangri-La, owned by a pimp and numbers runner, was what you would call a sporting bar. Numbers runners, numbers bankers, gangsters, off-duty cops, all hung out there. It was a real social place. Then there was Eddie's Palm Garden, owned by this Jamaican. There actually was a garden in the back. It was a swell looking place featuring a big bar and a back room for dancing. I enjoyed this spot for several reasons, not the least of which was the fact that Eddie welcomed cops in his joint. I could therefore run up a tab there. Near Eddie's a new jazz club opened, owned by some Jewish guy. It was a real sharp place, one that attracted a lot of girls. An Elks and Masons club located nearby had an area for guys to hang out, mostly to play poker. My friend Benny and I joined and were known to the older members as the "juniors." There were a few others further down as well which we didn't much frequent unless absolutely nothing else was going on.

You could relax in bars, have a few drinks, play some cards, run into people you hadn't seen for a time. I was not the kind of guy who'd go and buy a round of drinks for all, but I learned a technique to capitalize on such types. I'd see a guy who usually did this and right off I'd buy him a drink, quiet like. For the rest of the night he'd remember this gesture and keep buying me drinks and probably some for others as well. These dudes were always competing with one another, trying to outdo some other fellow who wanted to show he was an even bigger sport. The result—rounds of drinks for everyone. Buying that single drink might well keep my glass filled all night.

Girls came to bars, usually two, three, four girls at a time, hoping to find quality guys. These were by no means loose girls, and quite a few in fact were looking to establish serious relationships. The group that could pick and choose at will among the girls was the Londonaires. This small clique whose members hung out at Eddie's bar became the envy of all the single guys and girls in the area. Mail carriers, firemen, corrections officers, cops or gangsters (off duty these differences faded away), they were all the coolest studs you'd ever want to meet. They dressed impeccably, drove Caddies or Roadsters, had their own apartments, held steady jobs, and pretty much set the social standards in the area. To be able to hang out with them was everyone's ambition. The Londonaires were lovers; that was well known. Girls who wouldn't even let you hold their hand, much less kiss them, would go to bed with a Londonaire on the very first date. They were that sophisticated and decidedly in demand. The Londonaires sponsored all sorts of events—picnics, cruises, excursions, dances, money making affairs from which they benefited. So popular were these events that people forged tickets to get in. I never became a Londonaire (there were only about fourteen of them, all old-time friends) but they welcomed me into their circle, regarded me as sort of an associate member. In fact many of them used my apartment when I was away at work to play cards and craps. Once a week they'd be up there. I provided cigarettes, stocked the refrigerator with beer and snacks, (as well as cleaned up the place when I got home). They'd put aside some cash for me out of every pot. I could pocket up to a hundred dollars a week, pretty much paid my rent with this money.

The Londonaires were always going places, continually uncovering new spots where guys could have a good time. I enjoyed taking such trips every so often. For example, a friend and I took ourselves down to Washington, D.C. for a memorable expedition one long weekend. We had ourselves a great time with the "government girls" down there, who thought us northern boys to be oh, so fine. Word got around that some of the Londonaires had been traveling up to Canada and having a hell of a time there. Blacks, they assured us, were treated exceptionally well by the Canadians. If the Londonaires endorsed Canada it was certainly worth checking out. The story was that after touring Montreal a few times they had, on a later trip, gone north and stumbled on a place, Shenungan Falls, where they had befriended a local priest who happened to be a rabid jazz buff. In exchange for jazz records he let them stay in the rectory. They came back raving about the place. I soon found out why.

Three of us left New York on Friday afternoon and headed for Canada, first stop Montreal and the Queen Elizabeth Hotel for the night. Then the following morning we headed north. We had not forgotten to bring along several choice jazz records for the friendly priest. It was just as they said; a record for rooms deal was readily arranged (a bottle of whiskey thrown in as well—our priest, we had learned, was a drinker). Just what the attraction of the area was we soon saw for ourselves. It was, it seems, a timber region, and for two months each summer the men of the area left for the annual cutting. That meant all the women back home were virtually alone. They would gather, we were told, each day by the lake near the falls. Sure enough, they were there when we arrived, dozens and dozens of them. Few male fantasies could top this. Could paradise be any finer? Here we were, black guys, strangers no less, yet they welcomed us with open arms, invited us into their homes, cooked for us, competed for us. How could we not feel like conquering heroes? What more do I have to say? It was wild.

Having "discovered" this place we were not about to give it up. We came back (despite the length of the trip) several more times. Our priest was an earthy guy. He knew what we were up to, yet there were no sermons to us about abstinence or restraint. So long as we kept coming of course he got his records and his booze. Honestly, it wasn't just sex. These were genuine people, the friendliest folks I ever did see. (One of the guys ended up marrying one of the French Canadian girls.) Our being black seemed completely irrelevant to them. You tell me where in the United States that could have happened.

On some later trips we stopped in Montreal, where I enjoyed the gambling and some of the characters we encountered. Always we felt welcome. I remember distinctly the bartenders and cabbies confiding in us, insisting they much preferred to deal with Negroes than with white Americans. They were arrogant, always acting superior to everything Canadian, while we were gentlemen, they said. So comfortable were we, so hospitable were the people up here that some of us actually wondered about moving to Canada. But we were, most of us, cops. Giving up that kind of secure job would not have made much sense. To this day though, I still think about Canada. With such pleasant memories who wouldn't?

-IV-

The job, you hoped, would stay mostly routine but of course it never could. Even minor situations could blow up in your face. My unexpected brush with the mob was typical of the surprises you almost came to expect. I was working the Grand Concourse station in the Bronx this one morning. Though my midnight shift is about over, I'm still looking to catch me a few fare beaters and maybe a smoker or two. Smoking was banned in the subway system, but despite this there'd be people lighting up—cigarettes, cigars, pipes, it didn't matter. There was no easier way to meet your quota than to hand out summonses for smoking. We had a quota—don't you believe otherwise. All summonses were tallied on a chart at the stationhouse; competition was encouraged. Everybody could follow the score. Unless you handed out at least three a week they'd be on your back. You'd hear from them—"How come you're behind, Williams? Smith got twelve; you only got three. Don't you work the same job?" Of course Smith loved giving out summonses, really got a kick out of it. To me it was a pain. Then again, Smith's aching to make detective or plainclothesman. Those summonses are going to look good downtown.

Passing me on the platform is this young guy, real well-dressed, with a big cigar stuck in his mouth. He sees me all right, but the cigar doesn't move. If anything I detect a defiant turn of his head as he goes by. "Sir, don't you see that sign?"

(Something this obvious I couldn't ignore, certainly not on the Grand Concourse. A heavily Jewish area, the riders using this station were always writing letters to the Department complaining about or criticizing something or other.) "Put out your cigar. I've got to give you a summons." I might have just warned him had there not been so many bystanders around, obviously interested in how I would handle the situation.

It's clear this guy is not about to cooperate; no beat cop was going to tell him what to do. The cigar stays in his mouth. About five feet ten inches, he had the distinct look of a gangster—slick-backed hair, black coat with velvet collar, nails finely manicured, and sporting a thick gold ring. A nasty looking mouth matched a defiant attitude. Additional people gather, hoping to see what will happen next, before their trains arrive.

Then this guy ups the ante. "Well, what are you going to do, Officer?" On top of this there's a chorus of voices in the background telling me what I should do. "I'd give him a summons"—"I wouldn't let him talk to me that way." So there's pressure from two sides now. There is the defiant punk and there are interested onlookers expecting me to take action. What choice did I have? "You don't want to do this the simple way, so okay, you're under arrest." That I thought would somehow soften his stance but I was dead wrong. "You can't lock me up," he practically shouted. "You can't even put your hands on me. I'll be out of there in fifteen minutes, so why bother going through all this crap?" If he was trying to provoke me, he was well on his way, but I couldn't let him take charge. Already I'm thinking about the guys back at the station laughing themselves silly over this. Imagine arresting a guy for smoking! And then leaving a busy station in rush hour when I'm needed most to take care of a shit-ass situation and worse, to waste hours handling the nonsense. But then wait a minute, I'm thinking—this guy has a nasty attitude, he's defied me in front of a crowd. Too much to lose if I let him walk. Especially after he's shown disrespect to the uniform. Hell, I ain't backin' off.

I begin to cuff him. He wants to fight, I sense that, but he's not quite sure he can get away with that. If he resists I'll have plenty of witnesses tumbling all over each other to tell their story. I almost wish he had decided to challenge me. As angry as I was, I would have taken him apart. Back then we were instructed first to cuff all suspects, then to search them. I know all the T.V. and movie cops today put guys against the walls or cars and then start frisking them, but our instructions were that above all else first restrain your man. Another thing. Don't think cuffing is easy. You just slip 'em on. Not so. Unless the guy cooperates fully, which is usually not the case, it can get complicated, especially when he's moving around. Cuff a guy in front and you're in a dangerously vulnerable position. And cuffing his hands behind him ain't simple, believe me, especially when you're by yourself. And you've got to do it fast. Start fumbling about and you lose this air of authority and decisiveness. Fortunately in this instance (with a crowd looking on) it went smoothly.

The reaction in the squad room was no surprise—"Let the thing go." It took a fair amount of convincing to get them to let me bring him in. At the stationhouse he remained no less defiant than he was in the subway. "Nigger, you can't do this to me." And after his phone call, he let me know, probably for the hundredth time, that he was a "big shot," and had his "ins." I let it all roll off without reacting. The guy I saw was out of control emotionally. Confused and enraged, he'd likely say anything. (The guy, though, had balls, I have to admit that. While we're doing the booking what does he do but take out another big cigar and light up! He put it out though after someone pointed to the no smoking sign.)

It would take the better part of the day to process this guy. First off the van to take us from the subway to the stationhouse was late in arriving. There we were out in the street, both of us cooling our heels waiting for it to come. We arrived back at the precinct just as some of the guys were taking off for lunch. So it's another wait for them to come back. Next came the endless trip from the Bronx to downtown Manhattan. My prisoner would end up being arraigned in night court, no less!

The ride itself was a nightmare. Driving in traffic from the upper Bronx to lower Manhattan can take forever. Stop and go, but mostly stop. Even before we head into Manhattan though we had first to ride around to other Bronx precincts to pick up prisoners awaiting transfer to night court. Worse, I was obliged to ride in the police van along with the prisoners. God knows who was in there with me. Murderers, rapists, psychos, any and all of those might well have been my traveling companions. A driver and a helper were up front, but I might be dead before they'd manage to get to me. All this because I arrested a guy for smoking a cigar! The van is packed, it stinks, there's puke on the floor. The guys are angry, cursing you out, scared. But whatever shit they hand you, you have to stay calm. Can't put a hand on them. Too many questions will be asked. The ride was a horror.

It was not all bullshit; my gangster friend did have some "connections." When we got into night court already there was this very well dressed lawyer and two other guys. It made a difference. He brightened up considerably once he saw them there. Much of his former strut and arrogance returned. His "boys" were there to take care of him. "You won't hold me," he whispers. I never thought we would. After consulting counsel he pleaded guilty. The fine, fifty dollars. That was that. Case closed. I got my satisfaction (though it took me a whole goddam day to do it) and I suppose he had his—after all, he did walk.

I'd noticed but not paid much attention to the two guys with the lawyer. Tough looking characters, they remained expressionless through the brief proceeding. Had the organization sent them to make sure all went smoothly? As I headed down the corridor toward the exit I spotted them coming toward me. I tensed, my hand moving quickly in the direction of my service revolver. Was there to be retribution for mistreating one of their boys? Not at all. "Did he give you a hard time?" one of them asked, sounding concerned. "Was he an asshole?" the other chimed in.

"I know you didn't want to take it this far." These oldtimers would, I knew, never have gotten themselves into the position of this young hothead. They would have said, "Sorry, Officer," and immediately put the cigar away. If given a summons, they would have accepted it with a smile and an apology. The older gangsters knew how to handle cops. To these guys this young punk was an embarrassment, without the finesse of an earlier generation of gangsters. No doubt he'd get a reprimand or whatever it was they did to bring the young bucks in line.

"What's your name?" one of them asks. So well dressed and so well mannered were they that it almost seemed impolite not to respond. So I did, then realized I had been suckered, had let down my guard. The mob "made nice" to the police when it had to, but it could twist arms too, or even worse. Several days passed but I couldn't put the incident out of my mind. Then a letter arrived at my apartment. It carried no return address. Inside I found the final settlement. There were two tickets to Yankee Stadium, two to Rockefeller Center, and a couple of $100 bills. And a card, "Thank you very much," it said. No signature. Nothing else. My mind started racing. Are they setting me up? Do I keep the money? Do they want to have something on me? I looked for marks on the bills. All sorts of things go through your mind. I returned everything to the envelope and put it away for several days. But I had made my decision. The game at Yankee Stadium turned out to be terrific; the same with the show at Rockefeller Center. I never heard another word, though for a time afterwards I did find myself looking over my shoulder more than usual. But these were oldtime gangsters—they knew how to treat a cop.

Not striking twice in the same place may be true of lightning, but with police work it can happen. Not long after my run-in with our cigar smoker there I am back at the Grand Concourse station during rush hour. This time the problem is an old guy, Jewish no doubt, who's smoking a cigar. This I might have let slip by except that he was also fare beating, avoiding the turnstile by entering through an exit gate.

The old guy was very well dressed, had this sophisticated air about him. "I'm not smoking the cigar," he insisted when I approached him. "It's just in my mouth." But then he looked at it and saw, rather inconveniently, that it was still smoking. "It's a good cigar," he explained, "it doesn't go out immediately." "I'm saying it's a lit cigar," I replied. "You have to put it out." When he ignores my suggestion it's time to get serious. "I'm also going to have to lock you up for trespassing and evasion of fare." "Do you have a witness?" Right off the guy's letting me know he's no pushover, that he knows the angles. But his superior attitude just pisses me off more. I'm just some dumb black cop, he's figuring, no match for him. We know the type, have talked about guys like this back at the stationhouse, the wiseguys who shoot their mouths off, insist on their rights, are convinced no charge will stick. Be wary of these characters, we've been told, but don't back off. Concede nothing.

I'm taking the guy in but I don't cuff him right away. Again, I've got myself a crowd of spectators and naturally I'm getting advice. "Lock him up." "Let that old man go." "I saw him. Who does he think he is?" "I gotta pay my fare." I'm hoping a train will come and clear these people out. Were this a black guy chances are he'd start performing, trying to get the onlookers on his side. He'd call me all sorts of names, holler that I hit him, try to attract an even larger crowd in the hope that it might somehow get him off the hook. But not this Jewish guy. He won't be abusive or resort to name calling. No, he's the lawyer, better still, a Supreme Court Justice. No, his tactic will be to lecture me about his innocence, his rights, how the law works and why I've got no case.

Call in, tell them what I've got, arrange to meet them upstairs, then off to the station. That's standard procedure. I know exactly what I'm going to hear. Sure enough they want no part of this. "Forget it. It's a waste of time. Who needs this nonsense?" I'm not dropping this one, I tell them in no uncertain terms. But how do you explain why you're not backing off on this petty shit? So there I am trying to make my case when the guy lets me know he has a bad heart, then moments later begins moaning and screaming. "I've got a bad heart." (He is handcuffed now.) At which point he begins to slide slowly down the wall against which he had been propped up. The sergeant I'm talking to over the phone wants to know what I'm doing to the guy. "Did you hit him?" He's practically down on the ground now, his fancy camel's hair coat draped on the filthy floor. "Why is he hollering?" He's jiving me, I tell him; he's not flushed nor are there any other signs of distress, I add. But the sergeant keeps saying, "You gotta be careful with these people. You gotta be careful with these people. You don't want 'em to die on you. Is he cuffed?" "Yeah," I answer. "Well, take them off." "Don't worry about it," I tell him, but now the guy's really got me worried.

They're sending an ambulance. That might, I agree, be a good idea. Christ, maybe the guy isn't faking it. Wouldn't that be a bitch. Over a cigar and a fifteen-cent fare!! He's lying there, not moving very much, and breathing hard. And I'm hearing it from the spectators. "Why are you just letting him lay there?" "Why don't you pick him up?" "Why don't you give him first aid?" Still I'm not convinced. I let him stay there, moaning, although I do pull him up into a sitting position against the wall. With a crowd hanging around, I'm very careful now. "Put me down as a witness," one or two of them are already volunteering.

Finally the ambulance arrives and I uncuff him and get him in. The ambulance attendant looks a bit skeptical. The guy has got one hand on his head, but in the other he's still holding on to that damn cigar! We get him to the hospital and in he goes for tests while I wait outside. Then I see the doctor coming toward me. "Oh shit, I hope the guy's not dead." "Why the hell did you bring him in?" he says. "His heart's better than mine!!" Whew!! He's had his hospital visit; now he's got to face the court.

In court you know this guy is going to have a lawyer who will do his best to trip me up. We expect this; we're prepared for it. Sure enough I get a going over from the attorney, who concentrates on what's in my memo book. "What time did you record this information?" (Trying to establish the idea that I recorded it well after the fact and insinuating faulty memory.) "The first chance I had while it was fresh in my mind." (We're also taught to supply the right answers whether or not it happened that way.) "How much time elapsed?" Answer: "While I was transporting him to the hospital I began recording the events." If he can't get you here he'll shift his attack, look for some other loophole. There wasn't any. The Judge, after hearing the whole story, is openly angry at the guy for putting everyone to so much trouble. All he could do, though was fine him—five dollars. Yup, all it was, was a five-dollar case! (The original summonses, had he just paid it, would have been two dollars.) In court the old man seems perfectly fine. But something was missing. He had, I noticed, no cigar in his hand.

One had always to be prepared for matters more serious than curbing subway cigar smokers. Working the day tour on this one occasion I'm patrolling along the 47th and 50th station when I spot this enormous black guy (he had to be at least six foot four inches with exceptionally broad shoulders) walking along with this petite woman. From a distance she didn't seem to reach much beyond his belt line. Coming closer I could see that she was a frail little thing. Still this guy is slapping her around real bad. Whether she just wouldn't or couldn't scream, I couldn't tell. I hurried over. "What are you doing?" I'm no midget but I'm looking straight up at this guy. He dwarfed me. Up close I could see tears in her eyes and blood coming from her mouth. But she said nothing. I repeat, "What are you doing with this woman?" "She's my wife," he answers. "You ain't got nothing to do with it." "That's where you're wrong," I shout back. "If you're doing it out in public and in front of me, I got plenty to do with it." What I said seemed to make no difference to him. "Go take a flying shit," he tells me while grabbing her arm and starting to walk off.

22-SKOL

She's reluctant to move so he starts pulling her. She hasn't said a word yet. So I ask her, "Do you want to go with him? Do you want to press charges against him?" Her first words at last: "I just don't want to go with him." "Is this your husband?" I ask her, to which she shakes her head. "He is." Because it's clear that she doesn't want to go with him I get more aggressive now. "Let that woman go." He won't. "Then you're under arrest." He's not impressed. "Well, then, take me in if you can." I hadn't expected this. What am I supposed to do? But transit cops are expected to deal with situations like this, usually by themselves. This guy is huge. I can handle myself, but this is asking too much. Shit, just what I needed. But seeing him there beating up on this little thing, daring me to make a move, really got me steamed. Hell, he's big, but I'm tough. He's broad, but I'm fast as hell. I'm gonna take this bastard.

In all my years as a cop I never made a dumber move than I did now. To this day it's hard to believe my reaction. I unhooked my pistol belt and let it drop to the floor. Hell, this guy was challenging me—another man was demanding that I put up or shut up. Forget the "cop thing." I'd take him head on, man to man. Settle it with fists, not with a pistol. For the final time, "Let her go," I said, "or I'm going to kick your ass like you're kicking hers!!" Then somewhat inexplicably I found myself offering him a deal. "If you beat me you don't get arrested. If you don't beat me I'm going to put a hurtin' on you, and still lock you up." He's looking at me like who's kidding who. But I'm pushing him now. "Put it up," I tell him, "so that I can really do you in." My first thought was forget about a fair fight; the guy's too big. I started fingering the blackjack I (and most all the other cops I knew) carried. It's a deadly little device made of lead, the rounded head covered with leather. A spring allows it to snap into the target. Not much reason to aim this thing; wherever it hits it will do real damage. I probably would have hit him with it except that after just glaring at me and threatening to do me in he suddenly says,

"All right, I'm gonna fight you." I slipped the blackjack into my pocket, clenched my fist, and shot my right hand out.

I caught him flush in the jaw; he went down in a heap. I was shocked, not only that I had connected so cleanly, but that he had simply collapsed. Better still, he made no effort to get back on his feet. "I quit." That's all he said. At that point with my adrenaline overflowing it's not what I wanted to hear. I wanted him back on his feet so I could beat the living daylight out of him, but it's obvious he's not getting up. Meanwhile his wife, who watched him get hit and go down, is crying worse than before. "Don't hurt my husband, don't hurt my husband," she pleads. By now I've strapped my gun and holster back on and am preparing to cuff him. The cuffs barely fit, he's so big.

The guy's no longer the problem, his wife is. I've now become the brute. No surprise here. Every cop knows that in a domestic situation emotions run crazy so that even an abused wife can change her tune and rally behind her husband. As usual a crowd gathers, just as the wife is accusing me of hurting her poor husband, who's sitting helpless on the ground, his hands cuffed. Fortunately the change booth clerk has witnessed most of what has happened and has called for assistance. At this point the wife switches gears and begins pleading with me not to lock up her husband. "I started all of this," she's now saying. I'm thinking I'd better cover myself here so I ask if he feels I've abused him. "No, you were right, Officer," he says, "someone needed to kick my butt. I really shouldn't be beatin' on her." I'm listening to him and also writing his words down in my book. "Sign this, I say, which he does. That, I figured, gets me off the hook. So do we have a happy ending here? Possibly. I uncuffed him and they walked off together. But who the hell knows? He might have killed her when they got home. The clerk and I then got to discussing what just happened. "You were some fool," he says to me, "for taking off your gun." He was right, of course. Imagine the disaster had he grabbed for it and started shooting up the place. I had sure blundered and, in a fit of macho madness risked everything.

My explosive temper almost cost me my career. But sometimes you get lucky, and avoid disaster. So it was a happy ending for me at least, although the hand I hit him with hurt for days.

If there was a lesson in this incident, I didn't learn it, or at least not well enough. Because some time after this I found myself involved in another messy situation and my judgment once again, I think you probably would agree, was off base. I'm riding the lines in Queens when I get a call about a guy up in the control tower at the Queens Plaza station who's screwing up operations there. That's bad stuff, for it's the tower guys who handle all the track switching in the area. If they're distracted, you've got the makings of a real disaster. Sure enough, when I got over there the situation's not good. There's a black guy, apparently a nut case, roaming about the control room, getting in everybody's way and refusing to leave. The fact that I'm black doesn't seem to make the slightest difference to him. "Fuck you," he says when I start trying to talk to him and calm him down. "You're gonna have to kill me to get me out of here." I know if I pull my gun it's probably not going to make any impression on him; he's wound up so tight. And I'm not of the mind to punch him out and wipe the floor with him. Too many black guys have gotten that kind of automatic treatment from cops. As a black guy it's certainly not what I should be doing. I'm thinking let's show everyone that there is another way, that reasoning can work. I always thought of myself as a talker. I'll handle this guy with my mouth, get him to come along with me. So I strike up a conversation, try to find out what's disturbing him and what he's doing up there. But it's not working. He answers some of my questions, but is not a step closer to leaving. Meanwhile the guys in the tower are getting on me. "Cut the shit." "Get this guy out of here. We gotta get to work."

I'm still talking to the guy when suddenly two white cops, rookies who must have heard there was a problem up in the tower, burst in, walk right past me without the slightest acknowledgment, and head over to the guy. "You're getting out of here now, boy," one of them says. Now he does say it sternly, but by Jesus, that's all he said. And you know what our "crazy" man did? He said, "Yes, sir," and followed them as they led him right past me and out the door.

Do I have to tell you what this did to me? How I felt? The train guys in the tower, half of whom are black, are looking at me; they're not saying anything, but I know what they must be thinking. "You ain't much of a cop." Inside I'm raging. I've been made to look like a complete asshole in front of all those guys. Here I am a black guy trying to treat another black with some respect and restraint, and all he does is crap in my face. Then along come these two white rookies, ignore me, handle the guy like a piece of shit, and he goes, "Yessir," and just plain gives up and leaves. I'm being shown up, slapped down, and swept aside and sassed. All at once!

I chase after the two cops who have the guy in tow. "I'll bring him in," I tell them. No sooner have they left, headed away down the corridor than I tear into this guy and hit him repeatedly. He screams, bringing the two guys back on the run. It's all they can do to get me off of him. In that brief time I had managed to batter him pretty good. I had lost control. I was more than upset; I was in a rage. I hit him out of anger and shame. I wanted him to show me respect and he hadn't. I beat him to tell those white cops I would not tolerate second guessing my approach. I then turned to the guys in the tower. I wanted to tell them what the standoff had been about. "I saw in your eyes," I told them, "what you thought of me, but I was doing the right thing. You didn't see it that way because you were so hot to get back to work, but what I did works best, makes for less damage." I couldn't tell if they believed me, but they got my other message—that I wanted no further discussion of the incident now or behind my back. The subject was dropped.

But I couldn't get it out of my mind. For weeks afterwards I was sick to my stomach over how I had reacted. I was ashamed. I rehashed the scene over and over, wondering how else I might have acted. I should, I concluded, have been firm right off and first physically removed him. Only then should I have talked and tried to reason with him. Talking too soon and without effect left me frustrated and so I lashed out. And against a black man, no less. There was no excusing it. Instead I tried compensating. For a long time after, I leaned the other way, taking all sorts of needless abuse from civilians. That was my punishment.

Before you decide I was some brute picking on defenseless civilians, let me assure you I could on occasion rise to heroic proportions. Certainly it seemed that way the time I faced my most formidable subway felon. The incident happened at 42nd Street and 6th Avenue station, while I was doing the midnight to 8:00 a.m. shift. It was about 2:00 a.m. and I'm cooped out in an unused toll booth at one end of the station, taking my "lunch" break (we get an hour off during our shift), having myself a cup of coffee. I had informed both the clerk and the night porter that I would be there for maybe thirty-five minutes. It's wintertime, and once inside the booth I put the heater on, take my big horse blanket of a topcoat off, along with my gun holster and my shoes, lean back on the chair, and in no time I've dozed off. (I've also asked the clerk for a wakeup call in case I fall fast asleep.)

I should, of course, tell you that at this time the city was being terrorized by some loathsome character known as the "Paper Bag Bandit," who was on this crime spree involving assault and robbery. While committing his dirty work he wore a paper bag over his head. He struck mostly in the subways, usually hiding outside of ladies' bathrooms waiting for his victims. He had eluded all stakeouts set up to grab him.

It was one helluva wakeup call, a loud scream for help coming not too far, as I judged it, from the booth (which was on the mezzanine level) in which I was sleeping. I'm up in an instant, but my shoes, holster and topcoat are all off. And in trying to get dressed quickly I'm not doing very well. I do get my hat on, grab my gun and nightstick, and I'm off. The clerk has run to the booth, but like me he is hearing echoes and is confused about the direction of the screams. Anyway, I start dashing in the direction of the loudest sounds. Then I spot them.

What I see is this guy trying to take a bag off his head, while this lady is hanging on to his leg for dear life. Once he sees me he kicks her real hard. She lets go and off he runs. She's been beat up pretty badly, blood all over the place. He's got a good lead on me now. There's no way I can catch him, especially not with my shoelaces untied and flopping about. So I draw my gun. He's straight ahead, maybe half the length of the station away. But just as I'm squeezing the trigger there behind him is the token booth clerk. Shit! Too risky. I can't shoot. Too late. As I pull the gun up, it goes off and a thunderous boom blasts through the station.

A train is pulling in downstairs. I spot him heading to the platform level. Dashing down the nearest staircase I begin shouting. "Don't close the doors." But will the conductor listen? Other than my hat it would be hard to recognize me for a cop. The conductor sees me, looks confused, but doesn't close the doors as I dash by. I pass the motorman at the front of the train, who points to the stairs and up I go, but not before shouting, "Close the doors." I don't think I can catch the guy, what with my loose shoelaces and my equipment bouncing wildly up and down, getting in the way. But there he is! In what has to be the greatest piece of good fortune in my entire police career the guy has reversed direction and is heading back down the stairs right toward me. Was he confused? Did he figure he'd given me the slip or was he trying to get on the train? What difference did it make?

I figure it's got to be the Paper Bag Bandit. Of all places he's struck on my post. He's within reach. What a score! Running along with my gun out, I'm thinking am I justified in shooting him? Certainly I'm angry enough, having just seen the bloody face of that woman. He's about fifty feet away when I bring my gun down and take dead aim. My hand, I know, is shaking. I'm breathing real hard and I'm excited as hell. He sees this (knows I've already fired one shot) and promptly stops. "I surrender," he says, and throws his hands into the air and falls backwards onto the stairs. "Make a move and I shoot." He doesn't and I cuff him. Not only is he carrying a .45 automatic, but there in one of his pockets is a paper bag, the eyes cut out of it. I got him. The Paper Bag Bandit. The adrenaline surge is nearly overwhelming. The whole episode from start to finish probably took three, four, at most five minutes. Not to me though. I felt as if I had been chasing him for hours.

The clerk had called for assistance, and even as I was cuffing him I heard screaming sirens converging on the station from all sides. The call to "Assist Patrolman" always brings out every cop in the area. In the meantime I take him into the porter's room and cuff him to one of the steampipes. Now he's acting real defiant but he's also taken a shit in his pants and smells real bad.

Dozens of cops now pour into the area, followed not long after by reporters who've probably heard the news on the Police Band. With a case as big as this one every cop on the Force wants in on it, will figure some way to get cited for helping to capture this most wanted criminal. As they're arriving I know I'm going to have a problem. Still I had the perfect arrest—his gun, the bag, caught in the act, witnesses. But could I defend myself against the horde of opportunists who've flocked to the scene?

Leaving the porter's room I see the woman (an old Polish lady, it turns out) who had been beaten, talking to some of the cops. She'd gone into the bathroom, opened up the door to one of the stalls, and there he was, sitting on the toilet seat. He grabs her but she puts up a furious fight. "If he was going to hurt me, I was going to hurt him." (He had, I had noticed, a busted lip.) You had to feel for her. The cops, had they been alone, no doubt would have beaten the daylights out of him.

Cameramen are on the scene, getting their shots, most of which I notice are of this detective who's taken charge of the situation. I knew who he was, a rough Italian dude with a big reputation and plenty ambitious. They're taking pictures of him and some of those around him, even of the clerk and the porter.

Why isn't anyone taking a picture of me? Why aren't they crowding around me, listening to my story? I'm the arresting officer! Of course at that moment I don't look like a cop. I don't have a coat on, I'm wearing an ordinary shirt. I just don't fit the picture of a heroic officer. Leaving the scene I hurry over to the booth to get myself looking like a real cop.

When I return even more people are milling about. But the moment is slipping away. Worse, there's nothing I can do or at least nothing that I can think of doing. If there was any doubt, there was the captain telling me—"Earl, I'll take care of this." He did add, "You got a citation coming," but knowing this guy I wasn't reassured. He asked me to fill out the paper work on the woman and to escort her to the hospital (conveniently getting me out of the way). "But I'm the arresting officer," I replied. "Yeah, we know." (They had even removed my handcuffs from the guy and substituted someone else's.) Meanwhile reporters are crowding around everyone else and ignoring me. Not one fucking question do I get. I even got the guy's .45 in my pocket but no one's asked for it. Talk about being passed over.

Sure enough the newspapers gave the story big coverage. Guess whose name was missing? It was all about the detective and his men on stakeout when the Paper Bag Bandit struck. Caught him in the act. Nothing was said of shots being fired or of a gun being found on the suspect. So much for newspaper accuracy. A Transit Department secretary, a friend of mine, predicted that I would disappear from the record. "You know you lost it," he said. "You won't even see a commendation on this." He was right. Once again a black man had gotten the shaft. It's a bitch, I tell you. It was as if I had never been there. But there was some slight consolation. The guy I captured turned out not to be the Paper Bag Bandit but a copycat criminal. The police, embarrassed by all the hoopla surrounding the capture, offered this explanation. There was not one but several Paper Bag Bandits menacing New York. And they had rid the city of one!

But someone did know the truth about that night's events.

The woman who I had rescued called me soon afterwards and invited me out to dinner. The guy had battered her—she had lost several teeth and had her nose broken in three places—but she was a feisty lady, a tough, down-to-earth person who, you could tell, would recover and move on. We met at the restaurant. I brought her flowers and a box of candy. She presented me with two tickets to the theater. We drank wine, we ate, we had an enjoyable evening together. She couldn't thank me enough. That was just about all the reward I got. So it was all the more sweet.

For several years before retirement I was stationed on the Rockaway Line, teamed with the orneriest man you will ever see. You remember my friend Daly, I'm sure, and his explosive ways; well, this guy made Daly look like a Boy Scout. A loner, a bitter man, a brute, that was Mack. (What a guy like this is doing as a policeman is another story, but we attracted, I imagine, more than our fair share.) He couldn't get along with fellow cops and his treatment of criminals could get downright sadistic. Actually you needn't have been a "criminal" to earn his wrath. Say you were a fare beater and he caught you. If you happened to look at him the wrong way, he'd beat you up. Everyone knew it, but it didn't seem to matter. The Force protected its own; police brutality was an issue of concern only to civilians. Just where to assign Mack was a problem until they decided to put him with me. I had a reputation as a get-along guy. I had made peace with Daly; maybe they figured I'd somehow manage to keep Mack under control. We were given a rickety old squad car and assigned to patrol along the Rockaway elevated line.

Mack barely tolerated my presence. Actually it wasn't even that good: he didn't speak to me. We worked eight-hour night shifts and there was many a tour that not a single word passed beyond what was absolutely necessary for the job. Stopping for coffee, Mack would step out to get himself some and return to the car, slamming the door on the way out and again when he returned. Would he bring coffee back for me? Not a chance. I'd have to leave the car and get it myself. But we did carve out a "working relationship." Mack could write reports easily. I couldn't, so it was agreed that he'd handle this chore. Mack didn't like to drive, besides which he had a day job and enjoyed dozing at night as we moved about. So I did the driving.

It was a good post, usually quiet and manageable. Whatever action there was came not on the trains but from the many Irish bars located all along the elevated line. On Friday and Saturday nights there were the usual bands of drunks parading about. Fights would break out and cops would come by and separate them, then go on their way. There'd be few arrests because the cops regarded these tipplers as "their people," and meant them no harm. This one time I'm watching one of these typical weekend fracases from the station platform, but things are getting out of control. The drunks, there's lots of them, are beating up the street cops. In fact one patrolman has been knocked stone cold and is laying out on the sidewalk. I rush to the rescue and order everyone to step aside. No one resists. Seeing a black cop these guys know I'm prepared to dish out some real pain. To me they're drunks, and they're a problem. There's no kinship here.

Strangely it was just such a fracas that brought Mack out of his shell and led him to reveal the story behind his agony and despair. The incident took place at the Mott Avenue station involving six or seven Spanish guys who had become involved in a knife fight. Mack and I were nearby at the time having coffee when we heard sounds of a scuffle and rushed over. Without hesitating (he never did) Mack waded into the midst of it, using his nightstick with devastating effectiveness. I joined in; the two of us flailing away and subduing the troublemakers one by one. It was a scene always popular in the movies—"good cops" taking on a mob of evildoers and beating them into submission. Here we were in the heat of battle, standing together, protecting each other against real danger.

After this bit of heroics the change in Mack was remarkable. Why, it's hard to say for sure, but you have to figure that seeing me, a guy he wouldn't even talk to, fighting alongside him made him realize we were closer to each other than he would ever have before admitted. From that day on our relationship changed dramatically. There was no more slamming of car doors. He came back with coffee for himself and for me. He also got me the newspapers. And he began to talk. Did he talk, pouring out to me his troubles and his pain. His wife had left him. One son had married a Puerto Rican despite his opposition to the marriage. A daughter was working the streets as a prostitute, and his other daughter had married a black guy. That killed him, he admitted to me. That's why he resented every black he met. He had no girlfriends. He couldn't, he let me know, "relate to women."

Almost every night we talked endlessly about matters he had never before, he told me, discussed. Now he refused to work with anyone but me. My resentment and anger at him turned to sympathy and affection. We had at long last become partners. When I retired Mack was there, of course, came up to me that night and kissed me. Then he put his arms around me. "You were a great partner," he said. There was a time such words from Mack would have been impossible. Some time afterward he called me. He had accepted his black grandchild, he wanted me to know. Did I have something to do with that? I wanted to believe I had.

Yes, I said retirement. It was not something I planned, although I'd been thinking about it. I had, it turned out, no choice in the matter. It all began rather dramatically when I see this fellow jump the turnstile of the Mott Avenue station and I hear, "Stop that guy." As soon as he spots me he does a quick reverse, jumps back over the turnstile and bolts up the stairs and out of the station. I'm in hot pursuit. It's not, I can tell, going to be easy. It's wintertime and I'm wearing a very heavy topcoat, plus all the usual equipment. As I exit the station this fellow screams, "He robbed me," which helps explain what's going on. "Don't go anywhere," I shout to him as I run by. A cop always needs his witnesses.

It's not much of a contest. Try as I might I can't gain a step on this guy. One block, two blocks, three, I'm out of breath. Not only that, but all of a sudden I'm terribly dizzy. I can't stand on my feet. So I sit myself down on the sidewalk. It's at this point that I feel what seems like an electric shock go through me. The station clerk and another cop arrive, want to call an ambulance. "It's not necessary," I tell them. Just sitting there for a time seemed to work; I was feeling better. I even completed my rounds that day.

It's now three to four months later and I'm talking to a physician friend of mine at an ice skating rink when suddenly he says to me calmly, "When we leave the rink come right over to my office." I did, and he examines me, then explains why he had wanted to see me. "While I was talking to you at the skating rink you were having a heart attack." Seeing my eyes dilating had made him suspicious. My blood pressure was extremely elevated. I told him about my "dizzy spell" and shocked sensation some months before. He sends me to a cardiologist. That's when I got the bad news. "Are you a police officer?" "Yes." Then he started describing the scar tissue he had seen. "Well, I don't expect you'll ever work again." That was it. It had been over eighteen years since I'd joined the Force. Now suddenly it was all over.

I was retired. That would take some getting used to. But I had no regrets. Sure I'd had my difficulties and my disappointments but for me the years on the Force had been good years. I had been, to my thinking, a credit to the Transit Police. I had made a difference. I did my job and did it well. Conscientious, friendly, reliable, hard working—that I was. I had been there to assist and protect the people, and I had done just that. I didn't end up resenting the public or lining up with fellow officers against civilians. I didn't give in to the anger or cynicism you saw among many of the guys around me. I kept my cool, showed restraint and provided the public, which I had sworn to serve, with a sense of security. Year after year I got the job done. I had nothing to be ashamed of.

21 | I'VE BEEN DOING SOME THINKING

It's been many, many years now since I turned in my shield and retired from the Force. Feels like another life. Retirement for me was quite a new experience, satisfying, but in a different way. I remarried (after 10 years of bachelorhood), this time to a wonderful, intelligent, professional woman (a teacher), and together we raised three terrific children. We saved, we scraped and, unlike my mother, we made it out to suburbia, to a comfortable home, in an integrated community. I told you I was one of the lucky ones.

With my wife Dolores working, my retirement meant doing all the housekeeping and around-the-clock fathering. I survived though, as the kids all went off to college and I became a man of leisure, free to indulge myself and cultivate my garden. The indulging part never happened (my pension wasn't all that generous), though the garden, with the tender care I gave it, turned out fine.

I'd always been a curious fellow, you remember that, but mostly my early life was spent listening to others, being preached to by folks who had their own ideas. No more. I had, I figured, earned the right to my own conclusions, had seen much of the world, observed enough people to form a good idea of how it worked. And I enjoyed puzzling it out, putting the pieces together, uncovering the larger picture. Mostly my thoughts were about race, about the black experience in America. No surprise there. So much of my life turned on my being a black man in a mostly white society, a Negro in a country that long ago decided it had a "Negro problem." And the problem remains. Society simmers and sometimes explodes and millions of Americans of color continue to suffer lives that are bleak and too often brief. Fresh thinking—that's what we need. Truth telling. Honesty. A tall order, I grant you.

So what do I have to offer? I've been there—you know that now, and came to understand early on the terrible burdens blacks had to bear in America. My mother saw to that. She taught me for example that black boys had better learn how to deal with cops. (Do white parents even mention this to their kids?) She cried at news of lynchings and left the South because race ruled down there. Angry because of the stereotyping of blacks and the way we were presented in American history, she bought books in order to learn more about our past. Then too many of the older men who took me under their wing in my early years spoke about a repressive white society, made sure I understood that I was being victimized. (I didn't always buy it, didn't think I was doing all that badly.) To these leftists and Communists the system had first to be overthrown before I could go free.

I didn't need many reminders. Often enough white people didn't let me forget. The Irish gang which tossed me into the Hudson River didn't care whether I lived or died. The real estate agents who laughed at our efforts to buy a house in Levittown were part of a society prepared to keep us down and in our place. Same with the Lithographers' Union. It had no interest whatsoever in having me join the ranks. Certainly the U.S. Army was comfortable keeping us subordinate to white authority. Mistreatment at the hands of my fellow cops meant that even a badge and a gun would not change things much. I knew the score. Every black in America does. Every one of us spends a lifetime suffering indignities, defending ourselves against attacks, getting blamed, being belittled and feeling betrayed, hoping for acceptance and security—which usually never comes. That's all we want. That's all we ever wanted—to finally claim the birthright to which every American is entitled.

Had I understood nothing of my predicament, the black movement would have awakened me. Growing up I saw Garvey's followers march through Harlem. I listened to Adam Clayton Powell, Jr. insist we boycott stores along 125th Street. I picketed the Jamaica YMCA because it refused to admit blacks. I was there when the Army finally took action and ended segregated units. Along with a cadre of other blacks I swept into the New York City Police force and stood up to those white cops who resented our presence. I thrilled to Martin Luther King's call and to his dreams for a new society. Yes, I became part of the black awakening. Docility and resignation—Gone, Baby, Gone.

But why listen to me on racial matters? Is my voice any different from those who've long "analyzed" these issues? You of course must in the end answer this question, but do consider this. I'm black, always have been. It's to me all this stuff has happened and continues to happen. Talk about experience—I've got that. Heightened awareness—you bet. We've all had to watch the shit come our way, then duck, deflect, cope, bounce back and keep on going. Don't you think we've got most of it figured out, know how the game's played and what we must do to keep going? Credit us for some smarts here!

Schooling contributed little to my education. What I know I've seen firsthand, experienced directly. Experts don't impress me; I've reached my own conclusions. Lots of highly educated folks I know don't much credit such "life experience," but let me tell you—if you pay attention to what's happening, just don't let it roll over you and can piece things together—there's no better teacher. Hard knocks plus hard facts bring you to some plain truths. You'd be surprised how sharp you get out there just trying to survive. For a time that's all me and my mother were doing. Then there's little room for mistakes. But such desperation can also cloud judgment. Remember though, we got ourselves up off the floor and kept moving on and up—real poor—lower class—working class—lower middle class—middle class. Touch all those bases and you sure get perspective, get to know lots of different people.

And by and by I made it (without suffering setbacks, i.e., having to go two steps backward for every one forward, which is what happens to most blacks)—steady, secure job, two-earner family income—suburbia—kids all off to college. To really know life you've got to be living by your wits out on the streets. To begin to make sense of it, though, you need distance plus a level of comfort and stability. Comfortable I became, not secure though. What black man is?. Still we had our hopes. My mother and I were part of an era when we fully expected better things ahead. Dr. King's vision for America was our dream as well.

So let me tell you how I see racial matters here in this country. Long ago I stopped tolerating fools, quit believing what "people" said. When the usual bullshit starts flowing it actually pains me. I get headaches and become real frustrated because I see the poison doing its damage, see another chance to get at the truth lost. You've stuck with me this far in the book. Hear me out now.

I'm an angry black man, but I'm not hostile. I'm angry because of what's happened to blacks here in America. We've never known good times. What "good old days" are we able to talk about? Isn't every group at least entitled to that, to the right to be nostalgic? Most of us have never had a chance to get off our knees and to stand tall. It's been bad, real bad, almost from the start. Sure it's better now than before, but it's nowhere near where it should be.

Right off we were the victims—it's never really changed. Other folks came here for "good" reasons. In History they teach you about religious freedom, economic opportunity, adventure, escape. None of these apply to us. We didn't come, we were packed in and shipped, kicking, screaming in chains, dying at every point along the way. We were strangers, aliens, "heathens," "savages," brought by Europeans to satisfy their needs and their greed. No one much cared for us; or if they did, it was only because they wanted to exploit us. And so we were for over 200 years, as slaves—despised, feared, cut off from our past, from our original families and kin, stripped of most of our culture, considered not quite human. And once we were no longer slaves we were still black. And black was no good in a place where those who counted were white. In a "white man's" country we stood out as blacks, nowhere to hide because we were black—we couldn't just change our names. Told we were inferior, we were kept separate from most all others. Racism became like a narcotic—addictive, terribly costly, keeping whites from being able to think straight, forcing them to deny that we were able to think at all.

Racism felt good, especially to some white folks. Hell, if you were at the lower end of the pecking order, weren't going anyplace and feeling sorry for yourself, there were the blacks to get you out of your funk. Cheer up, white man, you ain't at the bottom; you're better than those niggers down there. Why sure enough I am. Already I'm feeling better about myself. People just off the boat (or plane) also take to this bogus booster business. Here they are, newcomers, feeling cut off, alone, having little, looked down upon by just about everyone else, and suddenly they discover the blacks. And in no time, in broken English they're talking all that racist garbage, certain that blacks are lazy, are hooked on welfare, and bent on crime.

Put blacks down and everyone, everyone white that is, moves up a notch. Not long ago I read where this immigrant landlord on Long Island turned away a couple that were looking for an apartment he had advertised. His explanation—we don't rent to blacks! Now ain't that something, foreigners telling you you can't live in "their" community. And then there are all these former immigrant groups telling you about how, when they first came over, they worked like dogs helping to build America—roads, canals, subways, mines, skyscrapers, tunnels—all that stuff. Hell, we've been building America right from the beginning, before all of these other people even got here. It was our hands, our muscles, our sweat that got things built in this country all along. Who's giving us any credit for this?

There we were, my wife and I, in a Queens store shopping for shoes for my daughter, who was all dressed up, sitting in the stroller. Nearby were two white teenage girls browsing through the stock. As I checked the shelves I glanced over and watched as one of the girls put a pair of shoes into a large pocketbook she carried. The two of them then left the store, walking casually past the checkout counter. Not finding the right shoes, the three of us prepared to leave. But before we could, there's a clerk stopping us, asking to check our shopping bags! Sure we were angry. What reason did they have to suspect us of shoplifting? Here we were, mature adults, well dressed, certainly respectable looking. No matter, we were black. That made us targets automatically. What satisfaction it gave me to let them know that while they were asking to inspect our bags, two teenagers had walked off with a pair of shoes, maybe more.

But there it all was—we blacks became scapegoats, are accused of bringing evil into the society. Sure you can fight this stuff, or let it roll off, become conditioned to it. But it happens all the time and just wears you down, gets you sick. The race card's been played for so long it's no wonder the deck is stacked against us. No matter that whites are the big time culprits, as involved in wrongdoing as anyone else; point your finger at the blacks, label it a black problem, blame the blacks, and you get whites off the hook. They're now innocent bystanders, or else victims of black misdeeds. (Same thing happened under slavery after white masters forced themselves on black female slaves, then blamed the women. It was, they explained, their irresistible sexuality that sent masters running into the slave quarters.) Welfare—you know as many if not more whites are on the receiving end (plus whites get most of the jobs in the welfare bureaucracies.) Still it's seen as mainly a black problem! Whites introduced, financed, distributed and mainly consumed drugs, but blacks also take the rap here. (Whites, usually better off, can hide their addictions easier than blacks.) Crime is everywhere, but black street crime grabs the headlines. Compared to whites we're nothing but petty muggers; major thievery—that's their game. White collar criminals rob this nation blind at every level. Take those riots in Los Angeles where whites, Asians, Chicanos joined in the looting, but wouldn't you know it—everyone "saw" blacks doing it all. No wonder we're disliked; we're evil!

Putting us down, making us scapegoats for lots that's wrong in the United States is bad enough. But worse, consider what our punishment has been over the years. Every generation of blacks has come under assault, had whatever stability it achieved undermined. Hell, we've always been an endangered species! There'll be some who'll tell you slavery wasn't all that harsh—"Look at those happy darkies a'singin' and a'dancin'"—but most will admit these were not good times for blacks. Endless labors, whippings, sadistic violence and slave auctions took up more time than the dancin' and a'singin'. But these same people will insist that once slavery ended blacks, now free, simply couldn't measure up, and so ended up at the bottom of the social system. They don't consider the lasting scars of slavery, overlook the abuse and exploitation that continued long after it ended. History becomes destiny. If you don't believe in history repeating itself just check out our story here in the United States.

For centuries blacks had worked for nothing, had nothing to show for it, and once freed weren't given a thing for all their efforts. They wanted land, sure felt they earned it. Nothing doing. Read about those former slaves who started farming soil abandoned by Confederate rebels. But once the war ended they were driven off, the property returned to these traitors. Tell me that's fair! During Reconstruction blacks did get a leg up in parts of the South, but most whites there couldn't handle it. So the Ku Klux Klan comes riding in with threats and killings, forcing blacks to run for cover. Then the "law" takes over to separate blacks from whites legal like. Segregation spread across the South, leaving behind two separate societies clearly unequal. Without their own land, most southern blacks were forced to become sharecroppers, usually desperate, always dependent. And when for all sorts of reasons southern whites became angry and frustrated, it was blacks who mostly paid the price. The roll call of lynching victims went on and on for years.

Talk about getting the breaks—for the last century and a half we didn't catch many. Once blacks began leaving the South they hit yet another wall, ran smack into Northern racism. After finally working their way into certain niches of the economy—for example as sailors, horse jockies, ship caulkers and in construction and catering—they end up getting the boot by other groups, aggressive and better organized. When they managed, against the odds, to build up business districts in various cities, it only made whites envious. "Riots" followed, along with the destruction of black sections of many a town. Organized white violence against blacks became pretty routine—something we don't much talk about. When workers formed unions it made little difference to blacks. Few were allowed in. It's no mystery why blacks stayed at the bottom of the economic ladder, stuck in menial labor and service jobs. When they washed windows, ran errands and shined shoes they threatened no one. "Blacks are lazy"—that's what you'll hear by way of explanation. Even when blacks rallied to the side of their country when it went to war, the record shows, they got no better deal here.

First we're excluded, segregated and brutalized, then, as if by way of explanation, out come the lies and the stereotypes to explain it all to generations of white Americans. Newspapers, magazines, vaudeville, radio and movies all played up the same negative images—blacks were feckless, foolish, thieving, lazy, uncultured, simple creatures, good for a laugh but not to be taken seriously. Black men were singled out, subjected to even more vicious distortions. They were sexually aggressive, prone to violence, criminally inclined, addicted to gambling, shiftless and unreliable. No wonder they were attacked by lynch mobs, picked up for vagrancy, abused by cops, jailed with regularity and fired with impunity. By contrast black women were considered to be more stable and reliable and less threatening. Rather than us, they got the jobs, were trusted (even with suckling white babies during and after slavery). What this did to the black man—that's easy enough to figure out. So when we march on Washington as we did, forget Farrakhan's foolishness and look at our faces, notice the pride and dignity still there despite it all.

We were here, no one denies it, since the early 17th century. Most every other group in America would love to be able to make such claims, would have used their presence back then to great advantage over the years. But blacks somehow have been left out of our history. We did nothing, accomplished nothing, contributed nothing—if you read most of the old history textbooks was any other conclusion possible? Nat Turner, Booker T. Washington, George Washington Carver and Jackie Robinson about summed it up. And yes, Satchmo, Joe Louis, and Duke Ellington. That's not much to show for almost 400 years! Blacks were planted in the soil of America early on, so how is it we haven't taken root? Belittle our roots, or better yet, cut them off and what comes forth becomes real fragile.

I'll grant you native Americans can paint a pretty grim picture. But aside from them (a much smaller group, most of whom escaped slavery) has any other people had so dismal a time of it in America? We were knocked down, kept down, stomped on, and then tripped when we tried to get up! That we survived it at all was a miracle. No one was rooting for us to make it. Most preferred to see us dead or departed from the country. I offer this little history lesson for those people who would tell us—Sure slavery was a bummer, but you've had well over a hundred years to get on with it and join the American mainstream. Hell, no! The shackles came off all right but what of the other "restraints"? In the years after 1865 we never got on the same starting line with our fellow white Americans. Whites, I know, refuse to see this, insist that for years it's been a fair race (or that we've been favored), but that just ain't so. Only in the last 30 to 40 years have we enjoyed a fighting chance to get in on some of the action.

You can't just ignore the long-term damage, overlook the internal injuries we've suffered. I know everyone is a victim these days and that lots of folks are out there claiming to have been denied and abused, but by God we are the original victims! We're legit; our credentials are impeccable. The scars are there; they haven't healed. When we argue for affirmative action to get us back into the game, consider what we've been through and what we still have to face. As usual, we're taking the rap, with affirmative action the latest whipping boy for lots of people who are understandably upset by other things going on. How many jobs have we supposedly made off with compared to the hundreds of thousands that just disappeared because corporate leadership moved to increase profits, downsize and go overseas? And the positions we're accused of occupying unfairly actually went mostly to women who rode the "rights" bandwagon, then jumped off once it got them where they wanted and deservedly had every right to go. The result was lots of angry white men. With fewer guaranteed positions and upset because women, now in decent jobs, were acting more independent than ever, these guys looked to place the blame somewhere. Of course it's got to be the fault of blacks! You know the expression "if it didn't exist we'd have to create it." Well we do exist—we're the all-purpose scapegoats.

And we still scare you. Now that's got some history to it. Even though slave rebellions existed mostly in slaveholders' fevered imaginations, the fear has never left. Revenge is after all simple enough to understand and worry about. Whites are uneasy when I'm present; I frighten them. And I'm not Willie Horton. I'm old, gray, rather respectable looking, still many whites find my presence unsettling. Just recently I had to pick up a set of X-rays from my doctor. While I'm waiting for the elevator two white women showed up, but when it opens they walk off, decide not to get on it with me. Just a day or two after that I'm driving slowly along a suburban street and happen to look in the direction of this baby sitter and the two or three-year-old kid she's watching. Would you believe the minute she spots me she walks over and picks up the child and heads toward the front door. I'm a child snatcher too, you see. Am I imagining things? Just ask any black man you know. Humiliations like those happen every day to all of us.

There's no getting used to it. And being middle class doesn't help much—you're still black. Cops follow your movements; taxis don't stop, restaurants seat you out of the way and the service slows. We're feared, mistrusted, forced always to be on guard. Knowing you're being observed, you can never relax or be entirely comfortable. So you expect it. You try to live with it, try to avoid potentially touchy situations, but it hurts and it takes its toll. Black Rage. Whites say they don't understand it or there's no reason for it. Really now!

It's a small step from distrust of the individual black man to fear of the black ghetto. Keep away; contain it. It is the home of the underclass and there's no hope for them. It's little more than a drug-infested, crime-ridden, decaying slum kept alive by welfare payments, drug money, lootings and periodic political handouts. The ghetto must be pacified, its violence kept from spreading into surrounding communities. For that you need the police. They are the front line of defense. Police forces must therefore not be weakened or seriously restrained, or the cops discouraged from making preemptive strikes to break up potential threats. And waiting to reinforce the police are the ranks of good white citizenry, (including especially the self-styled militia) allowed to arm and to defend themselves to neutralize any black uprising. Make no mistake about it—many of the gun control opponents are folks who fear us and who are armed, (with an incredible stockpile of weapons) prepared to shoot us down if they decide we're getting out of hand. Just read the hate mail our black leaders get each day. I know some blacks talk about armed uprisings and race wars but that's crazy, a fantasy, a guaranteed death wish. With all that firepower ready to blow us away, without any sizable areas that we control, without our own food supply, we wouldn't have a chance.

I know some of our wounds are self-inflicted and the result of internal divisions and battles that waste energy and spread confusion. Consider the black kids who get all over one of their own because he's taking school seriously, looking to get ahead, trying too hard. What's he doing become "white." I've already mentioned the tensions between black men and women. Black women, not feared as we are, are more likely to find jobs, get educated, move up. But you hear them complaining about not enough "worthy" black men, and see them get angry when black males up and marry white women. What's the matter, ain't we good enough for you?

Then there's those getting upset at blacks who "leave" for suburbia and end up living among whites. The charge—desertion, abandonment, escaping from responsibility. Probably they mean it but they're also jealous as hell. Hey, if you can get out, get out. Almost every other group in America has seen its successful people beat-it-the-hell-out to greener pastures. But blacks are uneasy about this. And some don't even believe it when they see it! I know about this, seen it happen when a black delivery person comes to my door. "Can you sign for this or is the owner of the house around?" Why doesn't it occur to him that I own the place or that I live in this neighborhood? I'm an impostor. I'm just visiting! "How in the hell can you afford this?" I mention some decent jobs, the two incomes and the sacrifices you make. I don't know if he believes me. And while on the subject, I've noticed blacks usually don't like working for other blacks. There's friction, there's tension—happens all the time. Watch the behavior of black store clerks. (Still I look for them, feel more comfortable dealing with them.) With whites they're likely to be polite, patient, helpful. Then a black customer arrives and they get uncomfortable, not sure how to relate or what to expect.

Color divides us blacks—that's an old story. The master was white, white was powerful, white was good, and black meant plenty of trouble and pain and worse. Light-skinned Negroes (encouraged and supported by whites) came to see themselves as better than their darker-skinned brothers and sisters. And if the lightness could be mistaken for whiteness, another opportunity opened up. You could pass, cross over, join the dominant group. Many, many did. People would be in for quite a shock if we ever totaled up these numbers. I don't blame them one bit. (Though you do remember how hurt I was by the actions of my mother's brother?) It was a way of saving yourself a heap of grief. But of course it divided us, weakened us, brought on a lot of anger, pain, and reproach. It also led eventually to a reaction and to the cry, "Black is beautiful." This was an important statement—it was prideful, combative, a breakthrough, a defiant answer to all the put-downs we suffered. But where it eventually led bothered me. To me what was beautiful was the miracle of our survival, the dignity with which we had endured, the belief in education and self-improvement, which we had kept alive. But "Black is beautiful" went, I thought, in the wrong direction. It pulled us away from the white society, even from the English language, along a black path, away from the mainstream. It played right into the hands of our enemies who had no problem with us heading off in our own separate way. Going it alone is not, shouldn't be, the answer for us in America. White society is where it's at, where most of the wealth, even our own money, comes from. We've got to identify with the majority, be fully prepared to join them (whether we like it or not) or we'll be left out on the fringes with little more than crumbs. We're Americans. We've got every right to our share of this nation's goodies.

Backing away from mainstream white society made some sense (what had it really offered us?) but was also surprising. Remember one of the real triumphs of the master white class was how they engineered the transformation of us original Africans. What a job they did. We came to be fashioned in their image. The WASP made us what we are. We are his cousins. He stripped away what we brought with us and replaced it with what He was.

He created us, made us one people out of the many that we once were. He formed us into Americans—authentic, original Americans. It was the greatest demonstration of the melting pot America had ever seen. He gave us his language, his religion, his names, his food, his clothes. We stayed loyal to his society, fought to defend his nation, accepted many of his individualistic values and in the end showed little hatred despite what he had done to us. We are, as I've said before, an exceptionally forgiving people. We even swallowed his dream. Certainly my mother wasn't alone in believing we could make it in America. If given a chance we could move right on up, take our place alongside him. When immigrant newcomers sneer at us, when they have the nerve to tell us to step aside, what do they know? Surely not that we were there at the start or that we are close kin to the WASP.

As I've said, it's just recently that blacks have seen some possibilities. It's not that years of resistance and protest, stretching back to Douglass, Dubois, Garvey, Powell, Thurgood Marshall, A. Philip Randolph and many others failed, but it was not until after World War II that it gathered some steam. The old docility began to fade and we felt freer to express our hostility, even our rage. Once we did, down went many of the old regimes of the South, out went legal segregation and in its place came a more progressive South, one more hospitable to blacks. Blacks sensed this and they began returning "home" and were welcomed—especially if they brought money along. I remember stopping in to buy a few items at this roadside general store in Virginia recently, and engaging the proprietor in friendly conversation. While we were talking, in came several white construction workers, tracking in dirt and looking generally scruffy and undesirable. Well, that guy let them know directly that he didn't want them in his store. And after they left he felt obliged to apologize to me for their presence. Imagine that if you will—a white Southerner sucking up to a black man while putting down a bunch of good old boys who he felt had no business being there. My, my, things do change.

Applauding the "new" black middle class is fine but believe me it has been around a long time. It's just that they've been overlooked, like so much else relating to blacks. I knew the black middle class in Harlem, and lived alongside them in that Jamaica, Queens project. Now these folks never had as much money as the white middle class, but they knew how to make do with less. Some challenge it was, but they did it. And they're doing it again today, large numbers of them are. Believe me, it's a struggle living that close to the edge, trying to keep a respectable lifestyle. Talk about your positive role models. You know who's come to really appreciate that fact? The white middle class. Layoffs of older middle level corporate employees have pulled the legs out from under lots of these folks. Now they're scrambling to keep afloat and are coming to know the sacrifices that it takes. The black middle class has known all about this; we've always been obliged to live that way. But you never hear us complaining much.

* * *

Well, by goodness, word is out now that we do have a past. There've been few more positive developments in recent years than the rewriting of our history based on facts, either long suppressed or simply ignored. (If you reduce our role in history that lets the white man add to his "credits" and limits whatever "claims" we might have based on our past contributions.) Wherever the white man ventured to in the New World we were there too, along with him, taking part in "his" accomplishments. We were in the North and the South and, yes, the West. We were pioneers, we were cowboys, we were outlaws and we were cavalry. Without protection provided by the "Buffalo Soldiers," the West would have been an even more dangerous place for the "palefaces." We explored the land, helped build this country, farmed this soil and fought for these United States again and again. We were educators, reformers, doctors, clergymen, teachers, writers, poets, inventors, politicians, judges, lawyers, reporters, professors and scientists.

We're getting to know much more about this. But there is so much more to do here, more information to uncover, to publicize and pass on to the next generation. Our people I know originated in different sections of West Africa, but those roots have mostly been cut away—too much time has passed; too little evidence remains. Almost all the original regional distinctions and cultural variations have been erased. I'm not for ignoring Africa but I'm far more interested in dusting off and exposing our American roots. Here is where we black folks really became brothers and sisters! Let us make known to all our long traditions here—where we've been, what we've done and how we managed. Above all else we are among the original Americans, so let our story be told and remembered and respected.

The white man made us in his image. Over time we began remaking the white man. Today more and more people realize that, a sure sign of the progress we've made. Mention music and you'll get absolutely no argument. The same with dance and style and art and literature, cooking and clothes and language and gesture, and yes, humor. Black culture exists—Hallelujah! Take black youth culture and how it's crossed over to white teenagers. Tough, defiant, macho, independent and aggressively informal—it's got that message young people want to send to us elders. Attractive black sports heroes dominate the field and monopolize the jock commercials, while black singers and entertainers are not far behind. Step aside, Aunt Jemima!

Still we're hearing all the time, especially in the media, how race relations are getting worse. I just don't believe it. Media pronouncements of course carry great weight and once they set the scene, they bring forth the images and the stories to support that point of view. Makes it real difficult to see matters in other ways. Good news, we hear, doesn't sell as well as bad. There's not many headlines in harmony. Mention friction and conflict and you got someone's attention. So the media prefers to see tensions in race relations. What could be simpler than black and white or having racial animosities to substitute for social class tensions which are more subtle and complicated and potentially more explosive?

Race relations are no way like they once were. People forget the bad old days, those times when decade after decade racial attitudes, the real ugly stuff, were fixed, unquestioned, right out in the open at all levels. It's not that way anymore. More facts have come out, especially about our history in this country. The schools are teaching about it and television too (where you do see plenty of black faces) is reporting more of it. There is no shortage of black writers telling our stories and large numbers of whites reading their words. More open and frank communication is taking place these days. Also intermingling and intermarriage (you probably don't even know about the magazines devoted to interracial marriages). I'm especially sensitive to that stuff, (we all were when it came to O.J. and Nicole, which was, before its tragic end, very much a story of interracial love and obsession.) And let me tell you, I'm seeing more and more of it out in the open. Even among the working classes where the racial divide is often hardest to cross. For sure the Simpson trial didn't do much to improve the intergroup dialogue but what struck me was how just about every group was represented in that courtroom. Ito, Darden, Fuhrman, Scheck, etc.—go down the whole cast of characters—it was one of the most politically correct dramas you'll ever see. And it took place in California where the racial and group mingling would astonish folks in other parts of the country. Once the color line blurs along the Pacific coast, expect that wave soon will spread out across the country.

What I believe also may help matters along is the large increase of Latinos. Most all of them are caramel colored people, blends of African, native Americans and some Spanish. These are attractive looking people. Now I know they're not without their racial hangups, but they're less uptight about them than we've been. They represent the middle way. And they are, and this is, the future.

So despite what we're told, I'm convinced that most whites

and blacks are becoming less prejudiced and are getting along better with one another. I also know there is a ways to go. Negative images still compete with coverage of black strivings, sacrifices and solid achievements. And watch white leaders regularly wriggle off the hook after being caught making blatantly racist comments. Putting down blacks is considered as harmless backsliding or excusable slips of the tongue. It takes time after all to kick the habit. Let a black, however, make an anti-white statement and there is public outrage and demands that the entire black leadership immediately apologize and disavow the individual. Sure blacks can be prejudiced and sometimes are, but racist? No. Racism to me requires more than genetic put-downs, but that you have the power to dominate others and systematically discriminate. Blacks in America have no such power. And they can't even talk as if they do. Outspoken or independent minded blacks immediately catch hell, become "irresponsible rabble rousers," and are "ordered" to cool it. White society comes down on them real quick (or looks for ways to buy them off).

Meanwhile black social and economic advancement continues, but never fast enough. Corporate America says it's gotten past tokenism, but it looks a hell of a lot like it when you count black heads in companies across America. When I think of black social mobility it reminds me of jumping beans—a few popping up and leaving the pack, but most stuck down below. School segregation—it's not the law but it's generally the rule in the United States. Blame segregated housing for a lot of it. (Blacks, you should know, are always letting "other" people move into their areas. The Chinese, Hispanics, Indians and Pakistanis understand they will not meet with resistance when they take up residence in or around a black neighborhood. We're hospitable people, you know. But let us just try to move in on others—watch out, baby!)

Money doesn't come easy to us. Try getting a mortgage from a bank. In fact qualifying for any kind of bank financing is a bitch. Getting started, whether it be a home or a business, and you're talking about a serious obstacle course. And even if we get some cash the terms usually are lousy. We have to pay more. In fact I'm convinced blacks ordinarily pay more for everything they buy. Blacks generally figure that one way or another they're going to get screwed out there. We all know about ghetto stores charging higher prices, but that's just part of the story. I've noticed that when I'm out shopping in stores or when I'm getting an estimate on work I need done in the house or I'm purchasing or pricing a car, somehow "specials" are never mentioned, higher-priced goods are pushed and lower-priced items I came in for become unavailable. What's going on? Should I just be happy they're willing to deal with me at all? Do they think I'm too stupid to know the difference? So we make less and are charged more. Some deal we got.

When I was a boy growing up in Harlem the streets were safe, the neighborhoods orderly, the sense of community strong. Sure we had our wiseguys, tough guys, hustlers and gangsters, but they knew their bounds, they had style and above all they had plans, most of them. One day they'd move up, go legit, get a business, even become respectable. It's another world, a war zone out there now on the inner city streets, chilling, heartless, terrifying, explosive, so much of it involving drugs and drug dealing, calculated killings, the "wasting" of innocent bystanders often by children callous and cold. Beyond anger and beyond remorse, beyond much of any feeling, it seems, these young men will kill or be killed, go to jail, then go back to the streets. There's no restraining them. The discipline an older generation counted on doesn't work today. These kids have no patience, no fear, no sense of any future. They terrorize their elders and are loyal not to any block or neighborhood but only to a circle of those who've banded together for protection and to defend their piece of the drug action. A minimum wage job, some low-level position which black kids and their parents once would have accepted and believed held out some hope, is for them not even worth considering. They are warriors and will fight for survival, only on their own terms. With them the light is flickering, leaving a nightmarish possibility for the future. Can this be the end of the line?

Some of this street toughness, defiance and swagger, does have its appeal. Watch decent kids, black and white, take on the language, the style and the look, then blast away with their rap music. They may do it to protect themselves, but it scares the shit out of the rest of us. When I spot these kids coming down the street (whether they are good kids or not I have no way of telling) in their getups, their hoods obscuring most of their face—I wonder . . . and I worry. So far the truly disaffected have spread terror and death on their own turf and killed mostly blacks. But consider if this violence were to overflow the black neighborhoods and take a toll among whites. That's when all hell will break loose along with your vigilantes. In would come the Army. But how reliable would it be? Would these troops, many of whom are blacks, fire upon their own? They probably would, but it's all very troubling.

Whites are real stupid people, many blacks will tell you that. What was gained by all this race bullshit? Look at the effort that went into setting up and maintaining this idiotic system. Think of all the resources that were wasted, all the talent that was denied and all the pain and suffering that went with it. What was the point of it all? What was accomplished? Well, the whites ain't that dumb. The smarter ones at least know full well what they were about. Don't forget the old pecking order. There's always a pyramid; every society has it. (Though in the United States discussions of class and social power make everyone uncomfortable.) Instead there's lots of loose talk of equality and equal opportunity in the United States—but there's no escaping it. You got this small number of folks on top, setting the stage and establishing the rules and calling many of the shots, and in one way or another keeping everyone else off balance and more or less down. Blacks have been the base of the pyramid from the beginning, and whites of all kinds have made it their business to keep us there. But it's the WASPs on top of the pyramid who've found this especially useful to their purposes. Keep the blacks at the bottom and you make, as I've said, a lot of down-and-out struggling whites feel better about themselves, make them willing to support a system that at least had the sense to keep blacks in their place. And of course should these less successful whites start complaining about their share of the pie, you change the subject and begin talking about hatred and fear of the blacks. They'll get off on that and stop asking other embarrassing questions. Yes, there has been method to this madness. (Jews should take comfort in these manipulations. Were there less racism around, don't you think the level of anti-Semitism would rise? That's long been a game with an easy target and a big payoff for those at the controls.)

But I'll tell you, the WASPs worry me these days. Up till recently they had done one hell of a job of running this country—and with their "associates"—most of the rest of the world. I'm not looking to replace them. I've never been big on toppling them. All I've been asking is to get in on the action, to be there on the same starting line. My generation was convinced that's all we needed to do—we could compete, we could take 'em (probably one of the reasons the whites were not eager to start the race together, have it all fair and square).

The WASPs seem to be losing their touch. They "won" the Cold War but don't seem to know what to do next. Under their lead the United States became the world's top economic power, but most of the world's people have not come along for the ride. The folks at the top got me a bit worried. They're not showing enough smarts nor understanding of what got us to be number one in the first place. Besides they're getting meaner, greedier, more shortsighted and looking back to a past that has few answers to what we're facing today. These WASPS are the past. Sure as hell ain't the future. Their kind will, in not too many years, slip into the minority in this country. The United States is "browning" for all sorts of reasons and many whites now on top of the heap won't take kindly to this. And when they look out across the world, whether in China, Japan, Southeast Asia or South America, they see even more people coming on—and they're not white either. Can we win their respect? Even our guns and missiles don't seem to scare people all that much anymore.

Faced with this our ruling groups don't seem up to the challenge. Republican Party policies in particular are off the mark, offering little to rekindle hope or restore a sense of fairness. Rather they seem eager to strip as much wealth off the economy for their corporate supporters as they can while offering most everyone else "feel good" patent medicines which don't heal a thing. For the poor the suggestion is that they survive largely on their own. Is closing off opportunities, overlooking serious training and retraining of workers, keeping wages low and allowing millions to go without health care coverage a formula for success? But that's what we're facing in the U.S. Instead of seriously thinking about opening up the system, becoming inclusive, using the talents and energies of everyone, making society fairer and more democratic, we are putting up barriers, blocking paths, dimming hopes, letting the wealthy take even more out of the pot. We're going backward.

I love America, what this country stands for, what this nation potentially can accomplish. Hey, believe it or not I'm rooting for these guys, the same ones who did me so much harm. I want them to wake up and to shake things up. Let me assure you that if they sense things slipping away—if there's a challenge from Hispanics, Asians, Gays, Women or far right Wackos or some combination of these groups—you know who the WASPs will turn to for support—you guessed it, the blacks. Why? Because we're so closely related. We accepted their ways and speak their language. In the end they will trust us to help bail them out. They know we've always been loyal.

You've read my story, taken your measure of me—understand my anger and maybe even accept the fact that I'm not bitter. I mean to be constructive. I want to see people coming together with blacks becoming full and accepted members of this society. But in spite of the progress made I'm not sure this will ever happen. There's a lot of history here, a lot of folks with a stake in the way things are, and so many changes that would need to take place. For starters consider these. White America has to 'fess up to at least some of what went on. It's got to own up not only to slavery but admit that even after that ended we blacks never really got much of a chance to join the mainstream. We've been playing "catch up" ever since and worse, we've simply been kept out of the game the whites have been playing. Put this in the history books. Especially let newcomers to America know what we've been through in this country. Remind them how, without much effort on their part, they've benefited from our struggles to gain some basic protections and some piece of the pie. As to compensation or reparations, why not? Aren't we owed something for all those years of free labor we gave you, for all the lynchings and destructive segregation? (Even if just a Holocaust Museum publicizing the horrors we went through. Of course this would put us in competition with the Jews who, to their great credit, have established many such memorials and centers to document that ghastly period. I'm troubled though by Jewish insistence on exclusivity here.)

Whose is the greater tragedy—what happened to the Africans during the course of the trans-Atlantic slave trade or Hitler's devastation of the Jews? Can you imagine a more futile and foolish debate? Yet that is what underlies these tensions. It's as if two condemned men took to arguing over who would have it worse—the one to be executed by firing squad or the other scheduled for the gas chamber. Millions upon millions of Jews died. Millions upon millions of Africans lost their lives. What's important is that each of us understand the tragedy that befell the other and work together to overcome conditions and oppose ideas out of which such depravities can arise.

Sure compensation is controversial, but haven't recent immigrants and refugees been given money and goods by the

U.S. government to get them going? Weren't the Japanese-Americans handed millions by Congress to compensate for our "jailing" them during World War II? Aren't American Indians getting certain exclusive privileges, being paid back because of the bad stuff the white men did? Why aren't we as deserving? Even a modest or token amount would do, would be just and honorable.

This payback must include some positive actions to get us off the bench and on to the starting team. Institutional racism—it's a fancy enough term, but what it means is that the deck's been stacked all along, that the usual paths to progress have been blocked for blacks. I saw how that operated. I watched teachers give up on black kids. I listened as employers told us there were no jobs when there surely were. I heard union bosses insist blacks had no business being in the union. I stood there while a police official announced he wanted no blacks on the force. Yes, the way's been blocked time and time again. I saw how other groups were favored, how they created exclusive pipelines and through nepotism primed the pump and moved their own along. We were never "in" anywhere, never were in a position to direct the flow, favor our own. Society has got to find a way to let this happen. Get us in, introduce some fairness into the system. We'll take it from there.

Groups usually look out for their own. Those who "belong" are comfortable with one another, prefer each other's company, keep outsiders at a distance and protect and defend each other at almost any cost. (Those whites disturbed at the delight of many blacks over the O.J. verdict should also recall and ask themselves about the demonstration of pride and support given during the trial of Mafia Godfather John Gotti by portions of the Italian community.) We've become very respectful of groups lately. We've come to appreciate the mutual support they provide and the unique cultures members share and preserve. We respect the "rights" they claim, and the political power they build. And Lord knows we blacks over the years could have benefited from greater cohesion and clout.

But I've told you why groups bother me. With groups come division, isolation, and indifference. Group members don't care much for "outsiders" or "outside" circumstances. Ethnic enclaves or "balanced" political tickets—for me they're a problem. But not to the powers that be. It's great for them when different people suspect each other, ignore common concerns. It's real useful to them when this diverts attention, provides a smokescreen to cover up the real centers of power and privilege. I'm for people mingling and mixing-for taking away artificial barriers. That's what should be going on here. That was the great promise this country made to newcomers. Come on in, join together—become part of this new blend, the true American. It is happening, although a lot of people don't see it or don't want to see it. Casual intermingling, mixed marriages, mixed neighborhoods—we're heading in that direction. Call it the browning of America—it's coming. With more and more people scrambled the race issue could just get lost in the mix. In the end the answer may not be enlightenment or conversion but simply color confusion!

America feels it has given us too much already, resents our asking for more. Whatever our condition, these folks say society is not to blame, we've brought most of our problems on ourselves. Lord knows we are not blameless. We've got faults, shortcomings too, but to point to us, the victims, and stop there is crazy. Still that idea sells, and the public continues to confuse consequences with causes and acts as if fixed negative character traits explain black failure.

We must at this point largely do for ourselves, accepting allies where we find them, but mostly working to get our own acts together. That's after all what Farrakhan's been preaching. The message of self-help is right out of Ben Franklin, Ralph Waldo Emerson and Booker T. Washington—is as American as you can get. Crusading against racism is passé. It will ease up, it already has, but it will never disappear—memories run too deeply here. Speak out against it and demonstrate. We need Al Sharpton and others like him to march against the latest outrage when it appears, as it almost certainly will. But let's not get hung up on this. And don't blame everything we've not been able to do on racism. For sure there's truth to it, but then it's also a copout, an excuse, a substitute for positive engagement. People are getting tired of that kind of talk.

Let us gather up our strength, especially our economic might. If white society won't give us the money to get businesses going and our people trained, let's reach into our own pockets, as Tony Brown and others have long been telling us to do. Co-ops, development banks, venture capital funds, even profits from the drug traffic-use it all to prime the pump. You'd get plenty of "bang" from those bucks. Let's spend our money in black-owned stores and enterprises. Let's encourage our churches to gather up their substantial funds and turn them as many have to matters of this world. Let them pay for training and for housing and to help restore our own communities. Let us get our people out there voting for blacks or whites who are with us and will help us get what we need. Let our politicians grow ever more savvy, able to play the political game with the same smarts that others have. We need more than symbols; it's time we had political pros working for us. Let us have our own leaders, not those chosen for us. If society is doing a lousy job educating our kids, forget integration for now and worry about getting equal funding and having our own schools and teachers ready to do the job right. Haven't the Black Muslims shown how it's possible to take young men, beaten in spirit, morally crippled, and turn them around, into disciplined, purposeful, positive human beings? And finally, if society's unwilling to tell our story or do it right, we should come forward with the facts and let them speak. Don't falsify, don't exaggerate—there's no need for excess here. Just set the record straight, tear away the falsehoods, fill in the blanks. That will be enough of a revelation.

We blacks were there when it all began. All along we showed

resourcefulness, skill and toughness, traits we're all proud of, when we helped build this nation. Whatever others may say, the truth is—we are as American as apple pie.